CW00971198

Teaching
Dance
Studies

Teaching Dance Studies

Edited by

JUDITH CHAZIN-BENNAHUM

Melinda Jordan, Editorial Assistant

ROUTLEDGE
NEW YORK AND LONDON

Chapter 3 is based on "From Improvisation to Choreography: The Critical Bridge" by Larry Lavender and Jennifer Predock-Linnell *Research in Dance Education* vol. 2 no. 2 pp.195-209 (2001) © 2001 Taylor & Francis Ltd.

Chapter 9, "Standing Aside and Making Space: Mentor Student Choreographers," by Larry Lavender and Jennifer Predock-Linnell, first appeared in *Impulse*, 4 (3--1996): 235-252; reprinted by permission of the author.

Published in 2005 by
Routledge
Taylor & Francis Group
270 Madison Avenue
New York, NY 10016

Published in Great Britain by
Routledge
Taylor & Francis Group
2 Park Square
Milton Park, Abingdon
Oxon OX14 4RN

© 2005 by Taylor & Francis Group, LLC
Routledge is an imprint of Taylor & Francis Group

Printed in the United States of America on acid-free paper
10 9 8 7 6 5 4 3 2 1

International Standard Book Number-10: 0-415-97035-0 (Hardcover) 0-415-97036-9 (Softcover)
International Standard Book Number-13: 978-0-415-97035-8 (Hardcover) 978-0-415-97036-5 (Softcover)

No part of this book may be reprinted, reproduced, transmitted, or utilized in any form by any electronic, mechanical, or other means, now known or hereafter invented, including photocopying, microfilming, and recording, or in any information storage or retrieval system, without written permission from the publishers.

Trademark Notice: Product or corporate names may be trademarks or registered trademarks, and are used only for identification and explanation without intent to infringe.

Library of Congress Cataloging-in-Publication Data

Teaching dance studies / edited by Judith Chazin-Bennahum.
    p. cm.
  Includes bibliographical references and index.
  ISBN 0-415-97035-0 (hb : alk. paper) -- ISBN 0-415-97036-9 (pb : alk. paper)
  1. Dance--Study and teaching (Higher) I. Chazin-Bennahum, Judith.

GV1589.T43 2005
792.8'071'1--dc22   2005001224

Taylor & Francis Group
is the Academic Division of T&F Informa plc.

Visit the Taylor & Francis Web site at
http://www.taylorandfrancis.com

and the Routledge Web site at
http://www.routledge-ny.com

Contents

Acknowledgments

This text has evolved over many years of teaching and studying literature and dance. In the world of dance, it was Antony Tudor who most taught me to be vigilant, to work through the problems of choreography and technique with irony and desire. Bob Joffrey instilled in me an energy of will and attention to style. Lillian Moore exacted an ethical sense of respect for the canon; Agnes de Mille smiled reluctantly when told the terms of a Broadway contract and then said, "No matter, we'll sell it." Danilova spoke of audience and seduction. It was the French author Michel Butor who knew that text could not be separated from the reader and Claude Senninger who provided me with a remarkable love of Romantic theory. Many modern dance teachers haunt these pages: Doris Rudko, Marian Scott, Pearl Lang, José Limón, Martha Graham, Merce Cunningham, Ethel Winter, David Wood, Yuriko, and Mary Hinkson.

More recently, I want to thank Larry Lavender for his insightful, kind, and wise comments on a text that builds confidence in our educational institutions. And I deeply appreciate all the hard work and wonderful editorial assistance from Melinda Jordan. Of course, it is the students who drive this discourse, the Paulettes, the Sarahs, the Melissas, the Bridgets, the Katias, the Mary Annes, the Teresas—the young women who wish to be seen, heard, and read.

Introduction

JUDITH CHAZIN-BENNAHUM

Our intent in writing a text on teaching dance studies is twofold: to fill a gap by offering suggestive models of how to approach teaching and learning in some of the major areas of academic dance education, as well as to help students to encounter these models in ways that are progressive, cumulative, and catalytic for fresh thinking. We hope that it contributes to the professionalization of dance education. Currently, among dance-teaching literature there are only a few recent books that explore the many different areas of dance studies. Our goal is to provide an updated and expansive text that will be used as a major tool in the classroom and will be required reading for graduate students in the field of dance. As such, it would be open to a very broad readership in universities, and perhaps studios, throughout the United States and abroad. This text will also be valuable to instructors or researchers who want to stay abreast of new currents in teaching as they are described by some of the very best dance educators across the country. We hope to encourage discussions about the relationship between teaching and scholarship and to promote the under-standing that teaching is integral to the development of knowledge. This volume features fourteen authors with long-established teaching and writing careers, each an expert in a particular field of dance.

Many young people graduating from universities with degrees — either PhDs, MFAs, or MAs — wish to teach at the undergraduate or graduate level in the field of dance. If they have attended good graduate programs, they may have had some experience teaching in the classroom, but more commonly their exposure has been limited to the studio. At conferences, we often meet these enthusiastic students, who ask us about teaching methodologies and texts to use. What we offer them are usually "quick-fix" workshops that cannot possibly prepare them to teach effectively and confidently. When they have graduated, these students often find themselves incapable of securing good jobs that they would otherwise qualify for, because of their lack of teaching skills and experience.

There is a burgeoning need at the level of higher education for research and training in teaching that is intellectually challenging and open to discussion, revision, and growth and that can become a topic of professional critique. While generic ideas have their place, for teaching to become intellectually respectable it must be taught in active, student-centered ways and be discipline-specific. Textbooks that hypothesize teaching methods arising from the materials themselves, in the diverse fields of the study of dance, are needed.

The art of teaching was revealed to me as I was sitting in my father's French Civilization class fifty-odd years ago, when I was a thirteen-year-old dancer wishing to be somewhere else. My father, Maurice Chazin, a professor of Romance Languages at Queens College, was voted the most successful teacher five years in a row. He had just introduced me to Professor Jacques LeClerq, the father of Tanaquil LeClerq, the famous Balanchine ballerina, who epitomized the goddess of dance to me. My father wanted me to go to college and thought that he might encourage me by introducing me to celebrated personalities, as well as by showing me how exciting university teaching can be.

There was an air of levity about the room as French philosophy and political theory were debated. The sound of my father's voice penetrated the intense atmosphere, and at times his voice became louder when punctuating an important point in his argument. He and all the students were speaking French, which I did not really understand. Words became heated as two men wearing army uniforms (many of the students were veterans on the G.I. Bill), began to defend their ideas, which left my dad with a smile on his face. The room was alive with conversation, questions, and vibrant gesticulations, but also with a sense of pleasurable safety. Everything I needed to know about teaching seemed to happen in those fifty minutes. The space opened up; suddenly the classroom grew to an infinite size, a space where thoughts and gestures thrived equally. The students entered the classroom prepared and ready for anything. The teacher nudged, informed, and guided. Everyone was learning and everyone was experiencing the topic at hand.

Those of us who teach dance and dance studies have had to develop and refine new languages to suit this ephemeral art form. When I first began teaching dance history, my mentor, Selma Jeanne Cohen, explained to me that universities were old, entrenched institutions that loathed changing their ways. Dance was not considered an academically viable subject, although the teaching of technique, choreography, and performance were highly valued. Cohen warned me, "It's going to be guerrilla warfare. First you conceive of an acceptable course (with extensive bibliography, exams, papers, etc.), and then you begin to invite yourself into other academic areas. Agree to lecture in Russian History on the Ballets Russes, French Culture on Louis XIV and his Académie de Danse, and English Literature on Romantic Ballet, and gradually you penetrate the Maginot line." This is what Selma Jeanne did and this is what most of us have done. We created the critical and theoretical frameworks common to other fields that serve as the foundation for teaching dance studies in universities and today, though still struggling to define ourselves, we have the solidity of well-researched historical and philosophical structures. As if this were not enough, dance instructors and writers are often called on to curate exhibitions, present dramaturgical commentary in programs, and produce themed festivals, and they are intellectually at the forefront of gender and race studies, as well as ethnographic interpretations of ritual and movement in global dance research.

Fortunately, a number of organizations support dance studies and the growing number of scholars and writers, such as the Congress on Research in Dance (CORD); the Society of Dance History Scholars (SDHS); Dance Critics of America; the World Dance Alliance; and the National Dance Education Organization, which has grown exponentially since it was begun in 1999.

Several themes thread their way through this text and shape the series of narratives about dance studies. For example, one cannot ignore the importance of Rudolf von Laban's pioneering work in the twentieth century and his theories, which have become an immeasurable framework for movement recognition and dance notation. Understanding that movement has cultural relevance underpins most of the writings in this text. Dance reflects culture and culture reveals itself through the medium of movement.

On a more personal level, our writers live in the complex world of the classroom, where the dynamics of interpersonal relations are in constant flux. The writers in this book seek to communicate about the essential relationships between teachers and students and the need to be flexible, compassionate, and empathic. They speak with reverence for the body kinesthetically and in the way it feels and senses movement, and of the activity of dancing as a way of knowing. And a few writers bring forth the idea of our "inner selves," that place deep inside of us that drives us unconditionally to dance.

As a way of entering this text, we begin the first chapter with a discourse on analyzing movement. Bill Evans describes the materials and methodologies for courses in movement analysis as they apply to dance. Evans has taught both undergraduate and graduate courses in Laban Movement Analysis and Bartenieff Fundamentals in university dance programs since 1986. Rudolf von Laban (1879–1958), a creative thinker who recognized movement to be the most basic of human languages, and Irmgard Bartenieff (1900–1981), a student of his who integrated his theoretical system into her own system of body re-education, provide dance students with the tools and knowledge they need to understand concepts that underlie all human movement.

Evans begins by caringly and carefully interacting with his students to help them to gain knowledge about themselves. At the heart of his work is his desire to help students understand their personal uniqueness through experiencing and reflecting on themselves in relation to fundamental evolutionary developmental movement patterns. In this journey, he prompts the student to learn dance techniques accurately and quickly. He encourages the student to use Laban/Bartenieff Movement Analysis vocabulary in order to discuss and write about dance more objectively in criticism, history, pedagogy, and choreography courses.

Chapter 2 poses questions about conceptualizing dance. Susan Leigh Foster, of UCLA, discusses the notion of theory as a hypothetical framework for evaluating dance's significance. In the tradition of Lucian and Thoinot Arbeau, Foster sets up a lighthearted dialogue between students of dance. Step by step, she offers different theoretical frameworks and highlights their merits and disadvantages. Foster explains the importance of accounting for the difference between dancing and writing about dance in any theoretical inquiry into dance. She also writes about how to assess the aesthetic and political implications of different dance theories. Furthermore, she sees the potential for texts written directly about dance and those written in related fields to mutually inform each other.

Moving on to issues surrounding the creative process, Larry Lavender and Jennifer Predock-Linnell put forth several important options for the teacher of choreography in Chapter 3. Traditionally, literature on the teaching of choreography depends on improvisation exercises that allegedly help students to develop diverse movement materials. Thus, improvisation as a spontaneous activity brings students in touch with their "authentic selves" and moves them toward developing their "singular" artistic voice.

However, Lavender and Predock-Linnell see the necessity for another step in the process of making dances: thinking, writing, and speaking critically about one's work. The role of criticism is elevated to a much higher station and is deemed necessary to the artistic process of choreography.

Musical instruction is essential to every dancer. In Chapter 4, Jeffrey Stolet, who holds an endowed chair in music at the University of Oregon, writes on musical studies and focuses on the essential attractions of dance to music and music to dance. He explores the technical aspects of musical study for dancers, emphasizing the five basic musical concepts — pitch, duration, timbre, volume, and location — as well as the key musical attributes, such as harmony, melody, counterpoint, and so on. He sees the enduring relationship between music and dance as a primal love affair and ascribes great importance to music's aesthetic, cultural, and philosophical impact on dance. Stolet reviews the exciting creative process involved in forging a choreographic work and discusses the meaning of music from a choreographic and performance perspective.

Like music and dance, film and dance sustain a strong interdisciplinary relationship. In Chapter 5, Beth Genné, of the University of Michigan, discusses how to teach dance on film so teachers can convey the complexities of the moving body through film images. She raises the important question, "Are we seeing dance as dance or dance as film, and how do we tell the difference?" Genné discusses the limitless possibilities and movements of the camera, editing processes, and lighting. She works with students so that they become aware of the so-called "choreography of the camera," and that magical stream of images that informs both the dancer and the audience.

As film records dance motion for posterity, so the history of dance creates ways of examining movement in the past. In Chapter 6, Linda Tomko, from the University of California, Riverside, explores ways to rethink the teaching of dance history courses at community college and university levels. She addresses the pressures that have been brought to bear on the very notion of dance over the last twenty years and thus, on dance history. Discussing recent conceptualizations of what is considered "dance" enables instructors to reframe ideas of how dance has figured in people's lives, and therefore, what may be learned when studying "dance." This chapter assesses the challenges posed to "history" by recent critical theory and suggests what can be gained by studying dance from a perspective that is concerned with change over time.

In Chapter 7, Mindy Aloff acknowledges that dance criticism cannot be separated from the history of dance in whatever time it was born. Writing dance criticism elicits many varied responses for the student learning about performance and presumes that the person writing about dance spends many active hours in the theater. Aloff emphasizes that in attending performances, we move away from the "joys and turmoils" of our personal lives in order to give ourselves over to something that is not us. She looks to see who is in the class and tailors the class accordingly. Her mission is to help the student write at least one paper in which he or she has come to terms with his or her own responses to a live performance and to the facts of the performance as validated by others who saw it.

The context of a dance, or its ethnography or anthropological perspective, has become an important topic to dance scholars. Professor Jill Sweet, of Skidmore College, addresses this topic in Chapter 8, based on the notions of culture, contextualization, and comparison through ideas such as cultural relativism, ethnic identity, worldview, and ethnography. She posits the idea that a knowledge-based definition of culture is important, particularly the notion of culture as *embodied knowledge.* Sweet emphasizes the students' investigation and experience of culturally diverse dance traditions through lectures, readings, exposure to films and dance, and opportunities in a studio setting to experience bodily what they are being taught. Finally, Sweet trenchantly warns us against the dangers of ethnocentrism and the anthropologist's duty to maintain a position of cultural relativism.

Teaching young dancers how to choreograph is one of the most difficult and challenging responsibilities at the university level — not only because the craft of movement demands many approaches, but also because the body relays such complex meanings and a dancer's identity relies in great part on the choreography that one chooses to perform. Does the neuromusculature of our bodies imprint on us a singular concept that differs from that of our friends and fellow students? And does this particular self-impression distance us from our peers, or unite us? Many years ago, when Mabel Todd's *The Thinking Body* appeared, I breathed a sigh of relief, sensing that this was a healthy counternarrative to the traditional canon of Aristotle's and Descartes' dualism of mind/body.

In Chapter 9, Lavender and Predock-Linnell continue their discourse on instilling confidence and sensitivity in the neophyte choreographer. Even if one is not teaching a course in choreography, one spends many hours watching and working with student choreographers. In mentoring roles, we are continually faced with deciding when, how, and to what degree to involve ourselves in the students' efforts. Naturally, we are ready to give substantive advice for handling complex artistic problems. At the same time, we must also "give the students space" to develop themselves as artists. In this chapter, the authors discuss a variety of challenges mentors face, such as the idea that the concept of the dance should allow for "emerging forms" to arise so that it does not limit the organic development of a piece. Above all, mentors carry the responsibility of nurturing the initiates so that they can move ahead in their creative work.

Keeping our dancers safe from physical harm is also an urgent goal in dance programs. In Chapter 10, Ginny Wilmerding, a professor at the University of New Mexico, describes the teaching of kinesiology and injury prevention. Every dance form creates its own unique physical demands on the body and brings its own set of problems to be analyzed and understood. Wilmerding advises us on the need for classroom lectures on biology, physics, and chemistry so that the student can better understand the physics of dancing many different dance forms and of dancing solo, as well as the unique demands of partnering. Like our other contributors, she recognizes the importance of understanding who is in the class and tailoring the course to the dancers' special needs — from the neophyte to the professional. She informs us that it is vital to recognize patterns of injuries and that their management and rehabilitation are essential to the college dancer.

Chapter 11 on teaching dance notation, or the ability to read and write movement, is a collaboration between Ilene Fox from the Dance Notation Bureau and Dawn Lille, a teacher at the Juilliard School. There are a number of methods that seek a scientific approach to reading and recording movement. We've chosen the teaching of Labanotation, as it has grown significantly in importance and credibility over the past fifty years. Labanotation, invented by Rudolf von Laban in 1928, constitutes the preservation of a dance and hence the ability to reconstruct movement. It is an exact means of teaching students to see rather than just look, to think concretely about what part of the body is moving, where it is going in space, at what level it is moving, and how long the movement lasts. Instruction begins with movement in the studio and proceeds to how to read and write that movement. What is immediately apparent in the teaching of notation is how deeply the body must be involved. It must do the movement in order to understand and relate to the symbols and motifs at the heart of notation. Applications extend to dance composition, dance history, technique, education, and therapeutic analysis.

If we are going to notate and save our wonderful dances, then we also need to archive them and to preserve them in proper conditions and in places where they are accessible to choreographers, students, and scholars, not just librarians. Elizabeth Aldrich, the chief archivist of the Dance Heritage Coalition in Washington, D.C., offers Chapter 12 on dance archiving. Archivists, librarians, and scholars play a leading role in ensuring the survival of America's dance legacy. Dance is documented and preserved by a wide variety of people and institutions, including, but not limited to, dance creators and practitioners, presenting organizations and festivals, specialists in new technologies, and members of many kinds of communities. Aldrich stresses the importance of documenting and archiving, and she addresses the different methods of taking care of documentation as well as covering the bases on how to begin an archival preservation program. Often we depend on dancers' body memory, which may not be accurate and may not last long. Thus, there is an urgent need to document these events so that the past is kept alive. Dance archiving also plays an important role by offering opportunities to students searching for ways to make a career in the field of dance.

Because this text privileges pedagogy, we conclude with Sue Stinson, who has taught dance pedagogy courses in higher education for almost thirty years at the University of North Carolina, Greensboro, an institution nationally known for its teacher education program in dance. In Chapter 13, Stinson speaks of the process of becoming a teacher — the journey rather than the destination — and puts herself in the position of a continuing learner, which allows her students to observe her teaching and critically reflect on it. Through lessons that are liberally illustrated with stories from her own experience, she teaches skills and brings insights developed in the context of relationships with peers and faculty, as well as with subject matter, one's students, and oneself. Each student brings her or his own experience in teaching and learning dance, and with preexisting cognitive structures, which profoundly affects how they understand theory in dance education. Stinson challenges them to construct new ways of understanding and to take risks as beginning teacher educators.

One of the most important ideas of this book centers on the fact that a good teacher is also a learner, and one who does not shy away from the same challenges that the student encounters. Teachers must have the courage to admit fault when they make mistakes in the course of the semester. Teaching and learning are about process and willingness to change, not only for the students, but also for the *ciceroni* or the person who guides the students. I hope our text on dance studies helps to enlighten you and to guide you toward that end.

CHAPTER 1

Teaching Movement Analysis

BILL EVANS

I feel very strongly that every serious dance and movement student deserves an opportunity to investigate Laban/Bartenieff Movement Analysis (L/BMA). It is part of basic dance and movement literacy. I have evolved a highly personal approach to the teaching of movement analysis. Without suggesting that you try to duplicate my specific methods of teaching this subject, I hope that these pages will provide a useful historical context and a clear overview of the possibilities I have explored.

As a professor of dance at the University of New Mexico from 1988 through 2004, it was one of my responsibilities — and genuine pleasures — to teach movement analysis to incoming undergraduate dance majors and minors during their first two semesters in the UNM dance program. During their precollege years, most of the students had learned to value inordinately the appearance of conformity, and most entered my courses wanting mainly to know the answers to the questions on which they would be tested. In class discussions they were initially willing to comment only when they felt certain they would be "right." To encourage the development of a more diverse and useful set of educational values, I created a two-semester sequence of movement analysis courses designed to facilitate (in the first semester) a process of self-discovery and (in the second) the acquisition of theoretical tools to be used in creative problem solving.

I invited students to participate in a process through which they could learn to understand and value their personal uniqueness. I then guided them through a process of applying the themes and concepts of Laban/ Bartenieff Movement Analysis as tools for self-initiated and personally meaningful change and growth.

Brief History of Movement Analysis

Rudolf von Laban (1879–1958) was a movement educator, choreographer, dance company director, visual artist, architect, scientist, and philosopher. He was born in what is now the Slovak Republic, but he worked throughout Europe as a significant participant in some of the major artistic proceedings of his era, especially the development of modern dance. In *Body Movement: Coping with the Environment*, Irmgard Bartenieff talks about her former teacher:

> He was in Germany during the Bauhaus and Expressionist periods, initiating and developing theatrical and recreational dance programs, schools and publications. In 1936, the Nazis forced him to stop, and he went to England, where he adapted his movement theories to wartime studies of factory workers, helped establish new schools for movement education and continued to publish his works. (1980, ix)

Laban was fascinated primarily with the *process* of movement rather than its outcomes, and he and his colleagues and successors have given us a complete theoretical system through which one can experience, understand, and describe movement in all its functional and expressive aspects. Laban's analytical theories (often called Labananalysis) are now categorized under the major headings of Effort, Shape, and Space Harmony. Any human movement can be viewed in terms of:

The inner attitudes which it reveals (Effort)
The process through which the body changes its form (Shape)
Its relationship to personal and/or general space (Space Harmony)

Labananalysis also includes Motif Writing, a graphic symbol language representing all major Effort, Shape, and Space concepts, which is used to record the observations of a Labananalyst. Motif writing can also be used to create a movement score that can then be realized; that is, it can be used prescriptively as well as descriptively.

Irmgard Bartenieff (1980–1981) was born in Berlin, Germany, where she was a student of biology, visual art, and dance before meeting Laban in 1925. She studied with the master and many of his collaborators and became a teacher of dance and of Labanotation (the system of precise and detailed movement notation for which Laban is best known, and which is related to but essentially different from Labananalysis; see Chapter 11). In 1936, Bartenieff fled from Germany to America, where she taught Labanotation and became a physical therapist. In 1943, she became a member of the New York City-based Dance Notation Bureau. In 1978, she founded the Laban Institute for Movement Studies (LIMS), also based in New York City (known since her death as the Laban/Bartenieff Institute for Movement Studies). A separate organization, the Dance Notation Bureau (DNB), was formed to promote the use of Labanotation. It might be said that the DNB deals mostly with the *quantitative* aspects of movement documentation while LIMS deals primarily with the *qualitative* or *expressive* aspects of human movement.

Unlike Laban, Bartenieff was not so much a theoretician as she was a hands-on practitioner, more concerned with investigating the unique movement patterns of an individual than with creating a conceptual framework. Nonetheless, her work (as refined by several colleagues and successors) constitutes the fourth major subsystem of Laban/Bartenieff Movement Analysis: Bartenieff Fundamentals (BF). Not only can we perceive a movement event in terms of Effort, Shape, or Space, but we can also choose to look at it in terms of what is occurring on the level of the body. That is, we can perceive a person's body-level connectivity: the kinetic chains he or she activates to make movement more or less efficient. We can also consider such fundamental issues as:

Where within the body is movement initiated?
How does it follow through to complete the phrase?
How does it sequence through the body?
What parts of the body are active and which are frequently held?
What is the prevailing body attitude?

Bonnie Bainbridge Cohen, a former student of Bartenieff's, has created a system of movement investigation, healing, and re-education known as Body Mind Centering. In recent years, several Certified Laban Movement Analysts — notably, Martha Eddy and Janice Meaden — have also become Body Mind Practitioners, and Cohen has generously allowed them to integrate many of her concepts and language into L/BMA.

Bartenieff Fundamentals, Body Mind Centering, Alexander Technique, the Feldenkrais Method, various forms of yoga, and other systems of fundamental movement awareness and repatterning — often known collectively as *somatic studies* — have been embraced by increasing numbers of dancers over the past three decades. Somatic studies encourage the student to pay attention to the messages the body is sending to the brain, to honor physical sensation and bodily wisdom. Because many of our traditional practices in ballet, jazz, modern dance, and other Western theatrical dance forms have encouraged an external approach to learning (i.e., copying the teacher, looking at ourselves in the mirror, concerning ourselves with "correct" positions and lines), the inclusion of somatic studies in dance training programs has begun to produce much-needed balance for many teachers and students.

One of the overarching themes of L/BMA is the need to balance the Inner with the Outer, or — as Peggy Hackney (2000) states it — "a lively interplay between inner connectivity and outer expressivity" (34). Western cultures have become increasingly concerned with the external image a person conveys; technological developments have also caused young people to become increasingly disembodied in the accomplishment of numerous tasks, which can happen instantly. Somatic studies remind us that physiological and psychological processes are essentially the same for us as they were for countless generations of our ancestors. Through somatic practices, we learn to honor the fundamental and timeless truths of what it is to be human; we develop body-mind patterns that are harmonious with our lifelong needs; and we learn to move (i.e., live) in ways that are healthful and regenerative.

My Personal Journey

My own process of self-discovery and self-acceptance — through which I was gradually able to overcome physical and psychological limitations and move forward in both my personal life and my career — was profoundly influenced by my study of Effort/Shape, Space Harmony, and Bartenieff Fundamentals. My exploration of these theories began almost thirty years ago when Peggy Hackney, whom I believe to be the world's foremost authority on the work of Irmgard Bartenieff, joined my professional Bill Evans Dance Company and the faculty of my school of modern dance, Dance Theatre Seattle. My investigation of L/BMA continued in the classes of Janet Hamburg, who taught in my Bill Evans Summer Institutes of Dance in the 1980s and early 1990s, and was more recently enhanced under Peggy Hackney again, with Janice Meaden, Pam Schick, and Ed Groff, in the Integrated Movement Studies Certification Program at the University of Utah. I am deeply and forever indebted to those extraordinary teachers and colleagues, who have become role models for the teacher I am and the teacher I wish to become.

Since 1976, when Peggy Hackney began sharing L/BMA concepts and practices in the day-to-day activities of my modern dance company and school, I have been evolving my own integration of L/BMA, modern dance technique, and choreography. In *The Wisdom of the Body Moving: An Introduction to Body-Mind Centering,* Linda Hartley articulates my own experience at the point in my life when I first encountered L/BMA:

> My instinct told me that I was all up in the air. I needed to place my feet firmly on the ground and relocate myself clearly in my body. I began to dance as a means to both embody and express who I am. I found I was also on the path of knowing in a new way that which I am. As I explored ways of making deeper contact with my body, my body was teaching me a new awareness of myself. (1995, xxii)

In 1978, another colleague/mentor entered my life: Karen Clippinger, one of the world's leading dance kinesiologists, became a faculty member of my Seattle school.

Ms. Clippinger helped me understand that, as she said in *Principles of Dance Training:*

> An application of scientific principles of training to dance is needed. Close work among the dance, scientific and medical communities is necessary to evaluate old methods and develop new methods. There is much work to be done to sort out the valuable dance principles which have been passed down through generations from the myths. Such a process can only yield better methods of dance training and provide a beginning for more effective injury prevention. (1988, 82)

The combination of hands-on applied dance science (which I learned from Karen) and the application of Laban/Bartenieff concepts (which I learned from Peggy) gave me a whole new lease on life as a dancer, teacher, and choreographer. Through the application of knowledge generated by my studies with Clippinger and Hackney, and numerous others in succeeding years, I have become a healthier and more fully functioning dancer; my choreography has become regenerative rather than destructive to my dancers' minds and bodies; and my students have learned how to develop the tools to take ownership of their own movement and of their well-being and expressivity.

In my years at UNM, I had the good fortune of collaborating with Virginia Wilmerding, another leading dance kinesiologist and exercise scientist. We took each other's classes and coordinated our teaching methods and course content to serve our students' dance science and somatics needs as we perceived them.

Movememt Analysis I

Early in the first semester, I would share with students an overview of L/BMA, by discussing its overarching themes, balancing:

Function and Expression
Stability and Mobility
Coping (Doing) and Indulging (Being)
Exertion and Recuperation
A concern for the Container (the Outer) with a concern for the Contents
(the Inner)

Students would discuss the relevance of these big ideas by making specific references to their current lives, and we would improvise around each idea.

Because I wanted my students to make deep contact with and learn from their bodies, my first-semester analysis course was organized around the six basic evolutionary Developmental Movement Patterns (Hartley 1995). In two-hour sessions held twice a week, we discussed and experienced these patterns, as they begin with cellular respiration at the moment of conception and proceed into early childhood through the overlapping stages of navel radiation, spinal, homologous, homo-lateral, and contralateral patterns of total body coordination. We studied and experienced these same neuromuscular patterns of body connectivity within the context of Bartenieff Fundamentals, as they serve us in our adult lives, as Patterns of Total Body Organization (Hackney 2000): Breath (both lung and cellular), Core-Distal, Head-Tail, Upper-Lower, Body-Half, and Cross-Lateral. We discovered that images derived from these patterns can travel at the speed of light to organize and integrate the entire body-mind in an instant to function more efficiently, different patterns facilitating different actions.

I assigned extensive readings in the books written by Bartenieff (1980) and Hackney (2000), and in journal articles written by numerous Labananalysts and educational theorists, as a preparation for my slow, gentle, thorough, and hands-on teaching of movement practices designed by Bartenieff, her colleagues, and successors. I would begin most classes by asking students to lie on their backs, close their eyes, and travel in their minds' eyes and proprioceptors through their bodies, acknowledging and savoring sensations and awarenesses as they made this leisurely journey. I would guide them with both anatomically and/or developmentally precise language and subjective imagery.

Later, I would invite students to improvise around each movement pattern, "listening" to their bodies' needs as they drew on the concepts and imagery I had shared with them to guide their explorations and choices.

They moved sometimes in silence and sometimes to music or their own vocal/body percussion sounds. Their improvisations progressed from internal breath-related changes, through small gestures and stationary actions, all the way to large motions through space. As they improvised, they examined the personal relevance of the concepts we were studying.

I assigned "study buddies," so that each student had a semester-long partner who provided intellectual and emotional support throughout the journey on which they had embarked. I frequently confirmed my belief that "it is a gift to be perceived," and students became increasingly appreciative of the thoughtful, caring, and honest feedback they received from their study buddies, other class members, and me. I devoted time in each class for students to reflect on their investigations and derive meanings from those reflections. I would ask them to record these meanings in their journals and share them with their study buddies and/or other members of the class.

I encouraged students to approach their investigations of these fundamental body patterns with their whole selves, engaging the four functions of the psyche — thinking, sensing, feeling, and intuiting — to perceive which body organization patterns were fully accessible to them as well as which patterns could be more available. Study buddies helped each other identify individual variations of and relationships to each developmental pattern, and I encouraged each student to ask: "What reflex behaviors have I patterned into my neuromuscular system?" "How do I think this came about?" and "How does it serve me?"

I often reminded the students that life is movement and that movement is change. We studied the process of change itself, learning to understand that growth requires change and that change is an ongoing, long-term process. In Hackney's words:

> … movement is a metaphor for change. But it is also an actualization of change. You are changing the habitual way you use your body and relate within yourself and to your world, as you practice moving in new ways. Your neuromuscular system is getting new information. By being actively involved in your own movement patterns, you can participate thoroughly and be in charge of your own change. (2000, 24)

I urged students to discover their personal meanings in relation to fundamental movement within the contexts of their own lives. I emphasized my belief that one can move with full psychophysical involvement — that is, one can be fully alive in the moment — only when personal meanings are recognized, investigated, and expressed. I stressed the importance of finding inner reasons for moving so that each of us can proceed in the world from an individual sense of core purpose. I explained my belief that, because the mind and the body are inseparable on every level, learning to move from the body's core allows one to move from a spiritual/psychological core as well.

We integrated these explorations of our neuromuscular patterns with a study of Howard Gardner's (1982) theory of multiple intelligences, learning to understand when and how each individual relied on bodily-kinesthetic, verbal-linguistic, logical-mathematical, visual-spatial, musical-rhythmic, intrapersonal, interpersonal, and/or naturalist intelligences to process information and generate knowledge.

I often sensed that students were troubled by feelings of having chosen an "easy" way out by having decided to major in dance. At such times, I explained my belief that good dancers are highly intelligent beings. As Howard Gardner says in *Intelligence Reframed*:

> I don't find it odd to speak of the bodily skill used by ... a dancer ... as embodying intelligence. The performances of these individuals are valued in many societies, and they involve an enormous amount of computation, practice and expertise. Snobbishness about use of the body reflects the Cartesian split between mind and body, and a concomitant degradation of processes that seem non-mental, or less mental than others. However, contemporary neuroscience has sought to bridge this gap and to document the cognition involved in action (and, for that matter, in emotion). (1999, 95–96)

I often perceived that dancers felt intimidated by those who possessed refined verbal skills, including me and other UNM dance faculty members. I encouraged such students to deliver their class presentations through movement and other nonverbal intelligences if they wished to do so. To help them to understand the wide variety of ways in which a dancer may become a successful teacher, I related such stories as this one:

> A few years ago I worked for a couple of days at a major Midwestern university, where I observed a faculty member conduct an advanced modern dance technique class. She came to the university teaching after a brilliant career as a performing artist and still dances with enormous skill and expressivity, and yet she was tentative and hesitant, knowing that I was watching her. Earlier she had watched me teach three technique classes, and had commented on my extensive use of language drawn from anatomy,

physiology, kinesiology, Laban Movement Analysis, and Bartenieff Fundamentals. I perceived that she lacked confidence teaching in front of me because she has not yet learned those words. Her students, however, revealed articulately the excellent results of her teaching, as they fully embodied a dance style which is often executed only superficially by such young practitioners. I felt bad that she was feeling linguistically inadequate rather than realizing that the bodily-kinesthetic, musical-rhythmic and intrapersonal intelligences which she embodies vibrantly are serving her students very well indeed. (2003, 55)

I shared this and other stories with students to encourage each of them to understand, value, and proceed from their unique strengths, even as they also recognized deficiencies they might like to work on.

I frequently mentioned that (as Bartenieff would say in response to many questions) *there are always many possibilities* (Hackney 2000, vi), and that no single way of engaging with the world is necessarily superior to the others. Instead of determining that a movement behavior was "right" or "wrong," we asked, "Is it appropriate? Is it serving my needs? Is it allowing me to function at my full potential?" If the answer to any of the above was "No," then the student could ask, "Would I like to invest in a process of change through which I might replace this behavior with another that could appropriately serve my needs?"

We learned to recognize that all movement patterns are taken into the neuromuscular system for legitimate reasons, and that a "good" person can embody an inefficient pattern. We learned that making judgments about such patterning was essentially irrelevant, and that what really mattered was understanding as fully as possible what each of us was doing and then examining that behavior within the context of one's life. I emphasized my belief that without context there is no meaning, and I encouraged each student to explore the impact of her/his fundamental movement patterns within various real-life situations.

There were usually around thirty-five students in Movement Analysis I. Instead of giving written examinations or requiring extensive papers, I evaluated students on the basis of their level of engagement in our ongoing investigations and on the basis of presentations, which each student would give to classmates and (when she/he chose) invited guests. During two weeks at midterm and the final two weeks of the semester, each student — with assistance from her/his study buddy — presented the results of her/his personal journey of discovery, reflection, and personal meaning-making. I strongly encouraged students to use words, movement, visual art, music, and/or the intrapersonal/interpersonal involvement of other class members in each presentation. I encouraged students to draw on their personal strengths but also to understand that this was a safe environment in which they could draw upon those aspects of themselves that had not yet been developed.

At midterm, students described how and when the Patterns of Total Body Organization and their multiple intelligences served them as dancers and in the rest of their lives. Most students discovered that their dance lives and daily lives were seamlessly connected. They discussed which patterns and intelligences were not fully available to them and — perhaps — why, often revealing childhood memories that had long been buried and unacknowledged. At the semester's end, students shared plans for future personal and artistic growth and strategies for facilitating positive change: for letting go of those behaviors they no longer needed and replacing them with patterns that would allow them to move forward in their lives toward personal and professional goals.

As I witnessed these presentations, I frequently felt goose bumps and was moved to tears. Most students shared stories of genuine transformation, some subtle, some involving quantum leaps of understanding and change. Many students described how the fear of being different, or not good enough, had caused them to hide, using movement to conceal rather than reveal who they really are. By being able to recognize and wrap words around their individual differences, they became able to claim ownership of those patterns and traits that make them unique.

Invariably, these recognitions of uniqueness were met with expressions of enthusiastic support from classmates. It was thrilling to witness students discovering and claiming ownership of aspects of themselves that had been hidden inside for years. I was not the only person crying, as students shared fears, doubts, and perceptions of themselves that they had discovered inside and were now able to celebrate, as they proclaimed, "This is who I am, and that's OK."

Even though this course was designed for dance majors and minors, I often had the pleasure of teaching students (and occasionally faculty) from a wide spectrum of disciplines: architecture, media arts, theater, music, athletics, visual arts, and education. Our midterm and final presentations were deeply enriched by the class members' diversity. Dance students were able to expand their horizons by witnessing the widely differing perspectives of students from other disciplines. We were reminded that life is movement, that movement is at the core of everyone's life, and that everyone has the right to learn about and express him or herself through movement.

One of the most surprising aspects of this process, for me, was that the students did most of the work themselves. My job was primarily to guide them into terrain that many of them had long ignored and then to get out of the way as they and their buddies engaged in the process of constructing self-knowledge.

During the semester, we often discussed the difficulties one encounters in this process of going inside to examine sensations, emotions, thoughts, and feelings. "Why is it so hard?" they asked. I found myself answering with the words that Elizabeth R. Hayes often spoke to me when I was an MFA student at the University of Utah more than twenty-five years ago: "Giving birth to anything is painful."

Almost always, students realized how short a time one semester really is and that the process of change they had embarked on had just begun. I often quoted Linda MacRae-Campbell (1988), who wrote in an article entitled "Whole Person Education," "Scientific research in neurology, psychology and education has etched expanded images of what it means to be human. There is an unlimited capacity for lifelong learning — and adults and children learn what has personal relevancy." (18)

Repeatedly, students asked, "Why didn't we know about this earlier? Why did we have to wait so long to go into our own bodies to discover these fundamental truths about ourselves?" I could only say that I believe it to be the birthright of every child in our culture to have the opportunity to know his or her body from the inside out and to construct this kind of self-knowledge. I made it clear that I was counting on them — our UNM dance majors — to create strategies for validating bodily knowledge and creating programs in movement education wherever they go.

One of the most important outcomes of this course, I think, was the creation of community. Because dancers were opening themselves so completely, supporting each other so thoroughly, and witnessing such genuine transformation, an unspoken bond developed among class members every fall semester. I was often delighted as I witnessed the positive impact of this bonding process — this shared sense of caring and trust — among students as they moved forward in the dance major curriculum over the following three or four years.

Movement Analysis II

For Movement Analysis II, I was given only two eighty-minute periods per week, and I chose to make that course relatively more formal and professional. The atmosphere created in MA I still permeated the proceedings, however, and the same sense of mutual trust and goodwill was almost always with us.

The second semester course revolved around the creation and presentation of two movement research projects. Students would deliver — individually or with their study buddy (for twice the time) — a midterm and a final presentation of action research in which they had applied a concept from Laban's Shape, Effort, or Space theory to an aspect of their personal, work, or artistic lives that they cared about deeply. Again, students were encouraged to deliver these presentations through as many of their intelligences as possible and to involve the intrapersonal/interpersonal participation of their classmates whenever possible and appropriate. As I did in Movement Analysis I, I required a written proposal from each student several weeks before the date of his/her presentation. On the days when the proposals were submitted, the class would sit in a circle as each student paraphrased this proposal verbally and then received feedback from class peers. My feedback would come in written form, and sometimes — if it was particularly delicate — in a private conference. I also required each student to give me a written outline before commencing his or her presentation and to provide a written response to each presenter immediately after each presentation, before we gave verbal feedback.

To prepare for these presentations, I guided the students through a process of investigation of the larger concepts within each of the LMA subsystems.

All investigations included some preassigned reading in Bartenieff's *Body Movement: Coping with the Environment* (1980), and/or various journal articles. Classes would begin with a short lecture segment during which students would take notes as I explained the theoretical concepts while writing their Motif symbols on a chalkboard and simultaneously embodying them. The lecture would often be followed by a class discussion during which initial questions were addressed. The most important portion of each investigation was always experiencing the new concept through improvisational movement. I also gave students a chance to utilize each new concept as the basis for an in-class solo or group creative project.

I gave students opportunities to apply each concept to guide observation, creation, and documentation in, at least, simple ways. Often, I would ask them to report on examples of each concept, as they observed them being embodied in other UNM courses, technique classes, rehearsals, and performances or at work, at home, at play, on TV, or in films. Frequently, we would use this observed and documented movement material as the basis for creative exploration and the composition of short movement studies. Again, I evaluated student work not on the basis of being right or wrong, but on the willingness to be fully engaged in both mind and body.

We began MA II by investigating Laban's Shape theory, because it is immediately accessible to most young dancers, and also relevant: dancers ordinarily spend a great deal of time considering the body's shape or form. Also, I would begin with Shape because it is relatively less personal than Effort and less mathematical than Space Harmony. In L/BMA, Shape refers to the process through which the body changes its form. Because life is movement, beginning with the growing and shrinking of each cell, the body is always changing its form: either growing or shrinking. Under the category of Shape, we studied:

Shape Flow Support: the breath-related changes in the size and shape of the thoracic and abdominal cavities that are ongoing throughout our lives

Still Forms: Pin, Wall, Ball, Tetrahedron, and Spiral

Shape Qualities: Rising/Sinking, Spreading/Enclosing, and Advancing/Retreating

Modes of Shape Change: Shape Flow (the body form changing in relationship to itself), Directional Spoke-like and Directional Arc-like (the body form changing to create bridges to points in the Kinesphere) and

Carving (the body form contouring to its three-dimensional environment)

Once students had a working knowledge of Shape, we would begin to explore Effort, which is what makes movement expressive. It is a basic component of artistry, and most dancers want to become more effective artists. I discovered that most students were thinking more of function than of expression when they used the term "artistic." That is, they often entered the course thinking that an effective artist was one who could lift her or his leg high, balance well on one leg, leap high, and/or turn rapidly. Therefore, we would usually begin our investigation of Effort by considering the difference between the quantitative aspects of dance (mentioned above) and the qualitative ones that we were about to study.

Labanalysts generally believe that at least 70 percent of our communication is nonverbal. Laban's Effort theory gives us inroads into seeing, discussing, and understanding the movement-level signals we are constantly sending and receiving but which are largely considered unimportant in most Western cultures. Laban categorized the physical properties of movement, which he called Motion Factors, and believed that each was related to a function of the psyche:

Flow is the ongoingness or continuity of movement, and is related to
  Feeling
Weight has to do with intention; it is the sensing, grounding, rarefica-
  tion or collapsing of one's physical mass, and is related to Sensing
Time has to do with a person's decision-making process and is related
  to Intuition
Space has to do with attention and is related to Thinking

Within each Motion Factor, there are two polar opposites, or Efforts,
which reveal inner attitudes:

Flow can be either Free or Bound
Weight can be either Light/Limp or Strong/Heavy
Time can be either Sustained or Sudden
Space can be either Multi-Focused or Direct

Free Flow, Light Weight, Sustained Time, and Multi-Focused Space are
inner attitudes that are often found together, or are affined. Laban called
these the Indulging Efforts. Bound Flow, Strong Weight, Sudden Time,
and Direct Space are also affined and are called the Coping Efforts.

The mover is not necessarily aware of the inner attitudes he or she is
revealing, and Efforts are hardly ever expressed one at a time. Almost
always, a person will be revealing two or three inner attitudes at any given
moment. Laban called the simultaneous crystallization of two Efforts
a State and of three Efforts a Drive. He named the possible two-Effort
configurations or States: *Dream/Awake, Remote/Near,* or *Mobile/Stabile.*
He named the possible three-Effort configurations or Drives: *Action,
Vision, Spell,* or *Passion.* On rare occasions a mover is simultaneously
expressing four inner attitudes: a Transformation Drive.

We would conclude our survey of basic Laban theory by looking at
Space Harmony, which has to do with the spatial architecture and geometry
of movement. This is the area of Laban's thinking that has the biggest
impact on my work as a choreographer. When I studied geometry in high
school, I struggled to see why it mattered. When I studied Laban's spatial
theories as a professional choreographer, I was immediately excited by the
infinite new choreographic possibilities it opened up for me. Nonetheless,
I saved Space Harmony until the latter portion of the semester so that students would be ready for the increased challenges it often presented; not
all students wish to be choreographers and many dancers are minimally
invested in using the mathematical-logical intelligence. (I developed a
third L/BMA course, Movement Analysis III, in which we studied Space
Harmony extensively, primarily for graduate students and as an elective

course for undergraduates who had developed an affinity for Laban theory in MA I and II.)

In Space Harmony, Laban gives us a framework through which to explore both personal space (the Kinesphere) and general space:

> We examine various possible approaches to and pathways through the Kinesphere: Central, Peripheral or Transverse.
>
> We study the Directional Matrix, Laban's description of 27 specific locations within the Kinesphere.
>
> We practice moving one-, two-, and three-dimensionally as we learn of Dimensions, Planes/Diameters, and Diagonals.
>
> We consider Spatial Pulls, Spatial Tensions, and Spatial Intent.
>
> We imagine that the Kinesphere is organized into various crystalline forms — Tetrahedron, Octahedron, Cube, Dodecahedron, or Icosahedron — and practice moving through these voluminous forms in specific sequences, which Laban called Scales.

I would often ask that students develop their own small-scale spatial forms (sometimes called the Platonic Solids). We would create a human-scale Icosahedron together, so that students could take turns moving within it to receive visual and kinesthetic reinforcement of this cerebral theory. By doing this, most dancers were able to travel along spatial pathways and to spatial destinations that they had seldom or never experienced. I believe that we open up new neuromuscular pathways by visiting new locations in the Kinesphere, thereby creating new possibilities in every aspect of our lives.

As students experienced and became fascinated by different aspects of Laban theory, they created research problems for themselves. For example:

> "How might using Laban's Directional Matrix impact my choreography for the ————————high school drum corp?"
>
> "Can I learn combinations in my ballet class more efficiently if I focus on the Modes of Shape Change being demonstrated (but not mentioned) by my teacher?"
>
> "Can my choreography for the upcoming UNM student concert be more interesting if I explore different Effort States and Drives within the phrases of movement I have already designed?"
>
> "What can I learn about my parents' ability to get along so harmoniously as they live and work together, by examining their Effort lives as they interact in various situations?"
>
> "Can I improve my alignment by focusing on my Spatial Intent in my flamenco class?"

"What will I learn if I interview a number of homeless people asking them about their relationships to their personal space or Kinesphere?"

Some students felt a need to investigate an aspect of Bartenieff Fundamentals in at least one of their MA II presentations, rather than an aspect of Shape, Effort, or Space Harmony. If a student could convince the class that this was appropriate, I would approve such a project, as I believe in honoring "aliveness" instead of sticking to a lesson plan even when it isn't serving students' needs and interests. One recent and memorable project involved a student who created a daily Bartenieff Fundamentals practice for her mother, who was obese, sedentary, in constant physical pain, and worked forty hours a week on a computer. The student made a videotaped interview of her mother at the beginning and end of the process and videotaped the two of them at regular intervals throughout the process of teaching/learning and practicing the Fundamental movement patterns. The results were deeply moving to all of us. The mother spoke of experiencing less and less pain as she learned and practiced more of the Fundamentals. Both mother and daughter — who had been somewhat estranged for a number of years — developed a closer bond than they had known for many years.

These MA II presentations usually included videotaped segments showing examples of "before" and "after," or a videotaped "before" and live "after." Almost always, the students ended up utilizing more L/BMA concepts in their research projects than they had set out to do. When one has this theoretical knowledge, of course, it makes perfect sense to use it as an opportunity arises, and their classmates and I always gave the students affirmation for any relevant application of Laban theory within their midterm and final presentations.

By applying L/BMA concepts in usually simple and direct ways to aspects of their lives that were of genuine importance, the students were able to understand the usefulness of these ideas and to gain confidence in their own ability to apply these theoretical tools to tackle other problems in their personal and dance lives.

Conclusion

Recently, a young woman who had just graduated with a BA in dance approached me. She thanked me warmly for having been her teacher over the past four years and said, "You really helped me to help myself grow."

I was deeply gratified by her comments, which confirmed some of the core beliefs that have guided me through the story I have shared in these pages:

> I am more effective as a teacher when I perceive each student as a whole person and a unique individual.
>
> Learning is most effective when the student is invited into the process and becomes an active participant.
>
> Increasing self-knowledge positively "… influences self-image, the single most important factor in determining an individual's success in any endeavor in life"(MacCrae-Campbell 1988, 18).
>
> Laban, Bartenieff, Hackney and the other creators of movement analysis have given us valuable tools to understand movement as an ongoing process, and to take control of our own positive change and growth.

I can happily report that most students completed theses courses having learned to value process at least as much as product, having lost the fear of not being "right," having generated significant self-knowledge and heightened self-esteem, and having learned that — within a supportive and caring community — they can use L/BMA tools to move forward in their lives.

References

Bartenieff, I. *Body Movement: Coping with the Environment.* New York: Routledge, 1980.

Clippinger, K. Principles of Dance Training. In Clarkson, P. and Skrinar, M. (ed.), *Science of Dancing Training.* Champaign, Il.: Human Kinetic Books, 1988. 45–90.

Cohen, B. *Sensing, Feeling and Action.* Northampton, Mass.: Contact Editions, 1993.

Evans, B. "The Multi-Colored Sky: A Call for Recognition and Validation of Differences through Movement." *Journal of Dance Education* 3 (1) (Summer 2003): 53–56.

Gardner, H. *Frame of Mind,* New York: Basic Books, 1983.

Gardner, H. *Intelligence Reframed: Multiple Intelligences for the 21st Century.* New York: Basic Books, 1999.

Hackney, P. *Making Connections: Total Body Integration through Bartenieff Fundamentals.* New York: Routledge, 2000.

Hartley, L. *Wisdom of the Body Moving.* Berkeley, Calif.: North Atlantic Books, 1995.

Laban, R. *A Vision of Dynamic Space.* Philadelphia: Falmer Press, 1984.

Laban, R. *Choreutics.* London: MacDonald and Evans, 1966.

Laban, R. *The Mastery of Movement.* MacDonald and Evans Limited, 1975.

MacRae-Campbell, L. "Whole Person Education." *In Context* 18 (Winter 1988): 16–18.

CHAPTER **2**

Dance Theory?

SUSAN LEIGH FOSTER

There are different genres of dance, from the simplest to the one
that is least so. They are all good, provided they express something, and the degree of their perfection increases with the variety
and scope of the expression. A dance that expresses grace and
dignity is good; a dance that creates a sort of conversation seems
to me better.[1]

"I don't think there is such a thing as 'dance theory.'"

"Great way to start: deny the existence of the thing you've been asked to
write about."

"No, seriously, there are dance theories or theories about dance, but I
can't imagine *a* dance theory."

"But is it just the singular versus plural that you're objecting to?"

"Well, maybe. Seems like the whole idea of what a theory is — a
hypothesis about what something is and how it works — implies that
there is more than one. Aren't there multiple theories about dance?
I mean, hundreds or thousands?"

"But if the use of the singular is your only objection, can't you just imagine 'dance theory' as the broader category that encompasses all theories?"

"Maybe. But now you've made me see another problem: To call it 'dance
theory' cordons it off as it own thing, separate from and comparable to

'dance history' or 'dance ethnography.' And I can't envision theory as operating at that kind of distance from either method or subject matter."

"Wait. You're saying theory is an integral part of research."

"It's woven into the entire creative/critical process."

"Maybe we should call it 'theorizing' instead of theory?"

"Ahhh. The gerund is always so satisfying. But seriously, theorizing can happen throughout the process of conducting research, whether one is making a dance or writing an essay. Theorizing is instigated whenever one asks oneself, 'What am I doing and why am I doing it?'"

"Nice work. You've managed to trash the title of your chapter, or is that why you insisted on the question mark? And you've opened up all these other issues, all in half a page."

"Okay. So, you have theories about what dance is and how it works, but how do you find out if they're right?"

"I'm not sure the purpose of theory is to be right or wrong. It's more like theories are either encompassing or reflexive, either broad or deep."

"I'm lost."

"So am I. Never mind. Let's think about it differently."

"But what if I have this theory that dance somehow reflects cultural values. How would I go about investigating it?"

"That's a good direction to pursue: the difference between theory and method. So, if you're thinking about dance and culture, maybe you would want to pursue an ethnographic method, looking closely at a given cultural situation, examining the significance of dance there, possibly comparing that situation to another that you have studied. But even as you're observing dancing in a given situation, you can be asking theoretical questions such as: 'What am I noticing about this dance and why: its spectacle? drama? intensity? organization? simplicity or complexity?' 'What am I taking time to write down about this dancing: the rhythm? the steps? the movements of bodies through space? the gestures?' 'What am I taking for granted, as being obvious or natural: the breath? the sweat? the dedication? the passion?' 'Who am I talking to about the dance and why?' 'How is my conception of culture influencing what I look at?' 'Am I imagining culture as cohesive and bounded: as porous? Migratory? As dominated by outside forces? And what difference does that make?' And, 'How is my presence as an observer changing what I am observing?'"

"You won't answer all those questions. You can't."

"But in the very act of raising them, you sustain a critically reflexive perspective on your work."

"You know what I think? A choreographer raises similar kinds of questions in making a dance."

"Like what?"

"Like, 'What's my conception of the body? Of expression? Of technique?' 'How do I want to represent gender? Community? The world?'"

"So, you mean you can reflect theoretical concerns in actions and not just in words?"

"Why not? Isn't that what Marxist theory implies?"

"But he makes a distinction between theory and something called 'praxis.'"

"But I don't think he meant that words are the theory part and praxis is the movement part, although many people have interpreted it that way. Often, theory and praxis are utilized to reinforce a binary between mind and body, or between thought and action. So, dance studio classes are often referred to as practical, and seminar classes are known as theoretical. But in my reading of Marx, he imagined these terms differently, as referencing an entire sequence of cultural productivity: from speculation to actualization. For Marx, and also for Gramsci, praxis is theoretically informed practice."[2]

"So, a dance class would be theoretically informed? But what theory is informing it?"

"I'm always asking that about dance classes. It seems to me that any dance class, through the activities or exercises it proposes, conveys certain ideas about what the body is. Does the class treat the body as a machine? As a vessel? As a precision instrument? As a source of ideas? As a vehicle for expression? How does the dancing discipline the body? Is physical pain considered to be a good thing, or an inevitable by-product of progress toward a goal? Is one body asked to compete with another? To support another? To partner another?"

"And you're saying that those attitudes reflect cultural values?"

"Well, that was on my mind because dances always say something about what it is to be a body, or an individual, or a member of a group. And then I was thinking about how other kinds of values are embedded in the choreography: whether the movement displays graceful lines and shapes; whether it focuses on rhythm; whether the dancers look identical or unique; whether they lift up and away from gravity or sink into it ... And I was reflecting on the process of making a dance, where the choreographer is always making choices about how bodies touch one another, how they repeat movements, how the movement relates to the music ... I could go on and on, but the point is that movement documents preferences."

"And so the question is whether these preferences resonate throughout other parts of the culture?"

"'Resonate'" is an interesting word choice."

"Well, the problem with the theory that dance reflects culture is that it makes dance a kind of passive by product or imprint of other more dominant cultural forces. But couldn't you also think about dance as producing culture, as generating cultural values through the ways in which it cultivates the body and brings people together?"[3]

"So does it do both?"

"I think theory encourages you to ask what is enabled by a given proposition and what is foreclosed."

"You mean, if I posit that movements are thoughts, what are the consequences of that?"

"Exactly. Many scholars believe that what is most important about dance is its ephemerality, the fact that it is intangible and vanishes. If that's your theory of dance, what does that imply about how you would study it or write about it?"

"Well, you would treat it very carefully. You would appreciate its transience and the fact that you can only imperfectly remember what you saw and felt. You might also pay a lot of attention to your own practice as an observer, asking yourself how and why you saw what you did."

"Psychoanalytic theories could help you with that kind of reflexive scrutiny. They consider how you might be projecting onto or otherwise transforming what you are seeing."[4]

"Alternatively, if you pursue the theory of dancing as a kind of thinking, then you notice and ignore different sets of things."

"You might look at how dancing is like talking, or how dance has language-like properties."[5]

"But this makes it sound as though you can never find out anything except what you already theorize to be the case."

"That's not what I'm arguing. On the contrary, theory helps you discover new things. As an integral part of investigation, it provides a flexible corpus of assumptions that are always subject to change depending on what you uncover during your ongoing research. I guess I tend to stress the role of theory in research because the emphasis on objectivity in Western culture over the past three centuries has obscured this dialectical back and forth between theory and inquiry that constitutes the research process. Proponents of an 'objective' approach have argued that the use of neutral observational tools would result in unbiased findings that could then be tested against other similar studies to determine their accuracy."

"That whole objective/subjective debate?"

"Exactly. I don't think there is such a thing as a neutral tool for looking at dance. Every checklist of movement features, every notation system devised, has values and preferences built into it that influence the resulting profile of the dance."

"Labanotation is a good example, isn't it? I don't understand how people can claim that it allows you to look at and compare the world's dances. For one thing, it organizes the body into center and periphery, and it privileges the movement of weight through time. How can you use it to look at contact improvisation? Or any improvisation for that matter?"

"Even the 'neutral' notions of space and time are culturally specific. Is space some geometric grid into which bodies move? Or is it produced by the interaction between body and environment? Is time metric? Cyclical? Steady or in flux?"[6]

"But don't you have to start out with some set of criteria for tracking the dancing? I know those features about choreography I mentioned earlier are culturally specific. They're obviously referencing central concerns of ballet and modern dance."

"But that's what's great about theory. It helps you take into account where and how you start. Theory encourages you to continuously reevaluate your own premises based on what you are learning."

"You make it sound like theory is everywhere, but I keep reading about specific theories, like feminist theory, or postcolonial theory. How do they relate to your idea about theorizing?"

"Those are catchall terms for various, sometimes contradictory theories, about … well, in the case of feminist theory, they are about gender; and for postcolonial theory, they address the condition and effects of having been colonized. But really, each of these terms represents an array of related hypotheses. For feminist theory, these hypotheses would address everything from women's role in the workplace to reproductive rights to whether or not there is something we can call women's experience, and if there is, how it could be represented.[7] And could it be represented across cultures and classes? For postcolonial theory, there are theories about what the nation is; how domination occurs politically, economically, and culturally; what constitutes resistance under such regimes; and what the enduring effects of colonization might be."[8]

"These are very important concerns, but it's hard to connect them directly with dance. We can look at who gets the more prestigious jobs in dance and why, or where the important venues are and who gets invited to present their work there. Or, when making a dance, it's obvious you need to decide what kind of gender roles you're going to invoke and who you want the ideal viewer to be."

"Dance scholars have been working on the same issues. They've used feminist theory to disentangle the biological body from the social body. Following feminist theory, they have proposed that gender is culturally constructed, and this has enabled them to analyze how male and female roles or masculine and feminine qualities are represented in dance.[9] They've looked at whether some kinds of dance or some kinds of work within dance are more masculine or feminine, and why.[10] They've examined how standards for the ideal female and male bodies operate, and how these reinforce or defy cultural norms.[11] They've considered whether certain genres of dance presume a gendered gaze from their ideal viewer.[12] And they've analyzed how gendered identity intersects with and complicates racial, classed, and sexual identities in a variety of different dance forms.[13] And similarly, with postcolonial theory, scholars have interrogated the exportation and importation of dance by colonial powers.[14] They've probed the ways that dance has been utilized in nation formation.[15] They've tracked the potential for agency under colonial conquest.[16] And they've even contemplated how dance history itself has been influenced by imperialist history."[17]

"What do you mean 'dance history itself'"?

"I mean the standard assumptions you find in many dance history books about the historical evolution of dance from 'primitive' to 'civilized.' All those dance histories that start with 'the origins' of dance as illustrated by African dance, and then 'spectacular' or 'courtly' dance as illustrated by Asia; and then they go back to the Greeks, as if 'Africa' and 'Asia' represented something more ancient than classical antiquity. Then they move forward through the Renaissance, the development of ballet in Europe, then modern dance in the United States... . These histories reflect a set of assumptions about progress and cultural refinement that were used to rationalize imperialist conquest."

"We're talking about how power operates, aren't we?"

"That's right. Theory helps you think about who has power and who is disenfranchised or marginalized and why.[18] Theory asks you to consider what a given set of assumptions will authorize and what they will repress."

"Seems like dance studies is often repressed within the academy."

"Yes, well, dance as an activity or as a subject in any form had a very rough time getting accepted into the university. I remember as an undergraduate going to the provost of my college and requesting credit for a dance class. He responded, 'Dance is a noncognitive activity, and has no place in the university curriculum.'"

"I've never experienced that kind of attitude, but it's true that dance is always sneaking in through the back door of physical education or theater arts, or sometimes music. Dance teachers manage to argue for its validity based on the idea that dancing offers a unique way of knowing the world — which is really a wonderful proposition."

"But then sometimes that unique identity for dance has been used to justify placing it on the periphery of academic studies. I remember that in my first job when prospective students were led past the dance studio, the guide announced, 'This is the dance studio where students come to blow off steam and relax after their academic classes.' And then there was the dean who informed me that 'Academic courses develop the mind, and dance classes develop the heart.'"

"I used to hear that more than I do now. But most students still explain their investment in dance as a passion."

"I think what's interesting about those kinds of statements is the organic relationship they presume between dance and other fields of inquiry. Instead of imagining that every kind of inquiry cultivates the mind, the heart, the body, and the spirit, they partition the person into symbolic segments, such as mind, heart, or body, and then assign talents and needs to each."

"So, it's a theory about the 'whole' person as made up of a bunch of different functions?"

"Precisely."

"So, where does music fit into that model, and what about music theory?"

"That's a wonderful question. I never thought about music theory in relation to the kinds of cultural and critical theories we've been discussing."

"Why not?"

"Well, music theory is the study of a given composition's harmonic and rhythmic structure. It examines the underlying principles of the scale, melody, and tonal progression and the structures of meter and tempo that are generating the composition. And it looks at forms the composition as a whole can take, such as a sonata or a fugue."

"So, the equivalent in dance would look at the basic vocabulary of a given piece, how the moves are related to one another, and then also how they are sequenced. And then also how a given composition develops through the use of theme and variation, or ABA, or story line."

"That's where the analogy breaks down. Music theory has focused exclusively on the internal structure of a given work with little or no reference to what it might mean or how it might signify something in the world. In fact, only recently have scholars who call themselves musicologists begun to forge connections between musical structure and structures of feeling, or even gender, and narrative."[19]

"And that's more what you think dance theory — I mean, theorizing — can do?"

"Yes, I suppose you could have a theory that the meaning of a dance was complete within its use of variation, rhythmic phrasing, repetition, and reiteration, etc. But the body always signifies so much more than that kind of formalist analysis would allow."

"You mean, it has a certain sex, or color, or personality, or a certain kind of intimacy with other bodies?"

"And music theory, at least as it has been traditionally formulated, doesn't address those kinds of valences. Mind you, the fact that music scholars make these claims about the sophisticated and complex internal structure of music, and also the fact that it can be notated so effectively, have given music a lot of credibility within the academy, especially when compared with dance."

"Music has mathematics and logic and form, and dance has …"

"Passion, evanescence, and spontaneity. Or at least that's the way the academy has often viewed it. Remember the provost's comments."

"And in terms of the theory part, departments of music have music theory as one of the subjects and music history as another?"

"Yes, and both of those fields typically focus only on Western classical music. Then they teach 'ethnomusicology' as a subject that addresses musical practices in the rest of the world."

"And what about popular music?"

"That's a whole other domain that music in the academy has only reluctantly addressed."

"I think it's a big problem in dance departments as well."

"And in dance studies. Concert dance, mostly ballet and modern, has been the subject of most dance studies. And again, dance anthropologists have looked at the rest of the world's dances."[20]

"Joann Keali'inohumoku tried to call attention to that in her essay "An Anthropologist Looks at Ballet as a Form of Ethnic Dance," didn't she?"[21]

"A wonderful text. Really inspiring."

"I'd love to see a list of the writings you think are foundational."

"I'm reluctant to make up such a list."

"Why?"

"Well, the very fact of establishing a canon of writings consolidates authority in a way that runs counter to the way of thinking about theory that I'm advocating. Theory isn't something to master in and of itself. It's there to help you out with a particular quest or predicament. Say, for example, you love salsa, and you don't understand why nobody has written anything substantive about its history and meaning. You can look to historiography and theories of history to think about why dance history has constituted itself in the way that it has.[22] And you can look to theories of race, identification, and popular culture to begin to understand how and why salsa matters to those who dance it."[23]

"Any given research project would engage with its own specific set of theories? Seems as though most of the projects I hear about are engaging with theories about race, or class, or gender, or sexuality, especially at this moment in history when we are discovering so much about how those categories of identity have been formulated in different places and for different political purposes."[24]

"But, still, theory is there to assist in interrogating power. It shouldn't claim power in and of itself."

"A while ago, you talked about cultural and critical theories as distinct from music theory. What do those terms stand for?"

"They're catchall terms for new paradigms of research that resulted from a set of epistemological upheavals taking place during the 1960s, '70s, and '80s. Prompted largely by Ferdinand de Saussure's and Charles Pierce's studies of language earlier in the century, a whole group of theorists, mostly French at first, began to question assumptions about what a text is.[25] They argued that all forms of cultural production are and can be read as texts: films, photographs, fashion—you name it.[26] Then they proposed that the author is really an effect created in the text, not somebody who created the text.[27] And they even argued that the reader is the author!"[28]

"You mean the viewer would be the choreographer?"

"Great translation. As you can imagine, this called into question all kinds of power relations that had previously been taken for granted. Scholars began to analyze all kinds of cultural artifacts and events as having the same degree of complexity and significance as verbal texts. And they began to look for cultural significance as the product of exchange and interaction among varieties of cultural production.[29] They dismantled the 'natural' connections between physical appearance and race, anatomical sex and gender, and sexuality and sexual orientation. And they looked critically at the role and function of the author in writing history or ethnography.[30] They even began to see individual identity as historically and culturally specific."

"And your ideas about theorizing come out of this?"

"Yes. That's their historical specificity."

"So, theories have a history?"

"Theories seem to come in batches. They share certain assumptions about the nature of reality at a given moment in history. Right now, scholars are still pursuing the ramifications of these theories about language that enable them to question the naturalness of equating sex with gender, or race with color. And it's been very productive to map out all the ways that those categories of gender and class and race and sexuality interact with one another."

"Sounds like all these theories constitute something like a paradigm. Thomas Kuhn wrote a wonderful book about how paradigms inform scientific investigation, and then suddenly they don't fit the data anymore, and someone comes up with a new paradigm."[31]

"Michel Foucault called them "epistemes," and he argued that they govern the production of knowledge in all fields during a given historical period."[32]

"So there are theories of history, and histories of theory. I like it."

"But how do you teach about this?"

"By asking students to undertake the same kind of translation you just did."

"You mean substituting dance for text?"

"Not just for text, but for any term that's being analyzed. I ask students to try to read about lots of different cultural phenomena and to try replacing the key terms under consideration with 'dance,' 'body,' 'choreographer,' and so forth. So, instead of Foucault's disciplining of the prisoner's body, think about disciplining the dancing body; instead of Mulvey's notion of the masculine, heterosexual gaze in film, the equivalent in dance, etc."[33]

"But what if it doesn't work? What if the theory doesn't fit?"

"That's when it gets interesting. That's when you see what is specific about dance as an endeavor and when you see what it can offer back as argument against or refinement of another subject's theory."

"So, again, the thing about what does theory elucidate and what does it ignore?"

"Yes, and what's great about focusing on theoretical issues is that you can talk with scholars and also artists who are each pursuing very different kinds of projects. The theory serves as a common focus for your evaluations of how it works or doesn't work."

"So, it creates a bridge between one's own and others' research? I like that. It means you can talk to one another even if you don't know the specifics of their project."

"Right. You can talk to them about the usefulness of the theories and methods they're using."

"But that can't be your only idea about how to teach about theory."

"Well, I guess one other important suggestion that's related to the idea about translation is to think choreographically about whatever it is you are observing or even reading about."

"Choreographically?"

"Well, you know the term 'choreography' first originated in the early eighteenth century, when it was used to refer to the writing of a dance in notated form, which is pretty interesting, given what we've been talking about. But, as far as I can figure, it started meaning the creation of a dance in the early nineteenth century. When I use the term it has more to do with the idea of how you make decisions about what the next move in a dance will be and why that matters. So, I'd ask a student to envision how bodies are moving; how they are relating to one another; what kinds of identities they are conveying; what stories they are telling; to look at how they are integrated into and/or framed by their surroundings; and to try to sense what their purpose is in doing what they're doing. Things like that."

"So, look at how the bodies are moving in the film or on the street or in the kitchen or wherever?"

"Exactly. And even try to imagine how they are moving in a text. So, not only the bodies being written about but also the author's body. Try to fathom what that body's posture is and how it's moving."

"You're crazy."

"Probably. But it does help elucidate what the author's theory is and what it's addressing and what it's ignoring. And while you're doing that, you should also notice how your own body is reacting to it all. Ask yourself what are you feeling, physically and emotionally, about what you're seeing or reading."

"And it's interesting that learning how to dance and choreographing dances might make you a more astute reader of texts."

"I just have one more question: What's this guy Condillac doing in this conversation?"

"Good close reading. I often start with the footnotes, myself. And the footnotes in this essay are certainly going to historicize my ideas about theory. Anyway, let's see … why Condillac? I've been reading him recently because he and Rousseau both come up with theories about the origin of language and its relation to gesture."

"Yes, it's always interesting to look at claims about origins, isn't it? Like Martha Graham claiming that if you have to ask yourself whether or not you should become a choreographer, you'll never be one, because only those who never ask will succeed."

"As though the origin of inspiration should never be examined?"

"Exactly. I find that really unhelpful. I ask myself every day what a choreographer is, and I think it's a good thing to think about. Anyway, what about these guys?"

"Well, Condillac thought that language was preceded by a kind of primitive song/dance. When people were afraid, or excited, or in need, they would spontaneously gesture and cry out. He contends that eventually people realized that these gestures were very helpful in signaling, say, the approach of a wild animal, so that everyone would know it was coming, and, even though they hadn't seen it themselves, they could see the gesture of the one who had and therefore protect themselves. Both speech and dance, he argues, grew out of this protolanguage."[34]

"So, it's natural to gesture/cry spontaneously in response to danger. And then speech grows out of this primal responsiveness, as the thing that it is not. That makes speech logical and contractual whereas the gesture/cry is natural and immediate?"

"Yes, and Condillac is perhaps the first philosopher to think about language in relation to the body this way. But what's also interesting about him is that he spent a fair amount of time discussing how dance, like speech, evolved into a standardized set of conventional signs that people use to express themselves. Like language, dance developed into a contractual system of signification. But then just a few years later, Rousseau stages the same origin, only he puts the cries first and the gestures second, and he dismisses the gestures by saying that a person would never be moved by someone merely gesturing their danger.[35] Only words can inspire sympathy."[36]

"So, just the opposite of Martha Graham proclaiming that movement never lies."

"Right. And also quite different from Condillac, because Condillac proposes that the cries and gestures each evolve into two distinct but equally persuasive symbolic systems, whereas Rousseau creates an oppositionality between them. For Rousseau, gesture can only express 'physical' needs, while language expresses a person's thoughts and feelings."[37]

"But what's your theory about all this? Why are you interested in it?"

"I suspect that around this time there was a paradigm shift in how Europeans viewed or learned the world's dances. They went from seeing the dances as different in degree to seeing them as different in kind from their own."

"Just like the contrast between Condillac's and Rousseau's notions of gesture and language."

"Right. And I'm hoping this could tell us something about how colonization worked."

"Or even what the body of 'the colonizer' would be like. But how do you investigate historical records to determine when or if this is the case?"

"I think historical inquiry is always motivated by the historian's own political and social circumstances. I'm trying to understand how all those histories of dance I was talking about earlier ever got written. What view of dance was authorizing them? How could we imagine a different way to write a history of the world's dances?"

"So, you want to redress the power imbalances implicit in the model that starts with 'primitive Africa' and ends with ballet and modern dance?"

"Theories are often motivated by a sense of social responsibility, a need to imagine how we could make the world better, or at least how we could understand what's wrong with it."

"Dances are often constructed in response to those same motivations. Choreographers want to present visions of what the body is or could be. They just utilize a different format for presenting the same concerns about power."

"And who's got what kind of power. That's why I prefer to imagine choreographers as theorizing corporeality and scholars as theorizing what dance is, and both of these pursuits as parallel forms of research, capable of mutually informing one another."

"So, the writing becomes a translation of the dancing?"

"Well, obviously writing and dancing are profoundly different endeavors, and you can't really translate the one into the other. But you can create a parity of status for each, so that the writing doesn't 'capture' the dancing, and the dancing doesn't elude the writing."

"So writing and dancing become capable of having a conversation?"

"A conversation — what a good metaphor."

"Should we call it a duet instead?"

Acknowledgment

Many thanks to Harmony Bench for participating in this "conversation."

Notes

1. Etienne Bonnot and Abbé de Condillac, [1746] *Essay on the Origin of Human Knowledge*, trans. and ed. Hans Aarsleff (Cambridge: Cambridge University Press, 2001), 118.

2. For a good introduction to Marxist theory, see Frederic Jameson, *Marxism and Form* (Princeton: Princeton University Press, 1974) and Terry Eagleton, *Marxism and Literary Criticism* (Berkeley: University of California Press, 1976). See also Antonio Gramsci, *Prison Notebooks* (New York: Columbia University Press, 1992). Many of Marx's theories about capital and commodification are explored in Lynn Garafola's pioneering study *Diaghilev's Ballet Russes* (New York: Oxford University Press, 1989).
3. Cynthia Novack proposed to study dance as culture in her study of contact improvisation. See *Sharing the Dance: Contact Improvisation and American Culture* (Madison: University of Wisconsin Press, 1990).
4. For a good account of psychoanalytic theory's potential relevance to dance, see Peggy Phelan, "Immobile Legs, Stalled Words: Psychoanalysis and Moving Deaths," *Mourning Sex: Performing Public Memories* (London: Routledge, 1997) 44–72.
5. Adrienne Kaeppler pioneered in this line of inquiry with her analysis of Tongan dance. See "Method and Theory in Analyzing Dance Structure with an Analysis of Tongan Dance," *Ethnomusicology* 16.2: 173–217.
6. See, for example, Jacqueline Shea Murphy's account of Native American conceptions of time in their dances in *The People Have Never Stopped Dancing: Native American Dance and Modern Dance History* (forthcoming).
7. Good introductions to feminist theory with specific relevance to dance studies include Teresa De Lauretis's discussion of film in *Alice Doesn't: Feminism, Semiotics, Cinema* (Bloomington: Indiana University Press, 1984); Judith Butler's conception of gender as performance in *Gender Trouble: Feminism and the Subversion of Identity* (New York: Routledge: 1990); and Susan Bordo's assessment of the status of the female body in contemporary culture in *Unbearable Weight: Feminism, Western Culture, and the Body* (Berkeley: University of California Press, 1993).
8. Good overviews of postcolonial theoretical issues include Dipesh Chakrabarty, *Provincializing Europe* (Princeton: Princeton University Press, 2000); Gayatri Chakravorty Spivak, *A Critique of Postcolonial Reason: Toward a History of the Vanishing Present* (Cambridge, Mass.: Harvard University Press, 1999); and Homi K. Bhabha, *The Location of Culture* (New York: Routledge, 1994).
9. These include Judith Lynn Hanna, *Dance, Sex, Gender: Signs of Identity, Dominance, Defiance and Desire* (Chicago: University of Chicago Press, 1988); Sally Banes, *Dancing Women: Female Bodies on Stage* (New York: Routledge, 1998); Christy Adair, *Women and Dance: Sylphs and Sirens* (New York: New York University Press, 1992); Ann Daly, *Done into Dance: Isadora Duncan in America* (Bloomington: Indiana University Press, 1995); Susan Leigh Foster, *Choreography and Narrative: Ballet's Staging of Story and Desire* (Bloomington: Indiana University Press, 1996); *Dance, Gender and Culture*, ed. Helen Thomas (New York: Palgrave, 1995); Ramsay Burt, *The Male Dancer: Bodies, Spectacle, Sexualities* (London: Routledge, 1995).
10. These include Ellen Graff, *Stepping Left: Dance and Politics in New York City 1928–1942* (Durham: Duke University Press, 1997) and Linda J. Tomko, *Dancing Class: Gender, Ethnicity and Social Divides in American Dance 1890–1920* (Bloomington: Indiana University Press, 1999).
11. These include Novack and Ann Daly, "The Balanchine Women: Of Hummingbirds and Channel Swimmers," *The Drama Review* 31.1 (T113) (Spring 1987): 8–21.
12. These include Susan Manning, *Ecstasy and the Demon: Feminism and Nationalism in the Dances of Mary Wigman* (Berkeley: University of California Press, 1993) and Susan Leigh Foster "The Ballerina's Phallic Pointe," *Corporealities: Dancing Knowledge, Culture, and Power*, ed. Susan Leigh Foster (London: Routledge, 1996) 1–24.
13. These include *Dancing Desires: Choreographing Sexualities On and Off the Stage*, ed. Jane Desmond (Madison: University of Wisconsin Press, 2001); Valerie A. Briginshaw, *Dance, Space and Subjectivity* (New York: Palgrave Macmillan, 2001); Susan Manning, "Black Voices, White Bodies: The Performance of Race and Gender in How long Brethren." *American Quarterly* 50.1 (1998): 24–46; Ann Cooper-Albright, *Choreographing Difference: The Body and Identity in Contemporary Dance* (Middletown, Conn.: Wesleyan University Press, 1997); and Thomas DeFrantz, *Dancing Revelations: Alvin Ailey's Embodiment of African American Culture* (New York: Oxford University Press, 2004).

14. See especially Marta Savigliano, *Tango and the Political Economy of Passion* (Boulder: Westview Press, 1995).

15. For example: Janet O'Shea, *At Home in the World: A History of Bharata Natyam* (Middletown, Conn.: Wesleyan University Press, forthcoming) and Avanthi Meduri, "Bharata Natyam — What Are You?" *Rasamanjar-i* 2.2 (Aug 1997): 22–43.

16. Rachel Fensham "Deterritorializing Dance: Tension and the Wire," *Discourses in Dance* 1.2 (2002) 63–84.

17. See Savigliano and also Ananya Chatterjea, *Butting Out* (Middletown, Conn.: Wesleyan University Press, 2004).

18. Dance scholars who have addressed this issue of power include Savigliano and Randy Martin in both *Performance as Political Act: The Embodied Self* (New York: Bergin & Garvey, 1990) and *Critical Moves: Dance Studies in Theory and Practice* (Durham: Duke University Press, 1998).

19. Examples of this musicological approach include Susan McClary, *Feminine Endings: Music, Gender, and Sexuality* (Minneapolis: University of Minnesota Press, 2002) and Jacques Attali, *Noise: The Political Economy of Music*, trans. Brian Massumi (Minneapolis: University of Minnesota Press, 1987).

20. For studies that redress this imbalance by focusing on several varieties of dancing, see Mark Franko in *The Work of Dance: Labor, Movement, and Identity in the 1930s* (Middletown, Conn.: Wesleyan University Press, 2002) and Ramsay Burt, *Alien Bodies: Representations of Modernity, 'Race' and Nation in Early Modern Dance* (London: Routledge, 1998).

21. See Joann Keali'inohomoku, "An Anthropologist Looks at Ballet as a Form of Ethnic Dance," *What Is Dance?: Readings in Theory and Criticism*, ed. Roger Copeland and Marshall Cohen (Oxford: Oxford University Press, 1983), 533–549.

22. See, for example, Hayden White, *Metahistory: The Historical Imagination in Nineteenth-Century Europe* (Baltimore: Johns Hopkins University Press, 1973) and "The Value of Narrativity in the Representation of Reality," *Critical Inquiry* 7.1 (1980) 5–27; Louis Mink, "History and Fiction as Modes of Comprehension," *New Literary History* 1.3 (1970) 541–558; and R.G. Collingwood, *The Idea of History* (Oxford: Clarendon Press, 1962).

23. Scholars who have pioneered in race theory in relation to dance include Brenda Dixon-Gottschild, *Digging the Africanist Presence in American Performance: Dance and Other Contexts* (Westport, Conn.: Greenwood Press, 1996) and *The Black Dancing Body: A Geography from Coon to Cool* (New York: Palgrave, 2003); Thomas DeFrantz, ed., *Dancing Revelations and Dancing Many Drums* (Madison: University of Wisconsin Press, 2002).

24. See Michel Foucault, *The Archaeology of Knowledge*, trans. A. M. Sheridan Smith (New York: Pantheon, 1972).

25. For overviews of this intellectual movement, see Fredric Jameson, *The Prison-House of Language: A Critical Account of Structuralism and Russian Formalism* (Princeton: Princeton University Press, 1974); *Structuralism and Since: From Lévi-Strauss to Derrida*, ed. John Sturrock (New York: Oxford University Press, 1981); Umberto Eco, *A Theory of Semiotics* (Bloomington: Indiana University Press, 1979); *Textual Strategies: Perspectives in Post-Structuralist Criticism*, ed. Josué Harari (Ithaca: Cornell University Press, 1979); Jonathan Culler, *Structuralist Poetics: Structuralism, Linguistics, and the Study of Literature* (London: Routledge and Kegan Paul, 1975); and Kaja Silverman, *The Subject of Semiotics* (New York: Oxford University Press, 1983).

26. See Yüri Lotman, *The Structure of the Artistic Text*, trans. Ronald Vroon (Ann Arbor: University of Michigan Press, 1977); Roland Barthes, *Writing Degree Zero*, trans. Annette Lavers and Colin Smith (New York: Hill and Wang, 1967), *Mythologies*, trans. Annette Lavers (New York: Hill and Wang, 1977), *Image, Music, Text*, trans. Stephen Heath (New York: Hill and Wang, 1977); and Michel De Certeau, *The Practice of Everyday Life*, trans. Steven Rendall (Berkeley: University of California Press, 1988).

27. See Michel Foucault, "What Is an Author?" *Textual Strategies*, ed. Josué Harari, and Barthes, "The Death of the Author," *Image, Music, Text*, 142–148.

28. See Roland Barthes, *S/Z*, trans. Richard Miller (New York: Hill and Wang, 1974).

29. In dance studies this approach is exemplified by Janet Adshead-Lansdale, *Dancing Texts: Intertextuality in Interpretation* (London: Dance Books, 1999) and Mark Franko, *The Dancing Body in Renaissance Choreography* (Birmingham, Ala.: Summa Pub., 1986).

30. See essays by Mark Franko, Lena Hammergren, and Sally Ann Ness in *Corporealities: Dancing Knowledge, Culture, and Power,* ed. Susan Leigh Foster (London: Routledge, 1996). See also Marta Savigliano, *Angora Matta: Fatal Acts of North-South Translation* (Middletown, Conn.: Wesleyan University Press, 2003).
31. See Thomas Kuhn, *The Structure of Scientific Revolutions* (Chicago: University of Chicago Press, 1962).
32. See Michel Foucault, *The Order of Things: An Archaeology of the Human Sciences* (New York: Vintage Books, 1973).
33. See Michel Foucault, *Discipline and Punish: The Birth of the Prison,* trans. Alan Sheridan (New York: Vintage Books, 1979) and Laura Mulvey, "Visual Pleasure and Narrative Cinema," *Issues in Feminist Film Criticism,* ed. Patricia Evans (Bloomington: Indiana University Press, 1990).
34. See Condillac 114–116. For his views on dance, see pages 118–119.
35. Jean-Jacques Rousseau, *Essay on the Origin of Languages,* ed. and trans. Victor Gourevitch (New York: Harper & Row, 1986) 240–241.
36. Rousseau 243.
37. Rousseau 243.

CHAPTER 3

From Improvisation to Choreography: The Critical Bridge

LARRY LAVENDER AND JENNIFER PREDOCK-LINNELL

We believe that the most important goal of dance education at the college and university level is to teach people to make dances. Even those students who aim to become something other than a choreographer — say, a performer, a critic, an historian, a Labanotator, a technique teacher, a designer, an administrator, or some other kind of dance professional — will do a better job for dance if they have had experience actually composing dances. Indeed, the work done by everyone else in the dance world is in a sense parasitic on that of the choreographer; if dance makers do not make dances, the rest are out of business.

When we talk about dance making, we have in mind the skills of *improvising* (both the "free" and "structured" sort), *composing* in the sense of shaping and forming movement material, and *criticism*: observing, describing, analyzing, interpreting, evaluating, and revising both the work in progress and the completed dance. These are complementary sets of skills. In fact, they are so intertwined that we would divide them only for discussion. Otherwise, as far as we are concerned, dance making simply is these three things combined: improvising, composing, and criticizing.

Among college and university dance educators who specialize in teaching choreography, it is widely agreed that this training should begin with improvisation. Indeed, semester- or year-long courses in improvisation are often required of students before they begin to work on choreographing full-fledged dances. No doubt a main reason for positioning improvisation as a starting point is that it is equally amenable to the artistic preferences both of teachers who believe that creativity in dance is primarily a matter of self-expression, and those for whom it is primarily a matter of form and structure. Indeed, the literature on the teaching and learning of improvisation and choreography is packed with form- and expression-based movement prompts and exercises. (We are thinking here of texts by Elizabeth Hayes [1955], Doris Humphrey [1959], Louis Horst [1961], Blom and Chaplin [1982], Alma Hawkins [1988], Sandra Minton [1991], Jaqueline Smith-Autard [1992], Daniel Nagrin [1993], Stuart Hodes [1998], and others.) Briefly, form-based exercises isolate and focus on such basic dance elements as space, shape, energy, motif, theme, and variation, to name just a few. Expression-based prompts, on the other hand, invite students to delve into their memories, beliefs, hopes, fears, and dreams, and then to generate simple movement sequences, or even whole dances, that symbolize or represent these facets of the students' unique identities. Dance educator Nora Ambrosia (1999) sums up the rationale often underlying the use of expression-based prompts when she writes that "Improvisation and creative movement are two dance genres that do not necessarily require participants to have a background in dance technique.... . These two genres are focused on self-expression and self-exploration" (87).

Interestingly, the literature is virtually silent on just how it is that improvisational work is actually supposed to function as a preparation for choreography. It just seems to be assumed that experience in spontaneously *exploring* basic elements and concepts of movement, and/or discovering the "self" in and through movement, prepares students later to *compose* dances. After many years of teaching improvisation and choreography and wondering about the connection between the two, we have come to doubt that skill in composing with movement follows automatically from experience in exploring movement or oneself through improvisation. This is because, in and of themselves, we find that improvisation exercises do not sharpen students' awareness in any lasting way either of their own aesthetic values or those of others, nor do they compel students (mentally or physically) to exercise and test their ideas about dance as art. In short, improvisational work — insofar as it privileges intuitive spontaneity and preverbal, nonreflective "thinking in movement," to use Maxine Sheets-Johnstone's (1981) famous expression — generally does not develop in students the kind of *critical consciousness* that we think is imperative to their future success as choreographers.[1]

In this chapter, we flesh out the thinking behind these assertions, and suggest how teachers can make sure the improvisation course will function well as a pre-choreography training ground. As a first step, we distinguish from three other pedagogical aims that might be served by improvisation the specific aim of preparing students for dance making.

Pedagogical Aims of Improvisation

Improvisation can be and routinely is practiced and/or "taught" with a variety of aims in mind. Often improvisation exercises are given to students in beginning-level technique classes to help them discover their capacities for moving and dancing in ways other than those with which they are already familiar—to develop a new and improved sense of their kinesthetic and somatic selves. Through this, it is thought, each student will develop an empowering sense of emotional, if not spiritual well-being, brought about through repeated experiences of open-ended movement explorations shared with others.

Improvisation is used within technique classes also as a supplement to standard warm-up exercises and class combinations. Here the aim is to develop versatile performers who can literally think (in movement) on their feet and respond spontaneously and unself-consciously to all manner of movement prompts, and thereby assist in the actual creation of new dances by generating movement material for a choreographer or director later to shape into a work for performance. Students who become skilled improvisers are able to come up with clear movement motifs and even extended passages of interesting movement virtually on command. Students who have developed these abilities in addition to a strong technical base are believed to have a noticeable edge in the competitive job market for dancers.

Perhaps seeking to capitalize on these two aims of/for improvisation, some teachers endeavor to teach students to spontaneously create full-fledged performances through free-form or structured improvisations. Rather than to think of improvisation merely as a tool for self-awareness and discovery, or for the creation of source material later to be crafted into a dance, these teachers think of improvisation itself as performance in its own right, equivalent in aesthetic merit and artistic import to reflectively crafted and repeatedly rehearsed dance. For these teachers, the crucial values achieved through improvisational dance are spontaneity, a sense of surprise (because anything may happen onstage at any time), and the liberation of the individual dancer from what is seen as a somewhat oppressive system of control by the traditional choreographer.

Finally, some teachers use improvisation specifically as a way of developing in students the skills of movement invention and development required for successful dance composition. While these teachers recognize and endorse the values of the other aims of improvisation, they direct students in improvisational work primarily to ready them later to design and compose dance works. This pedagogy focuses on the improvisational embodiment of specific choreographic concepts and artistic principles; movements and passages of movement improvised by students are used as samples for intellectual analysis, further bodily exploration, and as points of departure for focused and critically reflective exercises in dance design.

While the same kind of improvisational prompts and exercises may be employed in the service of each of these four "aims" of improvisation, success in student learning is measured quite differently in each case.

Students' success in learning improvisation specifically as a precursor to choreography is not appropriately measured by how much they come to know about themselves, or by how well they are able to perform as dancers in others' works, or by how much creative assistance they might provide other choreographers. As valuable as all of these achievements may be, they do not develop in students the critical consciousness necessary for choreography. To accomplish that goal, we argue that improvisation should be taught, and students' progress in it measured instead by the degree to which they are able to generate, manipulate, and develop movement material for their own choreographic works. Before developing these ideas further, let's think a bit about the ways in which dances are seen and valued within the Western concert dance tradition.

Expression and Form

We have noted that the literature on teaching and learning improvisation and choreography is packed with form- and expression-based movement prompts. Interestingly, regardless of whether a dance is created from one or another of these conceptual bases, or through some combination of them, finished concert dance works tend to be analyzed and evaluated primarily in terms of their form and structure rather than in terms of expressive power. Put another way, while the dance world (particularly in academia) has long been deeply invested in promoting the idea and value of self-expression, by itself the expressive power or emotional intensity of a dance is not generally considered sufficient to judge it as successful, or good. The well-designed dance typically is judged superior to the poorly designed one even when both can be said to "be about" or equally "expressive of" the same thing. Thus most choreography teachers regularly find themselves exhorting their students to edit, revise, and refine the form of even the most intensely expressive dances, because their works must be both emotionally powerful and well designed to earn critical praise.

The history of this dual criteria for the assessment of dance works extends at least as far back as the early decades of the twentieth century, when modern dance migrated into college and university curricula, and the notion of systematically teaching dance making first arose. Educational dance pioneers such as Margaret H'Doubler, who wrote the first curriculum for dance in higher education in 1926 at the University of Wisconsin, forcefully espoused a hybrid formalist/expressionist paradigm for the successful dance work. For H'Doubler (1925), art was properly defined as "the *adequate* translation of emotional experience into some external form" (11; emphasis ours). H'Doubler's ideas are echoed in virtually every text on the teaching and learning of choreography, and to the extent that these ideas hold sway in actual dance curricula, a greater pedagogical burden is placed on the shoulders of improvisation teachers who favor expression-based exercises than on their form-oriented counterparts. Specifically, if they expect their students to be recognized as "getting better" at dance making, teachers focusing heavily on expression must find ways to teach students not only to express themselves, but also how to shape their expressive impulses appropriately — or, as H'Doubler would say, "adequately" — as art.

Some teachers (and students) might reasonably resist this dual pedagogical burden on feminist grounds, characterizing the idea of "mastering" formal structures and adhering to "principles" of choreography as a tired legacy of modernist formalism, a tradition many characterize as one of patriarchal hegemony over art. To teach choreography in accordance with that tradition, it might be argued, is to send a message to dance students (the vast majority of whom are women) that formalism possesses or represents some "truth" about dance, if not about life and human experience generally. Against H'Doubler's paradigm of the dance work as a well-crafted and formally coherent unity, then, it might legitimately be insisted that what really matters is not aesthetic value at all, but rather the free expression through movement of one or another aspect or dimension of the artist's personal identity.

The feminist critique of modernist formalism raises very complicated issues, and there is insufficient time here to flesh them out adequately, much less to resolve them.[2] Suffice it to say that we agree that it is not right to teach improvisation and choreography strictly under the formalist banner; like every tradition, formalism cannot automatically be held to be universally valid or superior to any other. Thus it is never appropriate for teachers to espouse *any* rules or principles of art or dance as "the truth" about art. To do so would be to suggest wrongly to students that choreography is reducible to a kind of formula or recipe. We also agree that at the beginning of students' training in improvisation/choreography, the first obligation of the teacher is to help them become comfortable expressing themselves in movement (and in words). Indeed, unless students feel at ease with such expression, they will neither enjoy nor try very hard at dance making.

It does not follow, however, that improvisation and choreography students should be encouraged simply to ignore, or write off as "oppressive," such basic issues of dance craft as how to create an effective beginning or ending of a work, or how to utilize motifs, repetition, and contrast within a dance. These are fundamental and specific skills of *composition* in dance, and while what makes a beginning an "effective" one will likely be different in each dance, to create an effective beginning should be the aim of every dance maker. On the other hand, there seems to be no specific skill of "expression." Apart from identifying and praising visible aesthetic attributes of a work, there seems to be no way in which a choreography teacher might support the claim that a student is "improving" at expression.[3] In dance, as in other arts in which the work is experienced primarily through vision, the work itself as it is concretized in form is where a student's expressive accomplishments are or are not to be located.[4]

Edward S. Casey, in "Expression and Communication in Art" (1971), underscores this assertion through his analysis of the way that ordinary linguistic expression differs significantly from expression in the visual arts. Casey writes that the phenomenal surface of language "does not in itself typically engage our attention; what is presented to us phonically or in print — the 'vehicle' — is normally surpassed and even suppressed as we attend to the specific meaning conveyed by this vehicle." On the other hand, in the visual arts, "our attention is riveted directly onto the phenomenal surface; what we are looking for happens at or on this surface, not beyond or behind it. The expressive meaning is not experienced as detached from the presented gesture … it is felt as inherent in the phenomenal surface" (198). Following Casey's point, we hold that the specific pedagogical goal of the improvisation/choreography teacher is to help students enthusiastically put to use through conscious compositional acts whatever skills of movement design they possess at any given moment, and to gain these skills in the first place.

While movement concepts alone may serve as the basis for choreographic design, ideas and concepts from such other domains as literature, myth, ritual, psychology, politics, and so on also provide a wealth of possibilities.

Thus simply encouraging students to use ideas as the basis for choreographic design is not enough; they must also be helped to think broadly about what an "idea" even is. For many students, the concept of "having an idea for a dance" seems to mean the same thing as "feeling an emotion" — that is, sadness or jealousy or elation. Certainly, emotions can stimulate movement invention and design, and dances that "deal with" emotions are perfectly welcome. We would urge teachers, however, to widen students' notion of "idea" in every way possible so as to expand their awareness of the possibilities for dance. Some ideas for dances our students recently developed are: going to the bathroom on an airplane; a lone creature in a desolate landscape; moving in two directions at once. These ideas lend themselves readily to dance making because they suggest rich possibilities for expressive *motion.*

In asserting that expression is not a "skill," we do not deny that students' willingness to express their emotions and ideas, and their sense of confidence that their expressions are valid and worth sharing with others, might well be increased through expression-based improvisations. Our point is that the willingness and the self-confidence to express oneself are not so much skills as they are psychological attributes, the possession of which does not necessarily make a student able to choreograph more successfully (even by her own standards) than another student who lacks these attributes.

Similarly, it is certainly the case that the dances some students create often express what they, and we, consider to be more profound ideas or emotions than other dances express. But having profound rather than trivial ideas to express is not a skill, and there is no necessary correlation between that which is expressed in a dance and the quality or effectiveness of the dance as art. Obviously, it is important to help students develop their sense of the difference between profound and trivial ideas, and to help them self-confidently utilize as bases for choreographic design whatever they think are their most profound ideas. The key imperative, though, is to keep students focused on the specific issues of choreographic design.

Form without Formalism

With these ideas in mind, we argue for teaching choreography primarily as a skill-based formal craft. As already mentioned, we realize that no tradition, or set, of formal rules, values, or prescriptions may be held to represent the truth about art, so there is no danger in our pedagogy that values particular to modernist formalism will usurp other aesthetic points of view. But to neutralize the specific ideology of *formalism* does not necessitate a rejection of the artistic imperative of *form*. There is an important distinction to be drawn here. Briefly, as Bohdan Dziemidok (1993) explains:

> As an art movement artistic formalism may be defined as a theory according to which the value of a work of art *qua* artwork — its *artistic* value — is constituted exclusively (radical version) or *primarily* (moderate version) by its formal aspects. Its "meaning" or its (conceptual, cognitive, material, etc.) "content" has no important consequences for its value. Hence, only the formal aspects should be considered as criteria of artistic excellence. (185)[5]

Under the ideology of formalism, only ideas about form/design/structure count as "valid" ideas for art to "deal with" or to "be about." In other words, an artwork's form is taken to be its content, thereby shutting off further inquiry into its meaning. It follows from this that the significance of art comes to be seen as separate from and unrelated to the significance and contingencies of life. As Clive Bell (1914/1961) so famously put it, "To appreciate a work of art we need bring with us nothing from life, no knowledge of its ideas and affairs, no familiarity with its emotions ... nothing but a sense of form and color and a knowledge of three-dimensional space."(36–37) This sentiment was echoed years later by Clement Greenberg, perhaps the most influential voice of formalism. Greenberg (1961) wrote that content in art must become "strictly optical" and "be dissolved ... completely into form." (6) Not surprisingly, the desire of some artists to infuse through representational content the significance or the emotions of life into their works was rejected by Bell, Greenberg, and by formalist critics generally. Bell writes that in the artist, "an inclination to play upon the emotions of life is often the sign of a flickering inspiration," and in the spectator, "a tendency to seek, behind form, the emotions of life, is a sign of defective sensibility always." (39)

Obviously, dance — which is rooted in bodily experience and committed to the idea of the body as expressive of the range of human feelings and emotions — cannot adhere to such a disembodied theory of art as this. As an alternative to the formalist conception, art has often been construed as a matter not of denying but of bringing forward into the world the inner feelings, attitudes, and emotions of the artist, and — in our field — myriad aspects of the individual's somatic experience and identity. The risk here is that in her zeal to counter formalism's strict obsession with purely optical values, the antiformalist choreography teacher might overlook that the basic notion of *form* exists separately from the artistic tradition of *formalism*.

The danger, of course, is that she might forgo teaching skills of formal design in movement, directing students instead to concentrate on all manner of nonformal "content."

We think this is a dead end pedagogically, for no matter how they are prompted, the students' dances will adopt some kind of form or another; they could not be discerned as dances otherwise. Moreover, the forms these dances adopt will be experienced by viewers as clear, coherent, and appropriate for each work, or unclear, incoherent, and so on. The central question for the choreography curriculum is whether students are actually to be taught how to *compose* dances. Because we think they should, we argue that pre-choreography training — that is, training in improvisation — has to prepare students to deal with the compositional challenges they will encounter at more advanced levels; from the very start students must learn both to *form* their works and to *discern* form in others' works. These imperatives have nothing to do with the artistic tradition of formalism, for even works seeking to situate themselves outside of, or in direct opposition to, that tradition will possess some form or another.

In arguing for teaching improvisation and choreography primarily as a skill-based formal craft, we are not arguing either for the legitimacy or the primacy of any version of formalism. As far as we are concerned, dances and other works of art may "deal with," or "be about," anything, or nothing, at all. As concerns personal content, we are delighted when our students' works express ideas and emotions, or communicate "messages" of importance to them. But we are even more delighted when students can identify the visual aesthetic properties of their own and others' dances through which such expression or communication actually takes place. And we become positively ecstatic when they learn consciously to manipulate and control the form of movement in such a way as to modulate its expressive and communicative potential both in accordance with their artistic intentions and in an aesthetically gratifying way.

Thus, while we believe *coherence of form* is a primary value for teaching and learning choreography, we encourage teachers and students to challenge, violate, or ignore any set of formal "rules" they desire, and to invent whatever new ones they prefer. Our point is that regardless of what rules or principles (or antirules and antiprinciples) might govern the making of a dance, the work can be experienced and appreciated only insofar as it exists as a perceptible form that is strong or weak, balanced or lopsided, sloppy or neat, coherent or incoherent, or something else. And, we are happy for each artistic community — each choreography class even — to define the parameters of those sorts of value terms for itself. To teach choreography is to teach the crafting of movement into a perceptible form that possesses, hopefully, just those attributes that the artist desires it to possess.

Conscious and Critical Control

We would add one further qualification to our assertion that shaping and forming movement material comprise the essential skills of improvisation and choreography. As we have already implied, these activities need to be undertaken in a conscious and critically controlled manner — regardless of whether the initial movement from which the dance is crafted is generated improvisationally or in some other way. Here again, some expression-oriented teachers and students might disagree with us. Sensing (correctly) that we are construing choreography as just as much a "thinking" as a "feeling" process, some might argue that deep and authentic expression, if it is permitted to do so, will naturally find its own (perfect) form without the intrusion of deliberately analytical or intellectual effort. Embedded here is the Romantic idea of art-making as a kind of spiritual, or at least an inarticulable and intuitive, activity. On this view, the artist's dialectic with her materials is tantamount to an epic encounter with the forces of God or nature (or both). As such, art-making is seen as needing protection from the kind of reason-based, or rational, processes that seem implicit in the notions of "shaping" and "forming" and "conscious critical control." This view of art-making informs many choreography teachers and their students, leading them to resist any efforts to "intellectualize" the process of choreography. However, the very idea of a choreography *class*, and of *instruction* in art generally, entails gaining at least some measure of deliberate intellectual control over the artistic process.

Like artistic formalism, the Romantic conception of the artistic process can appear in a radical or moderate form. At one end of the scale are what we call "radical Romantics," those who deny that artworks require any shaping and forming process at all. Many beginning-level students adopt this stance when they suggest that artworks do, or at least can, come into existence through a spontaneous or entirely intuitive process. We find that what these students want from us is little more than a safe and nurturing environment in which to exercise, if not indulge, their ideas and emotions. Art, it is believed, will surely follow.[6]

Naïve as it may appear, the radical Romantic point of view is entitled to a serious response. In addressing it we readily agree that artworks can come into existence without any shaping and forming process at all. Indeed, it is a commonplace of contemporary art theory that virtually any object, whether or not the idea of "art" was included in its inception and creation, may be appropriated into the category of art. Even "pure ideas" can be, and have been, works of art. However, for specifically *pedagogical* purposes it makes no sense to consider "expression" and "art" as equivalent terms, because if they were there would be little reason to "teach" artmaking.

Underlying the teaching of art-making is the assumption that not just anything is art, and not just any process will result in a work of art. For pedagogical purposes, art is crafting, designing, shaping, and forming materials — in our case, movements — whether or not the process is inspired by or imbued with the artist's emotions and feelings. This is only to say, again, that powerfully expressive art is powerful *as art* precisely because of the strength of its form and design. We consider Antony Tudor's *Dark Elegies*, for example, to be a sublime work not because of the depth of the artist's revulsion against the destruction wrought by war. Millions of people feel just as Tudor felt, and they express these feeling sincerely, powerfully, and movingly in any number of ways. The difference between them and Tudor is that he was able to shape and form these feelings specifically into an artwork; it is thus not the feelings that were art, or even unique — it is the dance he made that is identified as such.

The moderate Romantic position, on the other hand, is taken up by many teachers with whom we have discussed choreography pedagogy. These teachers agree that not every intuitive expression qualifies as art, and endorse the general necessity for continuing to shape and form a work after its initial inception. These teachers part company with us, however, in holding that the requisite shaping and forming may be intuitive and unreflective rather than, as we argue, conscious and critical. Moderate Romantics with whom we have worked cite such examples as the Abstract Expressionist painter Jackson Pollock to make their point. Well-documented accounts, and even films, of Pollock's painting process suggest to some that while his works were indeed "composed" rather than having been the product of mere chance, or accident, they were composed in a manner akin to that of automatic, or stream-of-consciousness writing. Thus the moderate Romantic might assert that the compositional decisions, if one may call them that, which gave shape, form, and a unique quality to each of Pollock's drip-and-splatter paintings, were unplanned and spontaneous rather than reflective or deliberate. Using Pollock as a model, it might be suggested that shaping and forming a work of art may proceed without the direct intervention of the rational, planning mind.

While Pollock's case certainly raises interesting questions about the degree to which an artist's decision-making process in shaping a work is, or ought to be, reflective and deliberate, we find it simpleminded to think that his decision-making process was free of rational and reflective planning. His creative process appears unreflectively spontaneous because, by the time it had evolved to the point where anyone was interested in analyzing it, he had already spent years refining it — learning how paint "spoke" and learning to "listen" to it. Thus he was able almost instantly to predict how paint would behave from moment to moment as it was applied in various ways onto canvas. As his understanding grew of the relationships among such variables as the thickness of paint, its distance from the canvas when dripped or flung, its manner of coming off of different kinds of brushes, its ways of mixing with other colors at various stages of wetness or dryness, and the effects of his repertory of dripping, flicking, and splattering actions, he learned to control his painting process without appearing to do so. His control became so adept that his critical decision-making process became all but instantaneous, and thus virtually invisible, inviting the erroneous observation that there was no critical or conscious decision-making process at work.[7]

Thirty-five years of combined teaching experience have shown us that, like Pollock, students become artists through the development of a critical consciousness. In our field, this manifests itself as the ability to make specific decisions about the shaping and forming of dance materials, and to describe, analyze, interpret, and evaluate one's own and others' dances.

Choreography as a Critical Process

As an inherently conscious and critical process, art-making is an intelligent and somewhat systematic activity (see Ecker 1963 and Hanstein 1986). In composing a dance, we encourage student choreographers to try out ideas, stop along the way to analyze, interpret, and assess how these ideas are working — that is, how the dance is coming together — and erase, revise, and switch directions as many times as necessary. The artist must engage in a continual dialogue with herself and with the artistic materials with which she works. As all experienced artists know, artworks as they unfold tend to take on a will of their own; they begin to "speak back" to the artist. It is usually not long before the unfolding work-in-progress begins to suggest its own possibilities to the artist who must then "listen" to these and consider them in light of own intentions for the piece.

As Pollock no doubt experienced with paint, bodily movements, as they take shape and begin to be formed into dances, begin to announce their intrinsic aesthetic possibilities and limitations, and they compel, if not force, the choreographer to explore a variety of options to continue developing the work. In engaging with these options, artists often experience a struggle both between the intuitive and critical voices inside their heads (the sometimes contrary voices that embrace or reject various aspects of the unfolding work), and between their intentions for the work and the properties of the materials with which they are now working. These struggles are not to be avoided, for they are natural and appropriate; artistic creativity necessitates the experience of them. Indeed, one could argue that the real purpose of any art class is precisely to give students the gift of engagement with these issues. As the student gains experience, these struggles abate and may even become, like Pollock's, virtually invisible to others. This can only happen, however, if the student continuously exercises her critical judgment to work through these struggles; she must come to terms both with her aesthetic values and her evolving art-making skills to select from among the array of choices presented by the work as it unfolds.

Learning the critical process of dance making best begins in the improvisation class, because this is the pedagogical arena in which students first begin to experience the struggles inherent to artistic creativity. This means that improvisation students must be engaged at least part of the time in critically shaping and forming (and reshaping and re-forming) improvised movement materials. They must also spend time critically observing and discussing each other's work. The challenge for teachers is to facilitate students' engagement in these critical activities without compromising the spontaneity and freedom of improvisational work. The significance of this challenge must not be minimized, because while the basic structure of the choreography class lends itself quite readily to the inclusion of substantive critical activity, the structure of the typical improvisation class does not.

In the typical improvisation class, students are not generally expected either to design or to present dances-in-progress to the other students specifically for the purpose of receiving critical feedback. As we shall discuss, improvisation students are generally expected to *explore* movement rather than to *compose* with it. This, in a nutshell, is what makes improvisation not particularly useful as a precursor to choreography training; when improvisation is practiced as an end in itself, it does not do much to develop students' critical consciousness.

To remedy this, students should be expected to engage in the self-critical activity of composing with movement even in the improvisation class. Second, some of each student's improvised material should be considered critically both by the other students in the class and by the teacher. Hearing reflective critical remarks from others helps developing choreographers to see and understand aspects of their work that they may not otherwise consider. In addition, learning closely to observe and carefully to discuss the structure, movement qualities, and choreographic devices at work in others' improvisations helps students to develop a sharper artistic eye and thus contributes to their ability to see and evaluate their own work more substantively (see Lavender 1996).

Critical Training in the Improvisation Class

It remains to suggest how the improvisation teacher might facilitate the development of students' critical (and thus creative) abilities. Larry Lavender (1996) addresses the teaching of oral critical skills within the context of the choreography class, so we will not focus on that issue; we will discuss the development of students' *self-critical* skills. To teach self-criticism, teachers must, first of all, regularly put students in the position of experiencing the creative process as a fundamentally critical one. Students must spend a great deal of their time consciously engaging with aesthetic tastes and preferences by making specific compositional decisions with and about their improvised movement material. To initiate this, the teacher must make wise use of the primary mechanism she has at her disposal: the improvisational prompt, the instructions that she gives to students to stimulate their creative work.

Improvisational prompts may be framed as *exploratory* or *compositional* assignments, and teachers need to understand the difference between them. Exploratory prompts ask students to work within narrow and predetermined conceptual and/or aesthetic limits. These prompts have a definite end in view, and are designed to generate material without requiring the student overtly to make decisions about its shape, style, sequencing, or anything else. Exploratory prompts are often presented through a series of oral cues by the teacher. For example, the teacher might direct the students to begin walking in a random pattern around the room, paying particular attention to the way their weight is transferred from one leg to the other, as well as to such things as the length of each stride, the feeling in the pelvis and/or spine as they move, their speed, their visual focus, and so on. Through further instructions, the teacher may direct the dancers to walk (or run, skip, leap, gallop) sideways or backwards, on tiptoe, with bent or straight legs, or in any of a hundred different ways. In response to teachers' cues, students explore on a rudimentary level walking and other forms of two-legged locomotion. Through further cues, the students may include arm or torso movements, change energy qualities, add turns, and so on.

On the other hand, compositional prompts require students to make critical choices about the form and structure of their movement; at some point something has to be manipulated, deleted, added, repeated, or revised. For example, the teacher might instruct the students to improvise five clearly distinct body shapes. Next, the teacher may ask the students both to *alter* these shapes in some deliberate manner, and to *arrange* them into a sequence that the student considers as, say, beautiful, grotesque, smooth, or jarring. To accomplish this, the student must manipulate the shapes in accordance with her personal understanding of these terms. The student's aesthetic values come consciously into play as an influence on her artistic choices; the way she alters her shapes and the sequence into which she composes them will be, in fact, a concrete sample of her values.

Later, when discussing each other's sequences, the members of the class should articulate, to the best of their ability, both how their own sequence embodies their notion of the beautiful, or the grotesque, or whatever, and their assessment of others' sequences in accomplishing this goal. The point of compositional prompts and subsequent discussion is to compel students first to make specific aesthetic choices and then to gain consciousness both of the particular choices they have made and the reasons why they (or someone else) might make a similar or different choice. Developing this ability begins the growth of the critical consciousness that is essential for art-making.[8]

Another way teachers can stimulate the development of students' self-critical skills is to ask them regularly to write short, reflective assessments both of their creative process and its outcomes. Following the sequencing exercise just discussed, students could be asked to go home and write a couple of pages on how they created their original shapes (were they new to the student, or from some other dance they had seen or learned, etc.), and also to describe how they went about sequencing the shapes (was it random, or did they try several variations and then settle on one, or did they follow some other method?). Finally, the students can be asked to assess the relation between their sequence and their intentions. (If the sequence was intended to be grotesque, for example, did it succeed? Why or why not? What would need to change in the sequence for it to become truly grotesque?) These reflective writing assignments stimulate deeper understanding on the part of the students about what it is they are doing in class. By writing reflectively about their work, students discover how their feelings, intuitions, taste preferences, and rational mind are not really at odds with each other but, rather, form a multidimensional complex of attributes, all of which are necessary for art-making (see Lavender & Oliver 1993).

We have said that choreography is an activity consisting of the integrated skills of improvisation, composition, and criticism. It may be more accurate to say that criticism is the skill that bridges the other two skills. We are convinced that to make the improvisation class a meaningful first step in the development of choreographers, the critical skills of the students must be engaged and developed from the start. We hope the ideas presented here will stimulate others to explore the relationship between improvisation and choreography; no doubt there is much to be discovered.

References

Abrams, M. H. *The Mirror and the Lamp: Romantic Theory and the Critical Tradition.* London, Oxford University Press, 1953.

Ambrosia, Nora. *Learning About Dance.* Dubuque: Kendall Hunt Publishing Company, 1999.

Battersby, Christine. *Gender and Genius.* London: The Women's Press, 1994.

_____. "Situating the Aesthetic: A Feminist Defence." In *Thinking Art: Beyond Traditional Aesthetics.* Edited by Andrew Benjamin and Peter Osborne, pp. 31–44. London: Institute of Contemporary Arts, 1991.

Beckley, Bill, and David Shapiro, eds. *Uncontrollable Beauty.* New York: Allworth Press, 1998.

Bell, Clive. *Art.* London: Arrow Books, 1961.

Blom, Lynne Anne, and L. Tarin Chaplin. *The Intimate Act of Choreography.* Pittsburgh: University of Pittsburgh Press, 1982.

Casey, Edward S. "Expression and Communication in Art." *Journal of Aesthetics and Art Criticism* 30, 2 (1971): 197–207.

Danto, Arthur C. *After the End of Art.* Princeton: Princeton University Press, 1997.

_____. *The Transfiguration of the Commonplace.* Cambridge, Mass.: Harvard University Press, 1981.

Dickinson, Samuel. *San Francisco Kaleidoscope.* Palo Alto: Stanford University Press, 1949.

Dissanayake, Ellen. *Homo Aestheticus.* Seattle: University of Washington Press, 1992.

_____. *What Is Art For?* Seattle: University of Washington Press, 1988.

Dziemidok, Bohdan. "Artistic Formalism: Its Achievements and Weaknesses." *Journal of Aesthetics and Art Criticism* 51, 2 (1993): 186–193.

Ecker, David. "The Artistic Process as Qualitative Problem Solving." *Journal of Aesthetics and Art Criticism* 21, 3 (1963), pp. 283–290.

Greenberg, Clement. "Counter Avant-Garde." *Art International* 15 (1971): 16–19.

_____. *Art and Culture.* Boston: Beacon Press, 1961.

Hanstein, Penelope. "On the Nature of Art Making in Dance: An Artistic Process Skills Model." Unpublished Dissertation. Ohio State University, 1986.

Hawkins, Alma. *Creating Through Movement*, revised edition. Princeton: Princeton Book Company, 1988.

Hayes, Elizabeth R. *Dance Composition and Production.* Pennington: Princeton Book Company, 1955/1993.

H'Doubler, Margaret. *The Dance and Its Place in Education.* New York: Harcourt, Brace and Company, 1925.

Hickey, David. *The Invisible Dragon: Four Essays on Beauty.* Los Angeles: Art Issues Press, 1993.

Hodes, Stuart. *A Map of Making Dances.* New York: Ardsley House, Publishers, 1998.

Horst, Louis. *Modern Dance Forms.* San Francisco: Impulse Publications, 1961.

Humphrey, Doris. *The Art of Making Dances.* New York: Grove Press, 1959.

Irigaray, Luce. *This Sex Which Is Not One*, trans., Catherine Porter. Ithaca: Cornell University Press, 1985.

Jay, Martin. *Downcast Eyes: The Denigration of Vision in Twentieth-Century French Thought.* Berkeley: University of California Press, 1994.

Khatchadourian, Haig. "The Expression Theory of Art: A Critical Evaluation." *Journal of Aesthetics and Art Criticism* 23, 3 (1965): 335–351.

Lavender, Larry. "Post-Historical Dance Criticism." *Dance Research Journal* 32, 2 (2000–01): 88–107.

_____. *Dancers Talking Dance.* Champaign, Ill.: Human Kinetics, 1996.

_____, and Jennifer Predock-Linnell. "Standing Aside and Making Space: Mentoring Student Choreographers." *Impulse* 4, 3 (1996): 235–252.

_____, and Wendy Oliver. "Learning to 'See' Dance: The Role of Critical Writing in Developing Students' Aesthetic Awareness." *Impulse* 1, 1 (1993): 10–20.

McEvilley, Thomas. *Art and Otherness.* New York: McPherson and Company, 1992.

_____. *Art and Discontent.* New York: McPherson and Company, 1991.

_____. "I Think Therefore I Art." *Artforum* 23, 10 (1985): 74–84.

_____. "Art in the Dark." In *Theories of Contemporary Art.* Edited by Richard Hertz, pp. 287–305. New Jersey: Prentice Hall, Inc., 1985.

Minton, Sandra. *Choreography: A Basic Approach Using Improvisation.* 2nd edition. Champaign, Ill.: Human Kinetics, 1991.

Nagrin, Daniel. *Dance and the Specific Image: Improvisation.* Pittsburgh: University of Pittsburgh Press, 1993.

Root, Deborah. *Cannibal Culture: Art, Appropriation and the Commodification of Difference.* Boulder, Co.: Westview Press, 1995.

Sheets-Johnstone, Maxine. "Thinking in Movement." *Journal of Aesthetics and Art Criticism* 39, 4 (1981): 399–407.

Shusterman, Richard. *Performing Live.* Ithaca: Cornell University Press, 2000.

Smith-Autard, Jacqueline. *Dance Composition.* London: A & C Black, 1992.

Tatarkiewicz, Wladyslaw. "The Romantic Aesthetics of 1600." *British Journal of Aesthetics* 7, 2 (1967): 137–149.

Todd, George F. "Expression without Feeling." *Journal of Aesthetics and Art Criticism* 40, 4 (1972): 477–488.

Tormey, Alan. *The Concept of Expression.* Princeton: Princeton University Press, 1971.

Notes

1. The notion of "success" is of course problematic. When we speak of "gaining success" as a choreographer we mean (1) having one's dance works meet with one's own approval (personal success), and (2) having one's works meet with the approval of others in one's immediate dance community (public success). Every art-world community has a prevailing aesthetic, derived through consensus among its members. Through such actions as selecting students' dances for inclusion in concerts, and praising or not praising them in choreography classes, dance teachers create and sustain the prevailing aesthetic in their respective programs. Unless one opts to move into another community with a different aesthetic, public success will mean meeting or exceeding the aesthetic expectations characteristic of one's present art-world locale. Some students, of course, seek only personal success, which is a perfectly acceptable alternative; not everybody can, or should, strive for public success in art. Still, it is important for students to learn how their work stands in relation to public taste even if they are indifferent to it.

2. Christine Battersby (1991) laments that, in an effort to overcome the western aesthetic tradition, much feminist art criticism and theory has eschewed the very notion of "aesthetic value." In a critique of Griselda Pollock, whom she characterizes as too dismissive of the notion of "quality" in art, Battersby writes that within feminist art and literary history, "there has been no sustained attempt to develop a feminist theory of aesthetic value. Indeed, the whole topic has been neglected …" (34). In our field, a legacy of this neglect has been the supplanting of formal — i.e., visual — aesthetics by self-expression. No doubt this is related to the historically close link between visual aesthetics and patriarchy. See, for example, Luce Irigaray's (1985) rejection of the primacy of the visual in Western thought; Irigaray's stance has become a staple of feminist criticism in the arts. (For an encyclopedic survey of the role of vision in Western thought, see Jay 1994).

3. A student *may* improve in her ability to self-express through dancing; it may be that to *perform* a dance self-expressively is a skill that can be learned. But there is a difference between self-expression in performance and self-expression through *choreography*. Indeed, it is possible to choreograph a self-expressive dance and then not to dance it, or have it danced, in a particularly expressive way. Nonetheless, it remains true that choreographic self-expression may be ascertained solely through analysis of the visible form of a dance, and that this analysis might support the claim that someone has, or has not, "improved" at choreographic self-expression.

4. We do not claim that the kinesthetic or somatic effects, or impact, of a dance may not be experienced by the blind or by those whose eyes might be turned away. In placing dance among the visual arts and stressing its aesthetic form, we join a growing number of theorists who hail the return of the concepts, and the values, of "beauty" and "visual quality" into contemporary aesthetic and art-educational discourse. See, for example, Bill Beckley and David Shapiro (1998), and Hickey (1993).

5. Artistic formalism — most notably as espoused by Clive Bell and Clement Greenberg — has been widely criticized and rejected for its alleged promulgation of sexist and elitist values that either marginalize or attempt to assimilate the art of women, minorities, and non-Western arts traditions. See, for example, McEvilley (1991, 1992), and Root (1995). We think the ferocity with which "formalism" has been attacked has led many teachers to shy away from asserting that coherent form is an important value to impart to students in the arts, and that expressive power is a function of "form" broadly construed.

6. Most of the radical Romantic students we have encountered subscribe wholeheartedly to classic expression theory. Briefly, the theory holds that (1) in creating a work of art an artist is invariably expressing something, and (2) that the expressive qualities of the artwork are the direct consequence of this act of expression. That the theory is untenable has been demonstrated by a variety of theorists; see Todd (1972), Tormey (1971), and Khatchadourian (1965).

7. Pollock's case also raises the question of the degree to which skill in art is a matter of "genius," or native ability, as opposed to being something that can be taught and learned. The very notion of genius as we know it today is, of course, an outgrowth of Romanticism. Indeed, the notion has been criticized as a particularly "masculine" concept. Christine Battersby (1994) writes that "the Romantic concept of genius is peculiarly harmful to women. Our present criteria for artistic excellence have their origin in theories that specifically and explicitly denied women genius" (32). A question for further consideration is thus the degree to which the choreography curriculum (indeed, the dance curriculum as a whole) does, or should, organize itself around the traditional concept of genius, and what alternatives to this might be available.

8. Obviously, students' aesthetic values are informed by a variety of factors, not the least of which is their level of familiarity with different dance forms, and their knowledge of dance and art traditions, both Western and non-Western. While the systematic development and enhancement of these knowledge bases is not the ostensible aim of improvisation and choreography classes, it can be useful within these classes to expose students to any materials (for example, readings and videos) that might add to their basic working knowledge of dance, and thus contribute to the honing of their aesthetic sensibility (see Lavender & Predock-Linnell 1996).

CHAPTER 4

Wild Speculations and Simple Thoughts: Teaching Music to Dancers

JEFFREY STOLET

The intimate entwinement of dance and music has left indelible imprints on both art forms. The beauty of this artistic marriage arises from the essential attraction of dance to music and music to dance. In this relationship, music can serve dance as a subservient partner and accompaniment, or it can function as an equal component in a choreo-musical work, providing a sonic counterpoint to dance's visual action. Most dance, in fact, has a musical component, and if one considers silence in music to be the analogue to stillness in dance, then all dance—including silent ones—incorporates music into its realm. If all dance has music and coexists in a deep connection to and association with it, students pursuing dance studies are obliged to cultivate an understanding of music and the dance-music partnership.

The pursuit of knowledge about music and music's relationship to dance is a lifelong endeavor. Great musicians spend their entire lives developing their musical skill and knowledge. A ten- or sixteen-week course to develop musical skills and knowledge can only be a first step in this educational process. A music course for dancers could include concepts such as harmony, melody, consonance, dissonance, rhythm, tempo, meter, dynamics, and timbre. In relation to these fundamentals, associated musical terminology and methods for musical notation could be introduced.

Other relevant topics might include music history, musical structure, common musical genres, musical masterworks, issues related to music copyright law, and the uses of technology to create music for dance. In addition, the development of skills to communicate with musical collaborators and dance accompanists could benefit dance students. There is little argument that musical study can enhance the intellectual and artistic understanding of dance through the comprehension of a partner art, offer guidance with respect to the shaping of individual or group performance of dance, and provide a conduit through which a dancer can engage a musician to obtain collaborative and pedagogical goals.

Musical studies represent only a portion of the knowledge dance students need if they are to make sense of the complex relations between dance and music: significant thought about the dance-music relationship should be primary course material in any music class for dancers. This more comprehensive examination requires a free-ranging inquiry into the nature and fabric of the dance-music relationship, as well as an analysis of its various manifestations. Emerging from contemplations about the dance-music relationship, a course on music for dancers can illuminate the aesthetic and practical connections between music and dance, clarify the nature of the dance-music interaction, enrich the dialogue between dancer and musician, and give insight into the creative processes involved in making a choreographic work and into the choreographic and choreo-musical relationships of the greatest dance masterworks.

From a practical standpoint, a limited number of program hours can be dedicated to musical studies in a university dance curriculum. At the University of Oregon Department of Dance, where I served as music director for more than a decade, three courses were dedicated to musical studies: Fundamentals of Rhythm, Music for Dancers, and Dance Accompaniment. Not all dance departments, however, have such curricular luxuries and many may offer only one or two courses in music for dancers. Even so, given the infinite size of music as a topic, difficult choices have to be made about what to include as part of a music curriculum for dancers. What musical topics should be emphasized? How much music history should be presented? Should musical notation be used? If so, which notational principles should be introduced? If we include notational studies, what will we have to exclude? How should the course material be presented? These questions are difficult and endless; many of the answers depend on educational context.

My objectives in this chapter are to (1) suggest entry points to the study of music for dancers; (2) offer thoughts about the organizational structure of musical topics and pedagogical opportunities that might be employed;

(3) examine the dance-music relationship, thereby making this relationship more resonant; (4) and review music fundamentals as they are important in teaching music to dance students. I will first discuss some of the relationships between dance and music, and then examine the sonic attributes that every sound possesses, suggest how these attributes can be unfolded into concepts such as melody, harmony and rhythm, and identify ways that these basic musical formations are relevant to dance students. Finally, I will offer opinions about the practical aspects of teaching music to dancers, such as what specific material should be included in a course or curriculum on music for dancers, how the physicality of dance might be employed in teaching strategies, and what supplemental readings might be used.

Dance and Music: The Essential Attraction

One of the things I love about music is its connection to dance. There are many reasons for this marvelous, seemingly natural affiliation, some obscure and mysterious, others more obvious. I believe the study of music in the context of dance should begin with a broad consideration of these philosophical, perceptual, social, and metaphoric connections that bring together these art forms. It is not my intent to construct a complete theory about how dance and music are affiliated — that would be like formalizing a theory of love (an emotion that is similar to the attraction that dance and music appear to have for one another). There are, however, a number of observations that we can make that can give us insight into this association. Consider, for example, that music, beyond functioning as entertainment and aesthetic expression, is also directly connected to events such as weddings, funerals, and other religious ceremonies. We also have love songs, war music, music for sporting events, national anthems, school fight songs, and music for work in the form of slave songs. In addition, music is created specifically for dance, and is used to shape and provide social context (music played in nightclubs, for example, or Muzak played in elevators). My observation here is simple: Music tends to be intended for a particular context or occasion, or in association with other events.

In a subtle reciprocation, the opposite also seems to be true, that many events call for musical association — and it is truer today than at any time in human history. Audio-recording technologies, in their many manifestations, have led to what I call "the radical portability" of music. Radical portability is visible in almost every area of daily life, ranging from home stereos to the mall, from car radios to elevators, from handheld MP3 players to television. Whereas music was once significantly autonomous from pedestrian activity, music via its recently found portability attaches itself to our lives in every conceivable way, locale, and life context. As I write this paragraph, I am sitting in a Starbucks café. A car has just pulled into the parking lot with its radio blaring. The café is piping in some type of 1950s music through the entire restaurant. A student is working on her anthropology homework while grooving out to her tunes on an iPod. All of these activities call for all of this music. Today we have chosen to soundtrack our lives and, specifically, to soundtrack the physical activities in our lives.

Physical motion is central to playing music, and in many ways the performance of music often becomes a type of dance. Rock music from its earliest days has fused its brand of gyrating hip movement to the rhythmic character of the music. And rock musicians have known from the beginning that there is a vast aesthetic difference between simply playing a chord and playing the same chord while jumping wildly into the air. The best conductors use movement thoroughly and thoughtfully, both to guide the musicians in their ensembles and to lead the audience through the drama of the music. Further examination suggests that music may best be listened to when moving, which might explain our inclination to tap our feet when listening to it. This drive toward movement may also hold true when we simply think of music, as is suggested by a famous account of Beethoven near the end of his life: "In the living room, behind a locked door, we heard the master singing parts of the fugue in the Credo — singing, howling, stamping" (Thayer 1967, 851). It seems that in an effort to comprehend and give clarity to his own musical thought, Beethoven found the need to employ a parallel or corresponding physical expression.

Dance and music are both temporal art forms, and thus they unfold and engage one another in a time continuum. Often the dance and musical domains are coordinated in a tight association. The concept of *dancing on* or *placing a movement on the beat* is emblematic of how precise this coordination is. The difference of only a few milliseconds places a dancer precisely *on the beat* with his or her movement or in the netherworld between beats. The music and dance languages even have a precise term for how and when a note or movement can be placed between beats: *syncopation.* But concepts of syncopation require rigorous application. Not every time-point between beats is acceptable as a point when syncopation can occur. How syncopation may be applied depends substantially on the style of the music and the dance, but there are a very limited number of possibilities per style in comparison to nearly infinite numbers of time-points that are simply *off the beat.*

I bring these details into the discussion to amplify the closeness of the dance-music temporal relationship. If we compare music's temporal association with dance to music's temporal association with other events, such as weddings or sporting events, we find that there is a comparative crudeness in the nondance relationships. No millisecond demands exist in the music-sporting event relationship; time in these relationships is primitively measured in minutes or, at best, in five- to ten-second increments. In addition, the temporality of dance and music means that an enormous range of temporal correspondences can exist, extending from extremely tight note-for-note types of linkages to where the only correspondence is that both dance and music are occurring at the same time. It is not uncommon for a choreo-musical work to seek a middle ground where such things as meter, tempo, and some formal aspects have connections but where other elements occur in opposition to or in counterpoint with one another. Of course, it is not only the temporal coordination of dance and music that brings them together. Correspondences often exist in terms of emotional demeanor, balance between the choreographic and musical forces — how many dancers and how many instruments — and extramusical relationships (to name only a few other possibilities; Jaroslaw Kapuscinski [1998, 43–50] expresses some of these last ideas about correspondence in the context of sound and video image).

Music not only has this tight connection to movement, but the language used to discuss music is filled with examples where notions of space and movement are used, including many general references to the spatial domain, such as *higher* and *lower* pitches, or *wide* intervals. Musical language also references movement in general ways with phrases like *musical gesture* and refers to specific movements with language such as *leaps* and *jumps*, as in *leaps* or *jumps* in melodic lines. Harmony often is described in terms of types of motion (usually away from some starting point or toward some goal), and that counterpoint is often depicted as occurring in parallel, contrary, or oblique motions. I believe that it is music's invisibility, together with humans' ocular bias, that is largely responsible for the extensive borrowing of language from the visual domain to vivify the invisible domain of music.

While a variety of forces undoubtedly shape the connection between dance and music, there exist perceptual and experiential reasons for the success of this alliance, which work together and individually to create a complete experiential field. When I watch dance, a complete experiential field is formed from what I see, what I hear, and what I can vicariously experience based on what I know about the physicality of human movement. While the visual, sonic, and psychophysical domains provide information that overlaps, each provides unique experiential information. Music tells us what sight cannot; dance tells us what hearing cannot;

experience and knowledge about human physicality vicariously inform us about physical context beyond what sound and sight can articulate.

These elements function in distinctly different ways. If we consider the experience of seeing, we note that we do not see in a 360-degree circle. Instead, we control our field of vision, always taking in less than 180 degrees at any given moment. Often when seeing we narrow our focus tremendously to only a fraction of the 180-degree periphery. Reading text is perhaps the most extreme example of this narrowed focus; depending on the text's size, we can recognize and assimilate meaning from text only several degrees to the left or right of the point on which we are focusing. All this means is that we turn our heads and bodies to direct our focus toward what we want to see, thus eliminating from our visual field large portions of our periphery. We control what we see and do not see. Because we can direct our gaze, we feel and experience that we are looking outward and away from ourselves.

On the other hand, we receive sounds from a three-dimensional, 360-degree area around us. We find the location from which a sound is generated quite easily. Certainly this aspect of human perception is an important influence on recent development of surround-sound technologies that have found their ways into movie theaters and homes. We turn our heads and bodies but cannot direct our hearing and cannot hold back the advance of sound from all 360 degrees. Because we cannot direct our hearing in the same way that we can direct our sight, we feel and experience that sound comes toward us. This experiential opposition between the visual and sonic domains creates a wonderful bidirectional tension, which helps draw dance and music into spectacularly effective counterpoint. This bidirectional experiential opposition suggests that even in a work where tight correspondences in the choreo-musical relationship exist, the visual and sonic information would be drastically affected and enriched in its complexity by the manner in which the information is absorbed.

Humans, of course, live in and occupy space. We generally do not imagine existence outside of spatial realms. We also understand physical human abilities and limitations. No art explores and exploits space, or creates meaningful movement in space, better than dance. When we see dance movement, dancers and nondancers can vicariously appreciate the physicality involved in performing a dance, because as audience members we share a kinesthetic apparatus that is fundamentally the same. This vicarious appreciation is a substantially internal process, independent from what is being seen or heard. The collaboration between the eye and the ear that provides bidirectionally opposed data, combined with the distinctly internal and nondirectional vicarious appreciation of movement and physicality, renders a unique and complex aesthetic mechanism for human expression. The fact that dance and music are both time-based arts that share a time continuum, and that are interrelated in complex and sophisticated associations, further consummates their intimate bond. Together these factors contribute to the most successful relationship in all of the arts.

Five Sonic Attributes

Each time I teach a course to a group of musicians or dancers, I find that I spend a significant amount of time rethinking the topics I want to include and the strategy that I will employ to present the course content. Even after much review, I find that I return to a set of fundamental notions that guide the course content and the method of presentation that I ultimately choose. The first of these notions is that music is ultimately a time-based art form. We can't see it, taste it, smell it, or touch it, but we can hear it and we know that music passes in time. We hear, perceive, and understand that music is passing in or through time, one note passing to the next, one harmony progressing to the next. If there were no changes in these various musical parameters, we might understand music in a manner similar to the way we understand most traditional painting, sculpture, and architecture. It is only through the changes in these musical parameters that the passage of time is articulated for us. If there is no parametric musical change, there is no music. I believe that a dancer's study of music should begin with those musical elements that articulate musical change, that make the passage of time comprehensible, and that draw dance and music into the most compelling temporal correspondences.

Beyond a sound's placement in time (when a sound occurs), there are five sonic attributes that every sound possesses. These five attributes — essential musical components on which we need our students to focus their attention — are the articulators of time and are responsible for shaping fundamental musical constructs such as meter, harmony, melody, consonance, and dissonance, as well as more complex musical formations, such as phrase and formal structure. The five sonic attributes are:

Pitch
Duration
Timbre
Volume
Location

Every sound — my voice, your voice, a trumpet in the orchestra, or a car screeching around the corner —has a pitch component (or complex frequency spectrum). Every sound has a specific duration: it is a long sound, a short sound, or somewhere in between. Every sound has its particular timbre or tone color, which is largely responsible for allowing us to distinguish between a violin and clarinet when they are playing the same pitch. Every sound has a volume: it is a loud sound, a soft sound, or somewhere in between. Every sound emanates from a specific location. Your voice and the hum of your computer cannot come from the same spatial location. These sonic attributes are music's fundamental building blocks and the music's articulators of time. One of the true advantages of proceeding from these five sonic attributes to more complex musical formations is that a dancer can approach and consider every type of music without reference or bias to musical style or geographical point of origin.

Over the past centuries, the Western notational system has evolved methodologies for writing each of these sonic attributes. We use graphic strategies on a musical staff to notate pitch. We use symbolic strategies to notate rhythm (duration). We use text to notate timbre, and text and symbols to notate music dynamics (volume). In the case of location, this attribute has been largely ignored in Western music, but when it has been specified in a score, location is usually notated with text and phrases, like "off-stage trumpet," or is controlled by an a priori understanding about how musicians should be spatially situated. Issues of sonic location, however, play an ever-increasing role in recent developments in the electronic music discipline, where composers talk about placing a sound "in the stereophonic field" or "diffusing sounds in a three-dimensional space."

I will examine these five sonic attributes, consider how each makes its unique musical contributions, and suggest what about them could be introduced in a music course for dancers. In these discussions I assume a certain level of musical knowledge and therefore do not define or explain all terminology or concepts that I use. While I divide the discussion into separate parts, I believe that these five sonic attributes are inseparable and inextricably bound. The sonic attributes are bound so tightly together because every note in a composition has all the attributes. The result is that some discussions under one heading cross over topical boundaries to related areas. I have separated them only to aid in building conceptual clarity.

Pitch

We use the term "*pitch*" to refer to the human perception of a frequency of a tone, frequency being the rate at which a complete pattern of a sound wave is repeated. Pitches are said to be *higher* or *lower* based substantially on their perceived frequency. In traditional Western notation, we use a graphic strategy to notate the higher or lower pitches. In Figure 4.1, the five parallel lines are called the staff and noteheads are placed on the staff to indicate higher or lower pitches. This strategy is similar to what is used to indicate the rise and fall of a stock on the New York Stock Exchange.

The manner in which we notate pitch is a clear manifestation of music, through its notation, reaching into the spatial domain. The highness and lowness of pitches are sometimes, in fact, referred to as pitch or frequency space.

In music the specific pitch of a note may be less important than its relation to the other pitches around it. These relationships lead to the creation of many musical formations that we want to bring to the attention of our students. If, for instance, pitches occur in succession, one leading to the next and yet not occurring simultaneously, then melody arises. One of the most striking things about a melody is what we call its shape. The shape of a melody is the contour created by the changing pitches that make up a melody. Figure 4.2 demonstrates the concept of melodic shape; the line drawn through the noteheads indicates the melodic shape. In this example, there a clear progression from the first to the seventh pitch, the seventh pitch being the high point of the melodic shape.

The shape of a melody will be of interest to dancers, because it directs the journey of a musical phrase from its starting point to its pinnacle, and on to its point of relative repose. Melodic shape is also one of the most memorable aspects of a melody. It is often the part of music we replay in our minds when we think of a particular composition. Knowledge about

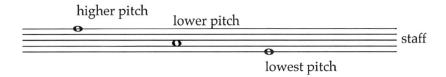

Fig. 4.1 Higher and lower pitches notated on a staff.

Fig. 4.2 Melodic Shape.

melodic shape can suggest how movement can be performed in relation to the temporal unfolding of the melody, or how movement can be placed choreographically into alliance or in counterpoint with it. The fact that much music has recurring melodies or melodic patterns makes observance of melodic events all the more important, especially in terms of musical form and structure. Certainly the concepts of motive and motivic development are tied to melody and melodic shape. An obvious way to vivify the concept of melodic shape to dancers is to have them create movement that mirrors the melodic shape of a variety of musical passages. This simple concept can be easily expanded so that students also create movement variations based on the melodic shape or develop the melodic shape as a kind of motive.

In contrast to melody where pitches occur one note after another, if pitches occur simultaneously (literally or conceptually), then harmony arises. The study of musical harmony is a vast, complex subject, and authors over the centuries have dedicated thousands of pages to the topic. Nevertheless, there are some basic aspects of harmony that are vital for the dance student to understand. First, a harmonic structure like a chord can and does occur in two basic manners: as a literal simultaneity or as a harmonic structure that temporally unfolds one element or several elements at a time.

Figure 4.3 shows the same harmony articulated in four different manners: In Figure 4.3A all the notes are presented simultaneously; in Figure 4.3B the notes of the harmony are presented in an ascending order one note at a time; in Figure 4.3C the notes of the harmony are presented like a waltz accompaniment; and in Figure 4.3D the notes are presented in a descending order one note at a time. The number of possible permutations is virtually infinite; however, in this infiniteness a new question surfaces: "What is the difference between Figure 4.3B and Figure 4.3D, shown as examples of harmony, and melody?" This is where it gets complicated. Melodic formations often have harmonic aspects and harmonic formations often have melodic aspects. It works a little bit like a crossword puzzle where a single letter may be part of an across word and a down word at the same time. We must understand that every note can function both melodically and harmonically, even though in a specific musical

Fig. 4.3 Four examples of the same harmony.

context a particular note may have a stronger harmonic function than melodic function or vice versa.

As part of harmonic theory, there exist concepts of consonance and dissonance. Consonance and dissonance refer to a qualitative aspect of harmonic structure that is highly context-dependent. How the terms "consonance" and "dissonance" have been used throughout history has changed, and there is much debate about how to characterize a musical trait that is so highly subjective. I won't argue for or against a particular definition here; however, I can say that consonance is often described with words like "stable," "pleasant," "accord," "agreement," or "relaxed"; dissonance, in contrast, is often evoked with words like "tension," "conflict," "harshness," or "disagreeableness." During the course of a composition, there is often an ebb and flow between relative consonance and dissonance. Any particular piece, section of a piece, or single harmony exists in a relative continuum between the most extreme consonance and the most extreme dissonance. In some music, dissonance resolves to consonance. In other music, there is no concern for the resolution of dissonance.

There are a variety of harmonic styles that have developed during music history, each having its own traits that distinguish it from other harmonic styles. Some harmonic styles are generally more consonant or dissonant than other styles. For instance, early twentieth-century Western art music is, relatively speaking, much more dissonant than the music of sixteenth-century Europe. Even so, within harmonic styles, listeners might very well expect considerable variation in how consonance and dissonance operate. The manner in which harmony is used and consonance and dissonance functions helps musicologists separate music into historical periods and makes understandable the development of harmonic style from period to period.

For dancers, the tracking of the evolution of consonance and dissonance in music can provide revealing information about a piece of music, and can guide dancers in performance and choreographic issues. One way to enhance students' understanding of consonance and dissonance is to ask them to create movement that reflects the patterns of consonance and dissonance found in music. This exercise should be done in groups, because consonance and dissonance develops from the relationships formed between and among pitches. Accordingly, we want dancers to become sensitive to the group dynamics that shape tension and resolution in both dance and music.

In many cases, the harmony in a piece of music is used as an accompaniment to a primary melody. Music with a primary melody and accompaniment is called homophonic. An example of homophonic music is shown in Figure 4.4, where the primary melody is presented on the upper staff and its accompaniment, harmony unfolding in time, is presented on the lower staff. In this context, the melody is said to be the primary musical object and the accompaniment is a secondary feature that supports the musical interests of the melody.

In contrast to homophonic music, some music exhibits the simultaneous occurrence of two or more melodic lines in counterpoint with one another. We call this type of music polyphonic and the simultaneous melodic lines counterpoint. In Figure 4.5, a melody begins in measure 1 on the lower staff, and in measure 2 the same melody enters on the upper staff. From measures 2–6 the two melodies are said to be in counterpoint with one another, and are considered to be coequals in the musical texture. Because the melodies share the same melodic shape, we call this type of music imitative counterpoint.

In addition to being the central agent in creating melodic and harmonic structure, pitch also has influence on meter and rhythm, such as in musical accent. Each change in pitch and harmony has the potential of creating accent. Accent is emphasis given to any note or harmony. That is why chord change is usually associated with the first beat of the measure. It is the point of harmonic change that causes the accent, and composers often place the beginning of the harmony at the beginning of the measure to create a natural correspondence. But a melodic line alone can cause accent. In Figure 4.6, we see an undifferentiated articulation of a single note on the

Fig. 4.4 Homophonic music: melody and accompaniment.

Fig. 4.5 Polyphonic music: imitative counterpoint by Zarlino.

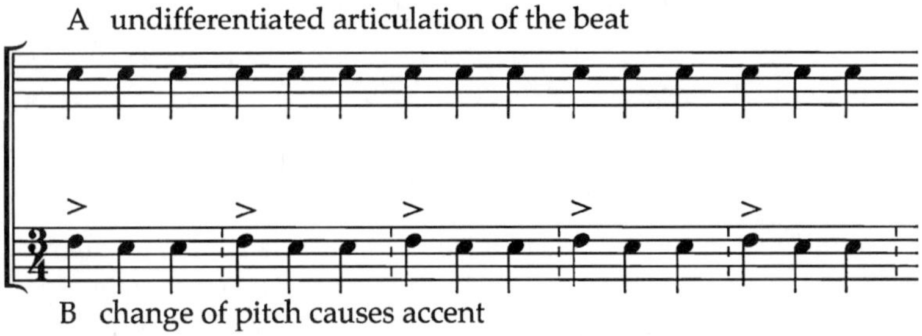

A undifferentiated articulation of the beat

B change of pitch causes accent

Fig. 4.6 Pitching change creating accent.

upper staff compared with a repeating pattern on the lower staff where every third note represents a point of change. On the lower staff of this example, the first of every three notes will seem accented (indicated by > marking) because it is the point at which the change in pitch occurs.

I believe that all of these pitch-related topics — melody, melodic shape, harmony, consonance, dissonance, and homophonic and polyphonic music — should be included in music courses for dancers and can serve as points of departure for more advanced discussions.

Duration

Because every note of a composition occurs in a time continuum and each note itself is a discrete length of time, duration is central to the temporal flow of music and to our perception of the division of musical time. Durational patterns — that is, the patterns of longness and shortness of notes — are largely what we refer to as rhythm. Rhythmic patterns surround us in the world each day.

The day-night cycle, the rhythm of tides, and the changing seasons are all natural examples of the division of time and recurring durational patterns: rhythm.

Rhythm in music encompasses all aspects of the division of musical time as well as the durational influences involved in creating metric accent and patterns of accented and unaccented beats: meter.

When a listener taps a foot in time with a piece of music, he or she is responding to a recurring musical pulse. We can graphically depict such a recurring musical pulse with a series of equally spaced noteheads. In Figure 4.7, the noteheads indicate the beginnings of time spans that are of equal duration. The noteheads are equally spaced on the page to indicate that the pulses occur at equally spaced time intervals.

The influence of duration can immediately be seen if we increase the duration of every other note to double its original value, so that the durational pattern becomes:

long——, short, long——, short, long——, short, long——

In traditional notation, this pattern might be realized as an alternating half note–quarter note rhythmic pattern with the quarter notes equaling one beat and the half notes equally two beats of musical time (Figure 4.8).

By virtue of the durational changes, the formerly undifferentiated and unaccented recurring pulse immediately becomes a triple meter with accents placed on the long notes: a triple meter with two levels of rhythmic organization. This pattern of accented and unaccented beats is shown in Figure 4.9.

In Figure 4.9, it would be equally reasonable for a listener to tap his or her foot on the beats as indicated by the "counts" above the notes, or in accordance with the measures as indicated by the "counts" below the notes. That is because two levels of musical time are in operation: one at the beat level and one at the measure level. When multiple levels of musical organization exist, one level "nested" into another as in Figure 4.9, we say that the music has hierarchical organization.

Hierarchical organization extends beyond the measure. In Figure 4.10, we see three levels of rhythmic activity (beat-measure-phrase): beats are articulated with the continuous quarter notes in the lower staff; measures are defined by the durational pattern (half note–quarter note) in the melody in the upper staff and the waltz-accompaniment figure in the lower staff; and the two eight-measure phrases are defined by the harmonic and melodic structure and concluding cadences.

Hierarchical schemes are a norm in many types of music. Understanding hierarchical meter and musical organization is essential when grappling with the organizational complexities of musical time. While this is not overtly true of all types of music, it is certainly true of Western music. Humans have proven to be quite comfortable creating temporal hierarchies. Sixty seconds comprise a minute, and sixty minutes make up an hour, and so on. In music we use a similar strategy, where a variable number of beats (short units of musical time) are grouped together to form

Time

Fig. 4.7 Recurring musical pulse.

Fig. 4.8 Durational pattern in traditional Western notation.

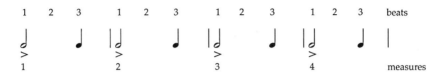

Fig. 4.9 Triple meter and two levels of rhythm.

Phrase one, eight measure phrase

Phrase two, eight measure phrase

Fig. 4.10 Three levels of rhythm.

measures (units of musical time composed of beats), and where measures are grouped together to form phrases. This type of organization is illustrated above in Figure 4.10.

The Western system of notation is organized to accommodate this hierarchical musical and metric organization. To depict these musical units we use a strategy where notational symbols specify relative duration (see Figure 4.11). In this system one whole note is equal in duration to two half notes, one half note is equal in duration to two quarter notes, one quarter note is equal in duration to two eighth notes, and so on. A series of symbols with parallel durational values called rests is used to notate silence.

As I have noted, rhythm and pitch do not function independently from one another, but are tightly entwined. That is because every note in a

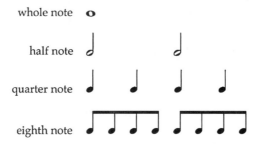

Fig. 4.11 Durational hierarchy of rhythmic values in Western music notation.

composition has both a durational and a pitch component. In the course of a musical composition, pitch and rhythm are often coordinated to shape melodic as well as harmonic formations. For example, the durational values of notes in a melodic line influence significantly our perception of that line. The classical techniques used in variation forms demonstrate fully the impact that durational and rhythmic facets of music have on the melodic aspect of music.

In addition, durational and pitch patterns together form the concept of motive. The motive is a compound musical formation containing both pitch and rhythmic elements, so in the course of the development of a motive, the melodic shape may remain the same while the rhythm may be subject to variation, or the rhythm may remain the same while the melodic shape may be varied.

A magnificent example of this type of motive development is contained in the first movement of Beethoven's Fifth Symphony in C Minor, Op. 67. Figure 4.12(A)–Figure 4.12(L) show the development of the primary motive at various points during the course of the first movement of the symphony. Figure 4.12(A) shows the primary motive, Figure 4.12(B)–Figure 4.12(E) show the motive's recurrence with intervallic variation and/or transposition. Figure 4.12(F) and Figure 4.12(G) show the motive ornamented with passing notes, while Figure 4.12(H) shows the motive in melodic inversion. Especially notable is how Beethoven squeezes the pitch contour entirely out of the motive in Figure 4.12(K) and in Figure 4.12(L) extends the motive to twenty notes, the climax very near the end of the first movement.

Different types of music evolve and transform motives in different ways. In my mind the ability to follow the motivic development in a piece of music is one of the most fundamental, interesting, and compelling ways to track the musical journey through a work without respect to style. The fact that in dance the motive and its development function in a similar

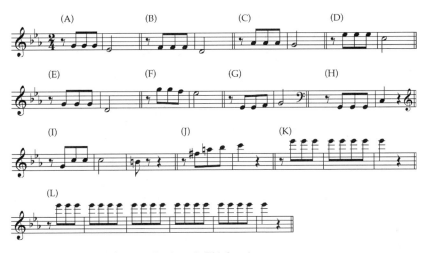

Fig. 4.12 Motivic development in Beethoven's Fifth Symphony.

fashion is all the more reason to make motive, a tangible fusion of pitch and rhythmic forces, a central part of a music course for dancers.

As we have seen, duration, the temporal aspect of sound, is central to virtually every aspect of music. Durational aspects of music create time-based formations like rhythm, meter, and hierarchical organization, and produce melodic and harmonic pitch formations. Accordingly, we want to give those elements of the temporal domain the appropriate prominence in their educational presentation. In addition, we have seen that the unique relationship between dance and music involves tight temporal relationships as compared with other music-event associations. When I have taught music classes for dancers in the past, I have delved into the issue of being "on the beat," different ways to be on the beat, different amounts of being on the beat, asking what it means to put movement on the beat, and asking if and how a dancer can move through and around beats. Inventing exercises that penetrate these questions could form an entire course on their own; however, several class periods dedicated to "on the beat" studies could benefit even our best dance students. For these reasons, I believe that all musical aspects related to the rhythmic aspect of music should be richly represented in music courses for dancers.

Timbre

Timbre (also called tone color) is the musical quality that lets us distinguish between the sounds of two different instruments when they play the same pitch. The frequency spectrum and the relative strength of each frequency component significantly influence the timbre of a sound. The wide variety of instrumental and vocal ensembles that perform music demonstrates the expressive musical potential of timbre. For instance, a work for string quartet has quite different timbral characteristics in comparison to a composition for brass quintet. The fact that musical ensembles can be made up of countless combinations of instruments that can produce an infinite variety of tone colors is one of the exceptional aspects of timbre in music.

As instruments have developed and evolved, the timbral possibilities granted composers have expanded. For instance, early string instruments have a vastly different sound from the modern violin, viola, and cello. During the twentieth century, composers became increasingly interested in new timbral possibilities. The prepared piano of John Cage, the airplane propellers of George Antheil, the sirens of Edgard Varèse, and the granulated, white-noise orchestra sounds of Iannis Xenakis all represent interest in timbral matters. The number of textbooks dedicated to extended instrumental performance techniques, which for the most part focus on new timbral potentials, confirms this intense concern with timbre. The emergence of recent electronic and computer music instruments with their immense capabilities to fabricate and modify sound provides even more opportunities for timbral explorations.

Timbre and the timbral characteristic of instruments and musical ensembles will be of interest to dance students pursuing music studies for a variety of reasons. First, different timbral qualities have different emotional affects. This simple observation might inform the performance of a dancer or guide the decisions of a choreographer. Second, the timbral fabric of a composition often corresponds to sections in the formal structure of a piece. Knowledge about such correspondences can inform the dance performer or choreographer about progression in a formal structure or composition. Third, knowledge about the timbral characteristics of single instruments or instrumental ensembles is certainly useful when seeking music for teaching or choreographic projects, and for communicating with dance accompanists or other collaborating musicians. Because students already possess knowledge about "tone of voice (timbre)," derived from early parental instruction, "Don't use that tone with me young lady (young man)," directing dancers to create movement where they also produce changing timbral vocal tones that serve as accompaniment, counterpoint, or mirrors to the movement can produce wonderful educational results.

Volume

In music we typically don't use the word "volume," but rather the term dynamics. "Dynamics" refers to the relative loudness and softness of music. (The term "dynamics" is used in entirely different way in dance and in music. While dynamics in music refers to the relative loudness and softness of music, dynamics in dance involves a combination of aspects of time and energy.) Dynamics is among the most primal of the musical elements. There is no theory for musical dynamics because none is needed. We learn very early in our lives about volume when our mothers say, "Shhhh," or when we as children quietly try to sneak up on an animal, bug, or friend.

The dynamic shadings in a piece of music provide great expressive potential, ranging from sudden dramatic change to long gradual crescendos, to nuanced shaping of melodic lines, to metric accents. It is worthwhile for dance students to learn basic dynamic markings so that they can follow scores and converse with musicians. Among the basic terminology and concepts that are useful to dance students are *fortissimo, forte, mezzo forte, mezzo piano, piano, pianissimo, crescendo, decrescendo,* and *sforzando.* We seem to correlate size and length with musical volume naturally: larger and longer with louder, smaller and shorter with softer. Exploiting this associative bias, we can devise movement studies that help define and demonstrate the concepts embedded in music dynamics. For example, with the resistance that a bungee cord provides, students can explore aspects of crescendo and decrescendo by gradually stretching and extending the cord for crescendo, and gradually releasing the length and tension in the cord for decrescendo.

Location

Sound emanates from discrete spatial locations in a three-dimensional, 360-degree sphere around us. This distribution of sound helps us to sort out and perceptually isolate sounds. The spatial location from which a sound emanates has during the course of music history been somewhat of the neglected musical parameter. There are, however, examples dating back at least to the antiphonal singing of chant or to the Gabriellis's spatialization practices at St. Mark's Cathedral in Venice, where the spatial disposition of instrumentalists or vocalists was significant. In modern contexts, there are instances when the spatial location of a sound does become important. For instance, the spatial distribution of instrumentalists in large ensembles is, in part, to facilitate the musical blending and isolation of various instrumental timbres. Spatial issues are central to the composition of electronic music, especially in surround-sound environments. Because spatial location has historically been less exploited as a sonic attribute, there may be reason to diminish its prominence in a music course for dancers. On the other hand, because dance deals so explicitly with space, creatively involving dance students' knowledge about the spatial domain can illuminate music's application of spatial concepts.

Practical Aspects: Content, Courses, and Method

It is probably clear that I approach the teaching of music by progressing from fundamental concepts to more complex ones. There are many advantages to proceeding in this manner. First and foremost, there is great clarity in a pedagogical organization of a course where central ideas arise from a limited number of sources. Virtually every musical concept can be traced back to the five musical attributes — pitch, duration, timbre, volume, and location — their unfolding in time, and the relationship between dance and music. As we have seen, the more complex musical structures such as melody, harmony, consonance, dissonance, rhythm, tempo, and meter, as well as basic musical terminology and musical notation, arise naturally from these.

As a practical matter, there will be a limited number of music courses that can be offered in a dance curriculum. Therefore, we will want to scale the material to be included in the music curriculum based on the number of music courses to be offered, and on such things as faculty resources and overall programmatic objectives. I would argue that, at a minimum, those musical elements that have close affiliations with pitch, duration, timbre, and volume in particular, and those that function as agents that coordinate dance and music, should be the central focus of a music course or curriculum. Focus on the basic sonic attributes alone would give students a way to approach any type of music. Beyond the five sonic attributes, my list of essential inclusions contains melody, harmony, counterpoint, consonance, dissonance, dynamics, rhythm, meter, tempo, and musical form. From these concepts, discussion could easily be extended to include aspects such as musical styles or genres of compositions.

If there is an affiliated music department as part of the college or university, it may be possible to augment the music courses offered in dance. "Arts and Letters" types of courses — such as Introduction to Music — are often required as part of the university general requirement and there is no reason why dance students cannot be encouraged or directed to take them. I don't suggest that these courses replace those dedicated to teaching music to dancers. Music courses dedicated to addressing the specific educational needs of dance students are essential to advancing the student's musical development. Courses offered in music schools or music departments probably have substantially different curricular objectives. Even so, if thoughtfully selected, the courses offered under the auspices of music may be able to augment students' exposure to musical concepts.

If there were three ten-week courses, as there were when I taught in the Department of Dance at the University of Oregon, I might suggest that the broad topic of music be divided into smaller subtopics, such as music fundamentals, music for choreography, and music for teaching. We used Fundamentals of Rhythm to introduce many of these essential concepts along with basic music terminology and notational concepts. Music for Dancers was a type of choreographic workshop where students could examine and discover relationships between music and dance within a guided structure. Dance Accompaniment was offered to provide a mechanism for students to learn about communicating and working with dance accompanists. If there is, say, only one sixteen-week course, then the amount of material would have to be somewhat reduced, perhaps with the content of the music fundamentals and music for choreography courses being collapsed into a single course. In this scenario, it would be desirable to include some discussion in a dance pedagogy course about how to communicate with dance accompanists.

I would organize the material of these classes along these lines:

Fundamentals of Music: This course would examine the five sonic attributes and musical concepts such as harmony, melody, counterpoint, consonance, dissonance, rhythm, meter, and tempo. The course would also introduce concepts of basic musical notation (with emphasis on rhythm), and basic terminology useful in locating music for choreographic projects, for communicating with dance accompanists and other musicians, or for pursuing scholarly research in dance and dance history. Elementary aspects of musical structure and form would also be introduced.

Music and Choreography: This course would present more advanced musical concepts through the prism of choreographic challenges. More advanced concepts of musical structure and the musical forces that generate it would be explored. By creating choreographic challenges for students to complete in relation to provided musical scores, students would gain new knowledge about musical style, form, and music history. More advanced terminology would be introduced as a natural by-product of the introduction of new concepts.

Dance Accompaniment: This course would create the opportunity for students to experience working as teachers with a dance accompanist, to develop effective and efficient techniques to communicate with an accompanist, to discover potential problems that may arise in communications, and to use musical terminology in manners that are helpful in such communications.

There are many effective ways to present course content to a class. Certainly different student populations and academic contexts will suggest different pedagogical methodologies and educational objectives. I believe that, in general, the most direct way a dancer can learn about music is primarily, though not exclusively, through the physicality of movement. There are several advantages to this methodology. First, using dancers' native tongues as the mediating interface for learning music allows students to bring most effectively their knowledge about dance to the study of music. Dancers can employ their knowledge about space and movement and connect it directly to the spatial and gestural metaphors used by musicians. Dancers can also bring to the music classroom concepts—such as counterpoint—that are jointly held between the two arts and find immediate and accurate meaningfulness. Second, approaching music through the window of dance helps bring into focus the dance-music relationship. Perhaps it is the pragmatist in me, but dancers take music classes to gain insight into how music can beautifully and wonderfully serve dance's aesthetic needs in performance and choreographic contexts. Using movement as an educational instrument directly serves this need. If one is inclined to supplement this focus on physicality, then there are also opportunities to enhance the basic course content through carefully selected outside listening and reading assignments. I would not discourage such supplementation.

There are many possible ways to frame this general methodology. When I taught these courses, I began by trying to make direct correspondences between the students' current knowledge and the new musical material I selected to present. After a few explanatory and introductory comments about the concepts to be considered, I would often pose questions to the class such as, "How could we physically represent the shape of this melody in movement?" This question can be answered with both verbal and kinesthetic responses. I consistently found that the Socratic method of teaching, question followed by answer, was especially effective at eliciting both an intellectual and physical response to the material being studied. Following from this method, the class could develop an understanding of pitch through creating individual and group movement that corresponds to melodic shape. The class could develop an understanding of timbre by vocalizing a tone of voice — then moving in correspondence to their own vocal tones. The class could develop an understanding about counterpoint through the creation of movement that demonstrates various contrapuntal relationships such as canon, diminution, augmentation, retrogression and inversion. Using this Q and A methodology we could also approach questions such as: What does it means to dance *on the beat, off the beat, or through the beat*? To me, the answers to these questions are given vividness not when they are answered with words and thoughts alone, but rather when dancers' movements find the "on, off, and through" of the beat.

When I have taught music for dancers' courses, I did not use a text. Instead I used musical scores or produced original material customized to serve my specific pedagogical aims. On occasion, I provided material from other sources that augmented and enhanced the topics under consideration. I am not sure how I would approach this issue now. There exist, however, some wonderful opportunities to enhance music courses for dancers through additional readings.

The Internet allows us to peek over the shoulders of teachers of music from all over the world, to learn from their pedagogical approaches, and to gain new knowledge. The material posted on the Web by my colleague at the University of Oregon, Christian Cherry, contains a number of interesting insights about teaching music to dancers. In addition, the International Guild of Dance Musicians publishes a scholarly journal that focuses on issues that arise in the dance-music relationship. Two years, 1991 and 1992, are posted as PDF files that can be downloaded. Among the articles posted there are "The Evolution of Martha Graham's Collaborations with Composers of Music for the Modern Dance," by John Toenjes, "Music and Dance, The Continuing Relationship," by Robert Kaplan, and "A Collaborative Process," by Larry Attaway, to name only a few. The Attaway article, in which he shares with the reader a daily chronicle of activities, is especially revealing about the creative interactions among artists.

In book form there is *Music for the Dance: Reflections on a Collaborative Art*, by Katherine Teck, which presents material primarily in the form of interviews with professionals working in the dance field. These interviews represent a number of perspectives from the ballet and modern worlds whose reading could be included in a course structure. Perhaps the most relevant in our discussion is her chapter "What Is Musicality in a Dancer?" where artists like Lou Harrison and Hanya Holm respond to this question (Teck 1989, 167–83). In additional to readings that focus on dance-music interaction it might also be reasonable to incorporate readings about the fundamentals of music or music history. Among the texts that might prove useful in this regard is Tom Manoff's *Music: A Living Language*. Manoff's (1982) extensive work covers the fundamentals of music, presenting them with sophisticated and advanced lines of thinking and in a manner easily understandable by dance and music students alike.

Bibliography

Attaway, Larry. "A Collaborative Process." In *International Guild of Musicians in Dance Journal.* Vol. 1 (1991), pp. 17–23.

Cox, Arnie Walter. *The Metaphoric Logic of Musical Motion and Space.* Dissertation (Ph.D.), University of Oregon, 1999.

Hodgins, Paul. *Relationships between Score and Choreography in Twentieth-Century Dance: Music, Movement, and Metaphor.* Lewiston/Queenston/Lampeter: Edwin Mellen Press, 1992.

Horst, Louis. *Pre-Classic Dance Forms.* 3rd edition. Foreword by Henry Gilfond. Brooklyn: Dance Horizons, Incorporated, 1968.

Kaplan, Robert. "Music and Dance, The Continuing Relationship." In *International Guild of Musicians in Dance Journal.* Vol. 1 (1991), pp. 32–35.

Kapuscinski, Jaroslaw. "Basic Theory of Intermedia—Composing with Sounds and Images." Originally published in *Monochord. De musica acta, studia et commentarii,* (Torún: Adam Marszelek Publications, 1998), Vol. XIX, pp. 43–50.

Manoff, Tom. *Music: A Living Language.* New York: W. W. Norton & Company, 1982.

Rosen, Charles. *The Frontiers of Meaning: Three Informal Lectures on Music.* New York: Hill & Wang, 1994.

Sawyer, Elizabeth. *Dance with the Music: The World of the Ballet Musician.* Cambridge, New York: Cambridge University Press, 1985.

Teck, Katherine. *Music for the Dance: Reflections on a Collaborative Art.* New York: Greenwood Press, 1989.

Thayer, Alexander. *Life of Beethoven.* Vol. 2. Revised and edited by Elliott Forbes. Princeton: Princeton University Press, 1967.

Toenjes, John. "The Evolution of Martha Graham's Collaborations with Composers of Music for the Modern Dance." In *International Guild of Musicians in Dance Journal,* Vol. 2 (1992), pp. 1–10.

Yeston, Maury. *The Stratification of Musical Rhythm.* New Haven: Yale University Press, 1976.

CHAPTER 5

Teaching Dance on Film and Film Dance

BETH GENNÉ

In a perfect world, we could take our students to see live performances of the dance we study in class. But for the vast majority of us this is just not possible. Even in major dance centers like London and New York, the repertory on view does not always fit the needs of the classroom. We must rely on film, video, and, more recently, digital imagery to "illustrate" dance studies. In this chapter, I'll take a look at both the potential and the problems of using the moving image in the university classroom. And I'll offer some strategies that I've found to be especially effective, inside and outside, of the classroom. Of course, in time, you will develop your own.

Used correctly, the recorded moving image can be one of the most effective tools for teaching dance studies. The increasing availability of the moving image has been a significant factor in the development of our discipline. Film, video, and DVD make possible deep and sustained visual analysis, an essential skill that lies at the heart of the best dance scholarship. With the use of freeze frame, slow motion, and the rewind button, dance can be analyzed as never before in history. I am constantly finding new ways to use these functions to analyze movement and point out details that too often elude us in the rush of performance.

Freeze frame is a fabulous tool for showing your students what you mean when you talk about a dancer's "line," on the ground and in the air. With slow motion, you can pick out details and nuances that too often get lost. You can point out, for example, a choreographer's favorite movement motif or show how dancers can phrase and shape the very same movement quite differently from each other. The rewind button is even more impressive. Balanchine once said that the way to learn about dance is to see more of it. I require students to view dance works several times, and I often give assignments that require them to choose a telling moment in a dance work to see over and over and discuss, compare, and contrast.

Films, videos, and DVDs also make it easy to use one of the most effective visual teaching techniques: comparison and contrast. On the first day of my survey of European and American dance from the Renaissance to the present, I'll often take the student on a visual "ride" through the course. The unifying theme is the genre of the pas de deux, and in an hour and a half you can swing through several centuries of theatrical dance: juxtaposing couple dances from the Renaissance and Baroque with examples from the Romantic, modern, and postmodern eras to show not only stylistic and technical changes, but also how our attitudes toward gender definition and relationship have evolved. Or you can compare different performers: all the mad scenes from *Giselle*; the White Swan and Black Swan pas de deux performed by Russian, British, and American dancers coming from different eras and schools, and each with a different approach to the role; Martha Graham's performance of *Lamentation* with Peggy Lyman's, or Yuriko and Graham as the bride in *Appalachian Spring*. You can also show how dances in Bollywood movies combine gestures from classical and popular Indian dances (Bharata Natyam, Odissi, and Bhangra), as well as from American entertainers such as Michael Jackson and John Travolta. You can illustrate both the subtle similarities and drastic differences of classical dance from the neighboring Indonesian islands of Bali and Java. The possibilities are endless, and the more you teach the more you will find.

To Talk or Not to Talk

When I first began teaching dance studies, I regarded the film as a kind of sacred text. As with a performance, you didn't talk while other people were dancing. Over the years, though, I've found it particularly effective to point things out on the screen like an art historian and to highlight or anticipate certain moments. In a survey course, when time is scarce, students need this kind of guidance, and even though you have seen this performance many, many times, they still need practice to really see (and absorb) what is going by so quickly. On the other hand you can "overtalk" so students end up looking for so many details that they become overloaded. Thus it is best to suggest one or two major things for them to look for before the film starts and then indicate when they appear. Whenever you can repeat sections, do so. No matter what, there is always more to see.

In all cases the classroom experience should be supplemented with visual examples outside of class. At the University of Michigan, we have copies of the DVDs and videos used in class on reserve for the students to study, and we also have a large library with dance examples. I assign viewings as well as readings in preparation for every class and analysis of these viewings is the basis for many, if not most, of our assignments.

Some Limitations of Film, Video, and DVD Recordings of Theatrical Dance

Film, video, and DVD have drawbacks as well as advantages in the classroom, and it is important to make students aware of them. Even when we can find a visual record of a dance on film, there are many problems. Any dance created for the stage or another "real" space is transformed by the camera. The camera creates an entirely different frame for the dancer than the proscenium stage, and so drastically alters the relationship of the performer to the space in which he moves and to the audience that is watching. Thus, a new and "invisible" author is interposed between the audience and the creative team of the dancer and choreographer: the film director, whose choice of camera angle, camera movement, and lighting can completely transform our perception of the dance. The director adds not only another layer of movement to the choreography, but, through the juxtaposition of long, medium, and close shots, forcefully directs and redirects our gaze in ways the choreographer may not have intended. Another problem is that film is flat — two-dimensional — and the physical and emotional impact of a living, breathing human body moving through the air and space that you both share is lost. Gene Kelly describes it:

> What you do miss in motion pictures is, mainly, the kinetic force. You're with the audience in the theater. You look at them and you can embrace them and they can embrace you so to speak, or you can hate each other, but you get no direct response from the screen. It is so remote from the empathy of the live theater (Knox 1973, 47).

Films as Fragments of the Past

There are other reasons a film of a historical stage dance cannot always stand as an accurate historical document: the ever-changing nature of the dance itself and our methods of preserving it. In many ways, dance historians face the same problems as archaeologists, as they must painstakingly piece together a mosaic of fragments within a context of archival research.

Archeologists can't, for example, show you the Parthenon as it looked in the fifth century B.C.E when it was built; time and history have taken their toll. The ancient temple of Athena at the heart of modern Athens is roofless and stripped, for the most part, of its decorative sculpture, now many miles away in the British Museum. The once brilliant polychrome surface has long ago disappeared and pollution has blurred the definition of the marble carving. The gold statue of *Athena Parthenos*, which once dominated the interior, is long gone. Nevertheless, the shell of the structure is still intact and the surviving details can tell you a lot, though not all, about the missing pieces.

It is the same for dance. Until relatively recently, dances were never recorded systematically in any great detail. Without a standardized, universally accepted written system of dance notation, the tradition has been an oral one: dancers passing down choreography by teaching the roles to their successors. It is similar to the party game of telephone, where a message transmitted in whispers down a line of people becomes a very different message when spoken out loud at the end of the line. The more people who transmit it, the more the message changes. Notice that I'm using words like "change" and "transformation" and not "distortion." This kind of transformation or change is not necessarily viewed as bad. It was expected that each choreographer or ballet master add his own stamp or "update" a work to suit the evolving technique of the dancer and the differing interests of the audiences. I can show my class, for example, any one of a number of *Giselles* now available on film, video, and DVD. But the *Giselle* that we see today performed by the Royal Ballet, American Ballet Theatre, Bolshoi, or Kirov (all available on video and some on DVD) incorporates the changes and additions of several generations of choreographers, each with varying national backgrounds, training, and technical traditions, although, as with the Parthenon, the shell of the original work may remain, with some individual sections remarkably well preserved.

As a historian, I try to "channel" the *Giselle* that lies at the core of each new production overlaid by layers of change, but still there if you look for it. I point out that the production of the *Giselle* we see on film has far more point work and far less mime than the *Giselle* French audiences saw in 1841. I tell them that the ballet's ending has an entirely different feeling with Bathilde's elimination from the final scene. And I assign Gautier and Saint-Georges' original, far more detailed libretto for them to read, instead of contemporary "Stories of the Ballets," and have them study Marian Smith's marvelous discoveries about the inaccurate wedding of music and mime in the American Ballet Theatre production, for example (Smith 2000, 2).

It is critically important to let our students know that dance studies is shaped by what is, or is not, available to be shown in class. Every year, new dance videos and DVDs appear on the market, expanding the repertory that we can show in class. But in comparison with our colleagues in the history of art or music, we still have to make do with a very small and incomplete repertory. It is hard not to envy the art historian, who has access to reproductions of hundreds of paintings, drawings, and sculptures to illustrate the evolution of oil painting from the Renaissance to the present day or trace the work of Picasso from youth to old age. Or the musicologist, who can compare any one of Mozart's forty-one symphonies (in any number of different performances) with any one of Haydn's more than one hundred. We often have to make do with only one or two examples of a choreographer's work. And sadly, for many, we have none at all.

I can buy a videotape of Pierre Lacotte's reconstruction of Taglioni's *La Sylphide* with so much sustained point work that I can't believe it is very close to the original. But what about the Bournonville *La Sylphide*? It is not available commercially. I do have a videotape of *La Sylphide* made for television by the Royal Danish Ballet: Nicolai Hubbë is James, Lis Jeppeson is the Sylph, and Sorella Englund is a truly frightening and powerful Madge. I've been using this tape for more than ten years now, and it is getting increasingly worn and blurry. Videotape has a limited lifespan, so to save the original, about five years ago I made a copy of my copy. That means my class now sees a bad copy of a copy. Now that it is relatively easy to transfer video to DVD, I'll have a more permanent copy, but it will lack the luster and sharp definition of my original recording.

Even though I can now prevent further degeneration of my precious *Sylphide* tape, there is a bigger problem, as this production is not commercially available, and it is copyrighted. If I show this tape in class, am I breaking the law? Probably not. I have consulted with the university lawyers who deal with such things and they tell me that because I'm not charging admission and am using the video for educational purposes, I *probably* can show the tape in class. I *cannot,* however, copy the tape and put it on reserve in the university library for my students to study.

I *can* buy a copy of *Napoli* —which *is* available in the United States— and put *that* in the library as my one example of Bournonville's many ballets. But there is another problem. I really want to show the Bournonville *Sylphide,* and I want my students to be able to study it. I've been telling them about the extraordinary impact of this *ballet d'action* on its audiences and its powerful influence on dance in general. Of all the performances I can show, this particular one comes closest to proving that Romantic ballet is thrilling to watch — and not just for the dance. It has a good amount of vivid, subtle, and convincing mime by the whole of the Royal Danish Ballet. In my opinion, it comes the closest I know to the effect of the nineteenth-century *ballet d'action*. And my students, children of the computer and MTV age, can sense it, and they sense it in a way they don't with any other example I can show them. They start out by reading Bournonville's libretto (translated by Patricia McAndrew in Selma Jeanne Cohen's anthology *Dance as a Theatre Art*). At first, some of them think, "Who cares about this silly story?" But by the end of the first act they are completely drawn in and they love it. They want to see more, but we don't have enough class time if we are going to make it into the twenty-first century in fourteen weeks. Nonetheless, I can't put it on reserve.

For twentieth-century dance, more is available, but there is still not enough. In the 1970s, for example, the American Public Television series *Dance in America* documented much of the Balanchine repertory. Several, but not all of these tapes, were made commercially available. This means I can show Balanchine ballets that are from almost every part of his career and that, just as important, were filmed under his supervision. Balanchine was quite aware of the special problems of the small screen and worked with his directors on camera movement and lighting to get the best effects, with no jump cutting and hardly any close-ups, except in dramatic ballets like *Prodigal Son*. The Balanchine Foundation has been making videotapes of Balanchine dancers from all periods showing dancers in interpretations of their most important roles, and they have made these tapes (*The Balanchine Interpreters Archive*) available to university libraries. The tapes are expensive, but no more so than a series of lavish special-edition art or science books. Any good research institution should include these in its collection. This means that I can actually teach an advanced-level course in Balanchine and trace and illustrate the development of the career of a single choreographer over almost a lifetime.

Unfortunately, this is an unusual situation. What about Tudor, Ashton, Fokine, Nijinska, Massine, Dunham, and Limón? Thanks, in part, to the *Dance in America* series we can get some Graham, Cunningham, and Taylor, but far less than their stature might suggest. Most modern and postmodern choreographers are poorly if at all represented. In the United States, it is almost impossible to get visual records of British, European, and Australian modern and postmodern dance. The list goes on and on. And, of course, the further removed in history, the fewer examples we have, so that reconstructions of Renaissance, Baroque, and eighteenth-century dance are very scarce.

This is not the worst scenario. I've been talking about the European and American dance traditions, but what about dance in the rest of the world?

The second semester of our introductory course at the University of Michigan is entitled, for lack of a better title, "Topics in World Dance." In it we cover, as best as we can, a variety of dance forms from around the world; in this category, we are even more hampered by lack of examples. I need good commercially available videotapes of court dances from Java and Bali, to say nothing of the rest of Indonesia and Southeast Asia, and I need more tapes of Odissi and Kathakali from India. (Bharata Natyam is easier.) We lack videos of Pacific Island dance from Fiji, Samoa, the Cook Islands, New Zealand, and of ancient Hawaiian hulas. Videos of the huge variety of dances in Africa and South and Central America are also hard to find, and I'm desperate for examples of Chinese folk and classical dance. And I want a video of Kabuki with English subtitles and of Korean classical dance. To be sure, there is the "JVC Anthology of World Music and Dance," an invaluable thirty-videotape series of music and dance from around the world with accompanying explanatory booklets. (There is an English version as well as a Japanese one.) It is an extraordinary resource, but too often the examples are truncated and filmed without dance values in mind, with choppy editing and too many close-ups.

The crucial point is that what I can teach of dance history is shaped by what films are available. Until we get more repertory on film, we cannot teach the full spectrum of dance and are forced to draw a skewed and incomplete picture of dance history. The limited availability of dance images not only restricts our ability to teach, it also affects what we research and we write about. I'll return to this, which is one of the most important problems facing our field, at the end of the chapter.

Teaching Film Dance

In this section, I write about film dance that is made specifically for the camera and in which choreography and camera work play equal and interdependent roles to create a unified whole. The good news is that almost every limitation that I have discussed in relation to stage dance recorded on film or video is not an issue here. Film dance is a new art form, born in the twentieth century and still developing. From the very beginning, dance was a major subject of the new twentieth-century art form called cinema, which was first presented to the public by the Lumière Brothers in Paris in 1895 and soon after by Thomas Edison in New York in 1896. Film dance, for the first time in history, preserved what had been an ephemeral art form. Like painting and sculpture, film dance can survive the death of the artist and be shown to later audiences in approximately the original format.

This medium offered new visual perspectives on the dancer and chore-ography and was perhaps the biggest change in the way Euro-American dance was viewed since the invention of the proscenium frame stage. With the moving camera, the dancer and the dance could be seen from any angle and the special effects of editing, lighting, and, in the later years of the twentieth century, digital imagery, added a new dimension to dance and the dancer on film.

There are as many ways of making film dance as there are styles of chore-ographers. In film dance, the most important of the dancer-choreographers in the movies became *directors* as well, whether through their dance sequences (Astaire and Balanchine) or the entire movie (Kelly and Donen). Fred Astaire used the frontal positioning of the dancer on a proscenium stage as a model, but took advantage of the cinematic medium to create an "ideal" theater seat for the viewer, which moved on level with the per-former to keep the full body of the dancer at the center of the viewing experience. Astaire also experimented with the special effects only possible with film, employing the moving camera in outdoor locations, slow motion, and multiple image effects. It was Busby Berkeley, however, who completely abandoned the proscenium stage model to create a spectacle in which the camera roamed freely through space, above and below, around, and even between the bodies he filmed. At times, his camera was more active than the dancers themselves. He employed close and medium shots to isolate parts of the dancer's anatomy, and used special cinematic effects — dramatic lighting, dissolves, and surrealistic images — to create a seem-ingly infinite fantasy dance space unbound by the laws of physics.

George Balanchine and Gene Kelly (the latter working with Vincente Minnelli and Stanley Donen) combined both approaches — keeping the dancer's full body, for the most part, at the center of the viewer's experi-ence, but also judiciously employing the moving camera and rhythmic editing to enhance the impact of the dancer's movement. Taking full advantage of color film, Vincente Minnelli, working with Astaire and Kelly, pioneered special color and lighting effects by coordinating color and lighting changes tightly with music and dance. Bob Fosse quickened the pace of his editing, isolating body parts with his camera as well as his choreography to create as much momentum with his jump cuts as the dancers' own movements. (Rob Marshall followed in his footsteps in his film of Fosse's *Chicago*).

Contemporary video dances combine techniques from all of these dancer-director-choreographers. One of the most interesting things you can show undergraduates is how the videos that they buy or see on televi-sion have evolved from earlier dance by comparing Michael Jackson, for example, with his idols Fred Astaire, Gene Kelly, and the Nicholas Brothers (see Genné 2002, 2003a, 2003b).

If images of theatrical dance are scarce and hard to obtain, popular film dance (i.e., in the movies) is the opposite. A trip to most video stores — or a search of amazon.com — can bring you virtually the entire repertory of popular film dance, so that you can, for example, easily compare and contrast choreographers, directors and dancers from every era. And the same is true of video-dance.

Dances created for film, video, DVD, and computer that were developed outside of mainstream cinema are a different case. The film dances, for example, of unique artists such as Maya Deren, Norman MacClaren, Meredith Monk, and Pooh Kaye are less available than movies, but are slowly becoming more obtainable through independent film distributors, and sometimes even the artists themselves. This is such a burgeoning field that it is difficult to keep up, but the Internet can help. You can check out the latest film and video dance creations at annual dance film festivals, such as the one annually held at the Film Society of Lincoln Center in New York. Once you have their works, you have them in the format in which they were intended to be seen. One hopes that, as with the recent *Envisioning Dance on Film and Video* (Mitoma 2002), books will be accompanied by DVDs that give you a chance to experience the moving image as well as read about it.

Whether you teach popular movies or experimental video, you need to make sure that you pay as much attention to the movement of the camera, the rhythm and style of the editing, and the use of special effects, as you do to the movement of the dancer, and to be constantly aware of how the two (and the soundtrack, if there is one) interact. This is not easy to do. (Consulting a film encyclopedia — like *Katz's Film Encyclopedia* — along with a film studies survey text to introduce you to basic terminology and various ways of "reading" and analyzing film can be extremely useful.) The job of the film director is to make you forget the many facets of the medium and to concentrate on the whole that is created. One of the best and most effective ways to break down and analyze these facets is to turn the sound off and concentrate only on the movement of the dancer and the camera.

A Room of Your Own

Whether you are teaching dance on film or film dance, you need to be able to present it to your students in the best possible way. Just as a dancer needs a sprung floor or marley, a painter needs paints and brushes, and a scientist must have a well-equipped laboratory, the teacher of dance studies needs the proper space and the proper equipment to show films, videos, and DVDs. When I first began teaching dance studies courses, I spent a lot of time trundling a heavy cart laden with a TV, VCR, and DVD player from class to class. Before and after every session, during the ten minutes between the end of one class and the beginning of the next, I'd hook up numerous cords and press many buttons, try to angle the monitor so that most of the class could see it, and then run around the room pulling down shades — often tripping over the tangled cords snaked on the floor in the process. In the darkened classroom, pressing the right buttons on the remote could be hit or miss. It was, to say the least, a time-consuming and disheartening task.

Now I have a "room of my own" that is set up to my specifications for teaching dance studies. It took a lot of convincing, but it was worth it. This dedicated classroom has a wall-sized screen, a built-in video projector, and a blackboard at the side of the lectern that can be separately illuminated when the room is dark. I can operate the multistandard VCR and DVD player, Powerpoint, and CD and audiocassette players from a lighted lectern at the front of the class. The room is windowless (and air conditioned) and can be lighted from the front with either standard fluorescent classroom lights and/or incandescent lights spotted in the room at various intervals. These lights are on a dimmer, so that at any time during the class I can raise or lower the lights to the degree I wish. I can make the room completely black or I can raise the dimmer incandescent lights so that students can take notes.

I consider each one of the features to be absolutely essential to teaching a good dance studies class, but when I first proposed them to the university, I had to fight for every item. Do you really have to have incandescent as well as fluorescent lights? *Yes*, and here is why. Fluorescent lights, even if dimmed, spread a uniform glow of ghastly spectral light over the classroom, which can drastically wash out screen contrast and color. Incandescent lights spotted over the classroom focus soft light in directed pools over the students' seats so that they can take notes. (There is a no-light zone immediately before the screen, meaning you get an absolute minimum of reflected light on the screen.) Fluorescent and full-spectrum lights wash out screen color far more than directed incandescents. The effect is like trying to show a video outdoors on a cloudy day.

My classroom has two doors: one at the front near the screen and one at the back of the classroom. They are windowless so that light from the corridor cannot wash the screen out. You'd be amazed at how a stream of light, even coming through a narrow slit, can wash out the detail and color in a motion picture image. What you are aiming for is the absolute darkness of a movie theater. And as in a good movie theater, the size of the screen matters: the bigger the screen, the better. It means that every student has a good view of the screen and its detail. There is nothing more difficult than trying to follow a corps de ballet or a group dance on a small television screen. The features of this classroom are not unusual, and you can find them in art history and film studies departments in your university. Try to negotiate use of those classrooms until you, too, can have a room of your own.

Building Your Own Video and DVD Library

Any graduate student in dance studies has probably already started to collect videos and DVDs — not only those that are commercially available, but those broadcast on television, and not only from the country they live in, but from others as well. As you get to know your colleagues from abroad, you'll find it increasingly easy to exchange copies of videotapes and DVDs, not only from their personal collections but also from those available commercially in their own countries. This "underground" network is a crucial resource, and I can't overstate the importance of starting a collection and networking with colleagues to supplement your archive. The BBC, CBC, and European and Russian television have paid far more attention to dance than American broadcasters (with the honorable exception of PBS). It is extremely important to have a well-equipped classroom with multistandard video and DVD players so that you can show works recorded in various international formats: PAL, SECAM, NTSC, MESCAM, M-PAL, N-PAL.

For the Future:

As dance studies are taught in more and more universities, the problems I've been discussing should begin to lessen. I realize that it is not practical to urge the creation of more commercially available tapes and DVDs. Videotapes and DVDs, especially of less well-known dances, "won't sell." At the least, they won't sell until dance has as widespread an audience as music or art. The irony is that audiences won't get interested in dance unless they can see it in the first place. That, in part, is up to instructors. If we can convince company directors and archivists that it is in their interest to make records of their repertory available to dance educators and that it will expand their audiences and not deplete them, we could move toward solving the problems I've been discussing.

Anyone who has been to major exhibitions at the Metropolitan Museum or the Museum of Modern Art in New York will see tourists willing to stand patiently in long lines. I have never passed the Louvre in the summer without seeing a long line, and I know that to get into Florence's Uffizi Gallery during the summer without an advance reservation, you had better be willing to get up very early and fortify yourself with a cappuccino for a long wait. People are not kept away from these art galleries because they've all seen (and can easily buy) reproductions of the paintings and sculptures they contain. They want to see and be touched by the *real* Raphael, Botticelli, Michelangelo, Rembrandt, Van Gogh, Matisse, and their fellow artists. Many will have made their acquaintance with these artists in introductory courses in high school or college, and the reproductions that decorate their dorm — and later house and apartment walls — only increase their desire to experience the originals.

There is no reason that those same audiences could not be queuing at major dance venues in New York, San Francisco, London, and Paris to see choreography by Bournonville, Petipa, Balanchine, Ashton, Graham, Cunningham, Taylor, and their fellow choreographers, no matter how many times they've seen them on video or DVD at home or in the classroom. They need to know about them before they'll want to come, however.

That is our job. But we cannot do it without the right tools. If we can form an alliance of dance educators to negotiate with the holders of dance resources — companies, television archives, choreographers, private collectors, and libraries around the world — to make visual examples available to dance historians in the same way that slides can be bought by art historians and CDs by musicologists, we can make a significant impact on future audiences for dance. It is especially important now, because the technology exists to create a database of moving images that could be accessed through the Internet and sent to classrooms around the world. Of course, choreographers' and performers' rights must be protected, and I could certainly see educational institutions and libraries paying a fee to use this service, as well as the need for a password for the site.

Films, videos, and DVDs can be among the most effective tools in the teaching of dance studies, but we need to tell our stories as fully and richly as we can. It is our job not only to teach with what we have, but also to make sure that future generations have more to teach.

A final note: The medium of the moving image is probably changing more rapidly than any other. During my teaching career, I've seen DVDs supersede videotape as the easiest medium to use in quality of image, portability, endurance, and storage capacity. The future is limitless: Maybe in a couple of years we'll be able to carry moving images, as we now do music, in some moving image "iPod" that will access images as easily as we pull out music.

Bibliography

Altman, Rick. *The American Film Musical*. Bloomington: Indiana University Press, 1989.

Billman, Larry. *Film Choreographers and Dance Directors: An Illustrated Biographical Encyclopedia with a History and Filmographies*. North Carolina : MacFarland & Co, 1995.

Cohen, Selma Jeanne, ed. *Dance as a Theatre Art: Source Readings in Dance History* from 1581 to the Present, Second Edition (with a new section by Katy Matheson), Princeton: Princeton Book Company, 1992.

Croce, Arlene. *The Fred Astaire and Ginger Rogers Book*. New York: Outerbridge and Lazard, 1972.

Dodds, Sherill. *Dance on Screen: Genres and media from Hollywood to Experimental Art*. London: Palgrave, 2001.

Delamter, Jerome. *Dance in the Hollywood Musical*. Ann Arbor: UMI Research Press, 1981.

Genné, Beth. "Dancing in the Street from Fred Astaire to Michael Jackson." In *Re-thinking Dance History*. Edited by Alexandra Carter. London and New York: Routledge, 2003.

Genné, Beth. "Dance in Film." In *The Living Dance: An Anthology of Essays on Movement and Culture*. Edited by Genevieve Benahum. Iowa : Kendall-Hunt, 2003.

Genné, Beth. "Dancing' in the Rain: Gene Kelly's Musical Films." In *Envisioning Dance on Film and Video*. Edited by J. Mitoma, 71–77. New York and London: Routledge, 2002.

Hirschhorn, Clive. *The Hollywood Musical*. New York: Crown, 1981.

Katz, Ephraim, *The Film Encyclopedia*, 4th edition, revised by F. Klein and R. D. Nolen, New York: Harper Collins, 2001

Knox, Donald. *The Magic Factory: How MGM Made* An American in Paris. New York: Praeger, 1973.

Jordan, Stephanie and Allen, D., eds. *Parallel Lines: Media Representations of Dance*. London: Libbey, 1993.

Mitoma, Judy, ed. *Envisioning Dance on Film and Video*. London and New York: Routledge, 2002.

Mueller, John. *Astaire Dancing*. New York: Knopf, 1985.

Prevots, Naima. *Dancing in the Sun: Hollywood Choreographers 1915–1937*. Ann Arbor: UMI Research Press, 1987.

Smith, Marion. *Ballet and Opera in the Age of Giselle*. Princeton: Princeton University Press, 2000.

Stearns, Marshall and Stearns Jean. *Jazz Dance*. New York: Macmillan, 1973.

CHAPTER 6

Teaching Dance History: A Querying Stance as Millennial Lens

LINDA J. TOMKO

How should we teach dance history in the millennium? To grapple with that question we must recognize the challenges that current academic inquiry poses to at least three of the anchors that comprise the question itself: the very notions of what constitutes dance, history, and acts of teaching. Yet never was the cry for historical perspective more vividly voiced in contemporary culture than at this time of fact-finding commissions on why the United States went to war with Iraq in 2003. We may take this impulse and imperative from the quotidian as one kind of buttress for rethinking what it can mean to teach dance history for new waves of students in a new century. At the same time, I will offer here no universal formula for teaching dance history.

As a female, white academic whose deepest preparation has been in dance practices of European and U.S. traditions, I am keenly aware that this working knowledge addresses only part of the everyday experiences or cultural familiarities for the students I encounter on the most diverse campus in the University of California system. The challenge for me, as well as for my students, is to query dances past and present that exceed a Eurocentric orbit and to remap our views of what dancings matter, where and when, how, and to what ends. At the same time, no matter how diligent our endeavors, the day has waned for single scales of value or comprehensive conclusions about change over time in dance and movement practices.

In this chapter, I speak to challenges currently posed to notions of dance, history, and acts of teaching. These are framed in terms of the academy in the United States, the area of my familiarity. I then suggest several lines of inquiry that can serve as nodes for framing historical study of dance practices in cultures, and for querying the ends of historical inquiry itself. To acknowledge the partial character of knowledge, and of revisionary efforts, I articulate continuing questions that beset this process of rethinking.

Dance/History as Academic Enterprise

When "dance" entered U.S. universities in the early twentieth century, it was frequently housed in physical education departments. New dance curricula promoted the acquisition and deepening of movement technique that has become known as "modern dance." Instruction in modern dance composition was quickly added to this curriculum, a step that required the theorizing and articulation of compositional strategies where no such excursus had existed before (see Ruyter 1979; Ross 2000; Tomko 1999). These foci anchored dance as an academic field through the 1960s. The privileging of modern dance isn't surprising in retrospect, given two factors. During the Depression, many university dance departments participated in the "gymnasium circuit," supplying their studios, gymnasia, and theaters as venues for touring modern dance companies. And, the 1930s through the 1950s comprised the heyday of modern dance as a concert form in the United States, one that was challenged by "postmodern" initiatives in the following decades.

In the early 1960s, stand-alone or distinct dance programs and departments started to emerge and extend their range. From the 1960s, dance history courses began to be introduced, at the same time that dance reconstruction and dance notation gained curricular representation. Synchronic study of dance in non-Western cultures frequently fell to anthropology departments. To be sure, and to an extent little matched elsewhere, UCLA's Dance Department developed wide dance ethnology offerings, paralleling strong ethnomusicology focuses in the same institution. Euro-American foci tended to characterize dance history and dance reconstruction studies. Selma Jeanne Cohen's (1974, 1992) widely used *Dance as a Theatre Art: Source Readings in Dance History from 1581 to the Present* illustrates this emphasis. The text took shape in part to provide relief from voluminous photocopying needed when she taught dance history courses at various schools. Dance reconstruction took important stimulus from the early music and early dance movements of the 1970s and the spotlight they turned on physicalizing European court and theater dances from the 1400s to the mid-1700s. Labanotation asserted a wider sphere, claiming the ability to represent dance forms the world over. Launched from work conducted in Weimar Germany and then in other European sites, Labanotation's positivist and documentary cast aligned with that of dance history and dance reconstruction studies from the 1960s through the 1980s, in which issues of recovery and accessing dances past took prominent position. In this model, creation of new knowledge about dance history generally was positioned at the graduate level, where, like the allied field of musicology, original research was deemed to require discovery of new archival materials.[1]

From the 1960s, then, two lines of activity were fundamental to staking turf and sustaining claims to disciplinary existence for dance among the arts and humanities: on one hand, the concentrated study of modern dance techniques and composition; and, on the other, positivist recovery, physicalization of dances past, and development of documentary techniques for presenting research findings. They put substance on the table; they claimed a "stuff" for dancing. The nature of this stuff was clearly shaped by a modernist analysis that demonstrated dependence on several concepts (Tomko 1999). It conceptualized aesthetic production as works of art, and it distinguished between "high" and "low" art, high and low culture, assessing the serious purpose and worth of artworks along this gradient (see Levine 1988; Giroux 1992, 43–46). In a related vein, it categorized artworks in terms of genre, emphasizing classification and clear boundaries between types of endeavors. Linked to this was the valorization of rigorous form. In addition, it characterized works of art as apolitical, occupying a realm apart. This mode of aesthetic analysis treated the work of art, in dance the choreography, as an aesthetic artifact that was original and complete, not open to ongoing, subsequent revisions, despite the example to the contrary that the choreographer George Balanchine offered. Copies or adaptations made from the original had less value or were deemed inauthentic; the original comprised an essence that mattered as an essence. Furthermore, artwork that demonstrated coherence and unified meaning was deemed best, and the intent of its creator was scrutinized as a prime key to this meaning.

Historians vigorously pursued the origins of artworks and the nature of the creative process, entertaining something of a contradiction at the same time. While continuing to recognize genius and intuition as both rare and indispensable to creating art, modernist schooling in the arts continued to teach composition. This was likely a continuity from Progressive-era theory, where legacies from John Ruskin's thinking and programs inaugurated in urban settlement houses promoted creativity as widely available and innately human. For all that this model prized the particularity of individual artifacts, it also attributed to artwork transcendent significance and communication capacities — as in describing dance or music as a universal language.

Boundaries established by high/low assessments of artworks tended to privilege theater dance genres like modern dance and ballet as appropriate subjects for dance history investigation, and, as recent research has shown, racial divides operated in the United States to make these genres largely the province of white choreographers and performers (see DeFrantz 2001, 3–35; Manning 2004; Perpener 2001). To be sure, new scholarship followed resurgence in the genre of tap dancing, which enjoyed an extraordinary renaissance from the 1970s, led by younger tap choreographers who brought veteran African-American tappers to the concert stage. At the same time, the newer generations themselves mobilized tap movement vocabularies with compositional strategies and sensibilities drawing from modern dance and jazz musics.[2] But other U.S. dance practices remained less examined, particularly those that could be characterized as social dance, participatory dance, popular culture, or ethnic cultures.

The scholarly historical research on theatrical, high art dance, and dances past that issued from the modernist aesthetic model typically took the forms of biography, chronology, company histories, and choreographic analyses. Few essayed the centuries-long scope of Lincoln Kirstein's 1935 book *Dance: A Short History of Classical Theatrical Dancing*, a "history proper" in Hayden White's (1987) terms — a narrative that offered up a moralizing impulse as well. Most of the formats intersected a key tenet and procedure of academic history research, study of change or process over time. Yet their conceptualization as historical studies was often framed in what can be called "nested egg" fashion. That is, taking dance as a center nested in a surround of "context," with factors in that context adduced to explain change in dance. The twigs buoy the egg; flows of impact are one-way. The "nested egg" conception of history writing offers little stimulus to imagine reverse flows or reciprocal impacts.

Pressures to Shift Models

The racial, ethnic, and age divides that the high/low distinction helped put in place are quite visible from the vantage of the first decade of the twenty-first century. The modernist aesthetic model of analysis offered little incentive to examine the excluded or to ask the impact of the exclusions, however; nor did it impel rethinking what counted as dance and how change in dance should be assessed. Certainly, within concert dance, 1960s cohorts of "postmodern" dance makers inaugurated new choreographic and performance approaches that challenged the definitions and instances of dancing fielded by modern dance before them, and fueled several decades of choreography after them. The 1980s media coverage of break dancing's arrival on the urban U.S. scene promptly generated debates about whether it was, indeed, dance. The impact of break dance and the hip-hop aesthetic have only continued, such that the emerging practice styled "street dancing" has taken a large place in danced television advertising, in commercial dance studio offerings, competition teams at universities and colleges, and repertoires of organized athletics spirit and drill teams.[3]

Imperatives and resources for rethinking dance and bodily enactments have come just as importantly from several shifts in models for historical and critical thinking in the academy. These include, without giving priority to any one or claiming to name all, the advent of social history, its analysis of exclusion, and its intersection with feminist analysis; the vacating of "foundationalism" in inquiries about being and knowledge; shifts to analysis of society that position power and discourse at the center of inquiry about society, social order, and organization; and rethinkings of the character and basis for subjectivity and identity.

The advent of "social history" inquiry during the 1970s and 1980s turned a different eye on the typical subjects for academic history research. Not the "great men," nor the wars they fought, in political history terms, nor the impact of ideas per se, in a history of ideas sense, but the actions and traces of people's lived behavior — from all walks of life — supplied the focus for social history inquiry. While people might write or say one kind of thing, the logic went, their actions bore scrutiny as well. And to assess the history of those who left no texts or self-disclosing documents — whether they were forbidden to write (slaves), untrained to do so, or from groups without archiving rationales (conversion narratives, common in Puritan New England, were not the norm in colonial Anglican Virginia) — investigation of people's actions as revealed by property exchanges or bailiff records or fertility rates promised to greatly extend the identification of historical actors and the kinds and causes of change. Propelled by social history inquiry, the experiences and agency of women, slaves, people of color, and the working classes were sought out and written back in to the historical record that had silenced them. (Just two examples of social history analysis are given by Blassingame 1972 and Sklar 1973.)

Social history analysis intersected powerfully with feminist analysis in the United States that has burgeoned since the 1960s and that limned, historicized, and sought to theorize the subordinations of women, and also how to stop them. Women's history, and, subsequently, the histories of masculinities and femininities, have realized that gender definitions themselves have changed over time and are not pre-given or biologically imperative. Furthering lines of inquiry opened up by Michel Foucault's (1978/90) work on the history of sexuality, writers like Thomas Laqueur (1990) and Londa Schiebinger (1989) have illuminated the social and discursive construction of bodies and sexualities, how they were thought in their own times to operate (differently in different eras and places), and the burgeoning of "science" as a domain endowed with authority regarding bodies and sexualities. For dance history scholars, these analytical shifts stimulated questions about the sexual division of labor in theater dance traditions, for example, and efforts to historicize attributions of gay sexualities to male ballet dancers (Burt 1995; Jordan 2001).

Sweeping interest in the insights of poststructuralist critical theory have led researchers in many disciplines to rethink the sources of authority and the courts of appeal for all kinds of values in past and present society. Where modernist analysis tended to look for universal values or transhistorical significance, several veins of poststructuralist analysis have vacated what Henry Giroux handily calls "foundationalism," the appeal to transcendental values and sources of arbitration. To take but one vein, the work of linguists and philosophers like Jacques Derrida on the ways in which meaning is actually created through language has led to recognition of the arbitrary linkage between a given thing in the world and a given sound/word. A play of difference underpins the generation of linguistic meaning, which is a hugely important matrix for human communication. From another angle, the long-valued Enlightenment emphasis on reason as the modality for achieving and addressing change has worn poorly as scholars have pursued the connections between Enlightenment liberalism, colonial subordination, and oppressions of capitalist economic organization (see Giroux 1992, 52–77). For dance history scholars, the philosophical relinquishment of transcendent bases for value impels the historicizing of procedures for making meaning and the warrant for bodily enactments in particular historical periods. The valorization of theater dance, for example, can be seen as a modernist value whose cross-temporal application may or may not be germane for the culture, country, and practices opened up to scrutiny by other interventions.

Veins of poststructuralist theory have also advanced alternative models for theorizing how societies and social experience work. The forays of

Michel Foucault have been extremely important in re-visioning the nature and location of power. Rather than power vested solely and continuously in government, bureaucracy, state, or ruler, Foucault proposed that power circulates and that it never resides wholly at a single point in a power relationship (see Foucault 1975/79; 1978/90; 1966/73). Antonio Gramsci's notion of hegemony buttresses this conception. Gramsci argued that in relations of subordination, the dominant parties have to secure the compliance of the subordinate, and that this compliance is never stable; it must be constantly negotiated and renegotiated (see Gitlin 1982, 205–07; Gramsci 1971/72).

According to Foucault, power is constructed discursively — that is, through systems of knowledge and language. One kind of discourse is the disciplining of the body; the corporeal realm is a locus where values and behaviors and ideologies are inscribed, made part of people's thinking and doing, expectations and practices. The priority given to power and discourse in social analysis has brought with it attention to representation— that is, modes by which one thing refers to, even parlays, another or others. Writings by Roland Barthes, and again Foucault, have been important in explaining how tropes and codes signal meanings and conventional understandings, and "how language indicates the modality of relationships between worldly things as signs" (Barthes quoted in Foster 1986, 235, n. 1; see also Barthes 1957/79). For dance history, such semiotic theorizing has opened up investigation of bodily actions, signs, and dancing of all kinds, theatrical or not, as enactors of codes but also creators of new codes.

The nature of individuals and formation of people as subjects in history and culture have been rethought in related ways. Foucault and feminist theorists such as Judith Butler (1993) and Iris Young (2002) hold that people are far from singular and coherent in their person and identity. Rather, individuals comprise themselves and are comprised in relation to many and varying discourses (Giroux 1992, 70; Haraway 1991). And they interact in many and many kinds of relations of dominance and submission — to name but some, in their gendered and classed and raced navigation of everyday life. Here it is the flux that characterizes people, their projects, their relationships, and their situation in their culture and society.

The shifting of social analysis to emphasize power, its discursive production, and people's multiply-fashioned identities and subject positions is of necessity painted here with broad strokes. The force of these critical rethinkings has brought to the fore the body and the corporeal realm as a dimension of social experience intimately involved with resisting but also complying with authority, protesting but also enacting roles exacted from individuals. These findings present dance historical inquiry with reasons to rejoin the connection that modernist aesthetic analysis severed between dance and politics. They promote reevaluation of dance — indeed, many kinds of bodily discipline and enactments — and relations of power in quotidian experience. Foucault pointed to military drill as a mode of fashioning citizen subjects. Dance analysts can assay, for example, the relations of power negotiated by violent bodily acts of racial exclusion, such as lynching, or the protest of assigned gender roles and political limitation embodied by suffrage parades and pageants. Dancing bodies past and present take on increased importance for telegraphing as well as challenging through their activity the very ways in which being and knowledge are construed, how relations of dominance and subordination are negotiated, and how new possibilities are imagined (Elias 1969/89). Thus, schooling in etiquette and dancing at the court of Louis XIV requires attention as both sign and technology of power rather than simply supplying a predecessor ground for the movement genre that became Romantic ballet. Blackface minstrel shows gain significance for the ways in which their movement codes, indeed the bodily register they deploy, instated racial subordination and promoted class rifts in the nineteenth-century United States (Lott 1993).

Challenges to Traditional History

The expanded inclusions, alternate models, and new theories for social, political, and historical analysis have offered invigorating possibilities for rethinking historical research and learning. At the same time, these imperatives have leveled severe critiques at the traditional academic enterprise of writing history. Key critiques admonish classical history writing for the truth claims it makes about its findings, the unitary and essential nature it attributes to historical actors, its commitment to finding origins, and its resistance to critical theory. These criticisms hit the mark in some respects and offer glancing blows in others (see Appleby, Hunt, and Jacob 1994).[4]

Because the study of change over time is fundamental to historical analysis, history writing and pedagogy have consistently endeavored to theorize causation. Economic determinants, ideas, and technological shifts are only a few of the causal factors that have been vigorously explored for several centuries. Nor has history writing held tenaciously to its interpretations as perduring truths. Historiographical analysis has been part and parcel of university historians' work in the twentieth century. These historians have reflexively inspected the models of causation and procedures for research used by "schools" and generations of writers preceding and concurrent with them. In U.S. history, to take one field, academics identify a "progressive" school of analysis from the early twentieth century that stressed conflict and struggle among historical actors (see Beard 1935/37). This yielded to a mighty "consensus" model of history writing that stressed factors that forged bonds or commonalities among people (see Hartz 1955). In the 1960s and 1970s, attention turned to people's "culture" — slave culture, working class culture, shop-floor culture — as seedbeds for agency and resistance to race and class oppression (see Gutman 1977). Some models of analysis have superceded others; histories of great men and political battles receive far less attention than previously, yet the "history of ideas" never seems to vanish.

Critical theory, on the other hand, has been slow of adoption by many historians, and this pace has at least something to do with the empirical bent that is a bellwether of twentieth-century historical analysis and teaching. This empirical bent requires that historians adduce past experiences and other data to sustain their interpretations or application of theories. The data must sustain verification by other researchers and the interpretations offered must bear up under logical scrutiny. These positivist hallmarks of traditional historical research valorize replicability, an indication of history writing's "objectivity" in terms of professional scientific method and a measure of its cultural authority.

At least two more factors fuel the enduring impression that historians do and endeavor to present truths. One is widespread use of an impersonal narrative voice in the presentation of historical findings, which absents the person and particular values of the given author. Another is the traditional decision not to voice as part of the historical argument itself the conditions, such as race or nation or class, that provide writers with access to materials or informants, access to platforms for publication, and thus cultural voice. Such matters of presentation, grown conventional across more than a century, naturalize the writing of history, and quiet ambiguities or unresolved features of interpretations. They defer questions about the part that histories play in perpetuating or contesting the system of social relations in which history writers, readers, and student participate.

Calls for Radical Pedagogy

Radical pedagogy, or pedagogies of freedom, in Paolo Freire's (1970/2000) words, fasten precisely on the impact that schooling can and does have in the sustaining of social and political orders and organizations in which people find themselves. The capacities for schooling to fashion in one class the workforce desired by another have already been identified by historians of the museum movement, for instance, and the advent of vocational training in the late nineteenth-century United States (Harris 1962). In this vein, Freire decries the "banking system" of education that locates all knowledge in the teacher and feeds information to students in one-way "deposits" that seldom cultivate their ability to question that which has been transmitted. Seconding Freire, bell hooks (1994) urges teachers to foster students' critical thinking so that they can question the rightness of "things as they are"; hooks also specifies the middle-class provenance of classroom protocols that narrow student engagement, mitigate against intellectual risk-taking, and reproduce middle-class points of view. These protocols teachers must change, she insists. Henry Giroux (Giroux and Roger I. Simon, in Giroux, 1992, 189) deftly articulates the ends of radical pedagogy as the promotion of students' abilities to imagine new possibilities that accommodate difference as the condition of contemporary culture. Education, which for Giroux happens out of school as much as in it, should be framed not to replicate the given. It should empower students to assess the prevailing circumstances and to conceptualize them differently, in order to pursue them.

A Proposal for Dance History Pedagogy

Shifts in what is deemed dance, upheavals in critical theory and history writing, and recommendations for radical pedagogy provide rich ground for revising the teaching of dance history at the turn of the twenty-first century. Where genre and notions of the work of art supplied a modernist lens for writing and teaching dance history, I propose four lines of inquiry as a millennial lens: scrutiny of bodies; compositional strategies; representations forged; and modes of support. These lines are guided and tethered by articulation of an "endgame," or outcomes we might seek for students engaging with dance historical questions. And the lines pull and tug at some knotty problems still to be resolved.

Dance history teaching in the millennium should enable students to assess dance in their own lives, both in their present and in the trajectories over time for their families and communities of affiliation. It should offer students strategies for encountering dance practices new to them, so that they might ask how unfamiliar dancing is configured and conducted, and to weigh the force, if any, that such dancing tries and has tried to exert on its communities, countries, and across borders. This pedagogy should equip students to query how "local" dance practices have moved with regard to larger scales and frames of reference, across time and borders. Here the state sponsorship of folkloric dance companies is immediately relevant, as is the recognition granted "dancesport" — the rubric for competitive ballroom dancing — as an official category for Olympic Games competition (McMains 2001). Dance history pedagogy also should abet the efforts of students who want to make new dances or ways of moving in the world. This could include, for example, students who investigate how past dancing constructed gender roles because they want to challenge gendering through new choreography.

This cluster of outcomes proceeds from the view that dance and movement practices constitute, enact, and sometimes challenge social and political relations that are fundamental to people living in groups. In this dance practices provide means both to enact and challenge ideologies. Thus dance history pedagogy should prepare students as well to assess the restagings, recyclings, samplings, or translations of dances past for their ideological effects, realizing that aesthetic dimensions do not exist apart from ideology.

Four Lines of Inquiry

In the stead of genre, pure chronology, or geocultural focus, I propose the posing of four lines of inquiry as a framework for teaching dance history in undergraduate history courses. These lines are scrutiny of bodies, compositional strategies, representations forged, and modes of support. While they receive separate treatment below, consideration of each actually impinges on others.

Scrutiny of Bodies

As a first line, nothing should be taken less for granted than the bodies that proffer and enact what societies variously call dance and movement practices. To be sure, the phenomenal experience that individuals have of their own bodies supplies a kind of base for empathetically comprehending and also generalizing to other human bodies. But this knowledge does not necessarily apply to all bodies, to bodies across time, nor to the virtual bodies that are joining quotidian experience via computer games, screen technologies, and interactive media. Thus a fundamental query about dancing in culture and across time is this: How were bodies — human, mechanical, and/or virtual — conceived and thought to operate?

The activation and restraint of moving bodies depends on the kinds of capacities attributed to it. This is vividly illustrated in Joseph Roach's (1993, 23–57) research on acting techniques in late seventeenth-century England and the economy of "humors" then thought to govern the body. Capable of quicksilver change, the humors could all too easily overcome actors in motion, so thespians practiced techniques to control their shifts, to wield them at their command. When the concept of a nervous system replaced that of the humoral economy, acting techniques changed in response. We should encourage students to ask what conceptions of bodies operated in different times, never to assume that those conceptions match present understandings. We should prepare students to consider the possibility that competing conceptions might well have coexisted, with shifts between paradigms not necessarily resulting completely or instantaneously. And we should promote students' investigation of training systems of all kinds as crucibles for bodily articulation.

It is equally crucial for dance history students to ask which bodies danced and which were excluded, which were consigned to dance in what ways and not others, which were deemed appropriate to signify for others. The gains of critical race and feminist analyses have made such questions nearly automatic by the twenty-first century, but even such naturalization needs to be underscored. Analyses of Romantic ballet offer a case in point. For years the significance of Romantic ballet was cast in terms of the literary topoi it utilized, its emphasis on expression of feeling, and also the new physical feats made possible by the innovation of toe shoes, which served so well the period interest in things supernatural. With the advent of feminist analysis, however, scholars have pinpointed ways in which Romantic ballet's narratives and movement design inscribed and performed the nineteenth-century ideology that assigned men and women to "separate spheres" in relation to the emerging premise of incommensurable male/female sexual difference. This was an ideology that still has force in wide swaths of the United States today.

In querying different conceptions of the body, teachers need to acquaint students with possible schemas or grids for analyzing depictions of bodies past and present. More widely known in dance departments today than thirty years ago, Laban Movement Analysis (LMA) offers frameworks for analyzing bodies as still forms and also bodily motion in space. In the first of these, for example, dance students can readily grasp LMA's parsing of the ways in which people organize the body's effort in terms of weight, time, flow, and direction (Davis 1970, 29–41; Moore and Yamamoto 1988). Brenda Dixon Gottschild's (1996, 11–19) analysis of Afrocentric movement offers another template for querying bodily mobilizations, calling attention to polycentrism/polymeter, high affect juxtaposition, ephebism, embracing the conflict, and an aesthetic of the cool. In a third vein, Richard Leppert's (1987) study of portraits of eighteenth-century gentry attends to the composition of grouping and the significance conveyed by individuals' locations at the center or margin of groups, the angling of limbs in and out of picture frames, and adjacency to architectural elements. This last resonates strongly with what follows about representation, but it is relevant here for helping guide students to appraise body-part deployment and orientation, and bodies as components of groupings.

Compositional Strategies

A second line of inquiry focuses on compositional strategies. In our time, football teams use playbooks in accomplishing game structures. Western middle class weddings tend to organize processional and recessional forays, sending parties of men, women, and children along central axes at typical paces toward a focal point in communal space, at which juncture words, promises, gestures, and physical tokens are exchanged before a reverse flow of people ensues. As Sally Banes (1985) showed in her pioneer writing about break dance, solos by crew members followed typical sequences of entry, footwork, spin, freeze, and exit with which dancers competed in a space ringed by their fellows and opponents.

I suggest as a working hypothesis that most movement practices deploy some kind of lexicon, or movement vocabulary, and some syntax, or sequence of what happens when. The identification of lexicon and the making of decisions about syntax may be conscious or unconscious; voiced, concealed, left silent; impelled by individuals, groups, collaboratively, through accumulation — or in other ways. Dance history pedagogy should encourage students to ask what concepts and traditions of "making" or composition informed practice in given times and places.

The most extensive analysis of dancing in this vein by far has been that of modern dance composition. This flows in part, I suggest, from the fact that modern dance as an emergent practice in the 1920s and 1930s famously distinguished itself by conscious search for choreographic methods. The writings of innovators such as Doris Humphrey (1959) and Louis Horst (1937/72) offer one kind of insight into the strategies they developed, from musical structures like rondo form or theme and variation to adaptations of affects and figuration from Renaissance and Baroque music as platforms for improvisation. Merce Cunningham and others have written about Cunningham's use of chance procedures and indeterminacy. In the late twentieth century, Susan Foster is unmatched in *Reading Dancing* for analyzing choreographic modes of selected modern dance, ballet, and postmodern choreographers, including Cunningham (Foster, 1986). Her recent work on Richard Bull's structured improvisation details a number of his strategies and offers lucid examples of their performance applications (Foster 2002). Together with Cynthia Novack's (1990) work on Contact Improvisation, Foster gives good grounds for students and teachers to continue questioning the long-held distinction between "improvisation" and "choreography," as these relate to binary oppositions of rehearsal and performance practices, choreographer and executants, origination and repetition. These questions can bring into focus the period's view of what is being made: its nature, how it is, can, and should be transmitted to others, and how its theory might be used to imagine another choreography, as Mark Franko (1993) has eloquently suggested for dances past.

In all this, it must be realized that the templates for analysis these studies offer may not, in fact, serve dance history studies that attempt to exceed focus on Euro-American practices. They nonetheless provide good reason to pursue these questions for other practices: Did compositional strategies obtain? What were they? Did they differ, and how did they differ, over time?

Representations Forged

The scrutiny of bodies and compositional strategies enables a third line of inquiry, the querying of representations forged. These may be representations attempted and intended by the period players themselves, but also the representations that investigators discern subsequently. In both veins, we should encourage dance history students to ask about the signifying capacity of movement structures, how the significations operated, and how they addressed the imbedded situation of being, knowledge, and power in the cultures where they circulated. Period documents offer students one kind of platform for pursuing these questions. Doris Humphrey's (1977, 238–40) essay on her 1935 *New Dance*, for example, parses the social meanings she sought to communicate by using particular spatial forms, deployments of dancers, and sequencing of action. At the culmination of the choreography, a closed, wheeling circle of dancers signaled the unification of individuals and forces that earlier in the piece had been disjunct and fragmented. Charts and textual explanations specify the action and intended meanings of gestural codes for various periods, as in John Weaver's (cited in Cohen 1974; 1992, 54–57) descriptions of pantomime gestures he asked of dancers performing his 1717 *The Loves of Mars and Venus*. Students can quickly determine that bodily codes are anything but transhistorical when they enact one of the gestures for jealousy: pointing the middle finger to the eye, which in the twenty-first century can rudely exhort viewers to a sexual act.

Retrospective investigation of how dances signified is just as important. Linking literary theory with paradigms for dance making, Susan Foster 1986, 234–36) in *Reading Dancing* identified four modes of representation in dance that offer students a springboard when querying "the choreographer's relationship to the body and to the dance and the dance's relationship to the world and to its viewers." Pairing literary and choreographic figures of speech and design, these modes of representation are metaphor/resemblance, metonymy/imitation, synecdoche/replication, and irony/reflection. They are derived from corpuses of Euro-American writing and dancing. Thus, when we encourage students to ask whether (and which of) these representational modes inform movement practices in cultures they investigate around the globe, we engage students in possibly discovering the limits for explanation the model provides. Limit testing also can demonstrate the need to create new theory.

In a third register concerning representations forged, we should introduce students to historiography, the study of how past dance history was written, the interpretations its writers offered, and the theories (causal or others) it invoked. Previous historical treatments of Ruth St. Denis offer a ready illustration. Suzanne Shelton (1981, 51, 55) situated St. Denis's early career focus amid a vogue for exoticism in the United States impelled by the likes of Edwin Arnold's book *The Light of Asia*, Eastern influences on American Transcendentalism, and world's fairs. Adherents of this exoticism took a type of "come-outer" cultural stance in which they distanced themselves from prevailing American culture. Pursuing a different tack, Jane Desmond's (1991) article "Dancing Out the Difference" on St. Denis's *Radha* invokes the perspective of Edward Said's (1979) book *Orientalism*. Said showed how a tradition of Western scholarship on the Middle East prioritized the ancient history and achievements of these "Oriental" cultures, reifying their pasts at the expense of their presents. Moreover, what was gained by this scholarly construction of the East was a sense of self for Western readers and writers, a self constituted by distance and difference from an exotic, sensuous, and past Orient. Eclipsing the radical come-outer view Shelton offered, Desmond positioned St. Denis as culturally rapacious, appropriating themes and visual looks from an Orient that the West racially denigrates in order to consolidate a Western identity, which itself is undifferentiated. My own work on St. Denis (Tomko 1999) has tried to unpack the several kinds of codes for femininity that she twined together in dances like *Radha*, invoking both the (conservative) spirituality expected of middle-class women by the separate spheres ideology still regnant and the (more transgressive) sensuous appeal she cultivated in her dancing and that period viewers inextricably linked with ballet girl dancing, employment, and social status. This gender approach positions St. Denis differently again, as a self and a performing identity both multiple and very much in the making as it tried to renew and reclassify the activity of dancing at a time of other attempted change in U.S. gender roles assigned to women.

By leading students to scrutinize historiography, we remind them and ourselves of the made-ness of historical accounts, the change over time that characterizes the accounts as well as the social experience they endeavor to parse, and the play and array of theoretical tools that might be invoked for studying and writing history.

Modes of Support

A fourth line of inquiry seeks out the support for dance and how it changed over time. Heeding the Watergate-era maxim "follow the money," dance history pedagogues should promote students' questions about the material conditions of possibility for dance and movement practices. We should encourage them to ask what or who paid to cultivate the bodily skills that practitioners deployed; how the fashioners of dance and movement practices subsisted; whether and when movement production was considered a commodity and in whom its ownership was thought to inhere. These questions are intimately connected with how dance movement practices operated and exerted force in their cultures. Timothy McGee's (1988) work on Renaissance dancing masters illuminates patronage as one configuration of support for dance professionals at a time when elite family structure and class considerations impelled the amateur pursuit of movement skills. Following up the tantalizing consideration McGee gives to the Christian conversion of two Italian dancing masters, the [Jewish?] Ambrosio brothers, we could encourage students to ask about the relation between occupation and opportunity, class position, and racism. Raymond Williams (1983, 30–48) models another question, indexing the reorientation required of "Romantic" artists when commercial markets replaced patronage models. While state sponsorship for theater dancing has a long history in Europe, the case in the United States is very different. Following barely four years of federal support programs for dance and other artists during the 1930s, the U.S. government inaugurated its longest-standing support programs with the founding of the National Endowments for the Arts and Humanities in 1965. Given the censorship efforts of NEA over the past twenty years and also the strong record of corporate sponsorship for televising dance and movement production today, we might encourage students to inspect Paul DiMaggio and Michael Useem's (1982) contention about elite [private] versus corporate sponsorship in the 1980s:

> Because of the importance of the legitimating function [that arts sponsorship performs for corporations], corporate boards, it may also be hypothesized, will be more concerned than élite [private] boards with the content of exhibits and performances, less ready to support risky artistic ventures, and quicker to censor offensive programs. If the *élite* mode of class domination set firm *social* limits on the diffusion of high art to the public at large, the *corporate* mode of class domination may instead set *ideological* limits on the content of the art that is presented (196; original italics).

DiMaggio and Useem's hypothesis makes explicit the interested nature of arts sponsorship in the late twentieth century, confirming that dance and movement production take action in and are acted upon in particular political and cultural and social situations. Students can fairly ask of any dance practice what financial conditions make it possible, and whose interest its aesthetic production supported. In tandem with this should run the questions of who or what wields disposition of the practices, what concepts of ownership prevail, if any, and whether/at what junctures practice has been commodified.

To take these four lines of inquiry in hand, teachers and students must face the questions: To which dance and movement practices, to which societies should our questions be directed? I suggest that this will and must be decided differently in different countries, in different regions of countries, and with the goal of serving the students who matriculate in particular institutions. First and simply, we need to decenter the Euro-American foci that have grounded much of dance history teaching for the previous half century. In support of an endgame for dance history pedagogy that prompts students to query the configuration of their own education, we need to include in courses dance practices that are marginalized as well as privileged, the better to ask how and why dancing confirms but also contests, complies with but also resists the power relations or racial ordination, gender channelings, or class positions that prevail.

In support of endgames that encourage students to query their own situation but also imagine new possibilities, we need to include in courses dance practices in which students engage themselves but also those they do not readily encounter. And to support students' abilities to parse the ways that local practices participate in larger swaths of signification, we need to include in courses some practices that have moved through time and across the globe. Will inclusion of widely varied movement practices in single courses actually permit the study of change over time? Yes. Courses can take as one kind of diachronic thread changes over time in the four lines of inquiry — that is, in bodies, in compositional strategies, in representations and their cultural operation, and in support. Other threads might be changes in conceptions of dance as property, shifts in identities formed or challenged through movement practices, or changes in phenomenal or virtual notions of space, contact, time, and sound effected, even countered, through dance. Will length of school terms and the number of dance history courses required for dance major students shape the selection of practices for given dance history courses? Absolutely. Will a new canon emerge? Possibly, though it might take several decades to coalesce.

The focuses and findings of current dance history, critical theory, ethnographic research, and academic discipline formation will always fuel the publications, visual as well as textual, that teachers can bring to the classroom. But what the students bring to the classroom should also inform focuses selected for courses. Should we be worried that dance history courses within a state system or country could be characterized by so much difference in the practices they pursue? No. Linked by commitment to parse change over time, the lines of investigation suggested here offer a sufficient analytical coherence.

Putting Lines of Inquiry into Action

How should these lines of dance history inquiry be taught? First and foremost, I propose the cultivation of a querying stance in students. By this I do not mean that we should organize class size so that a Socratic method of question and response can be implemented across the board. State budgets certainly militate against that in many public university systems, where rubrics for instruction tend to channel students into lecture-based and "delivery" format classes until late in their undergraduate education. At that point, "seminar" frameworks that enable lively and consistent discussion among small groups of students prove more possible. We are unlikely to see change in this situation in the next decade or two. The cultivation of querying stances pivots on turning aside the "banking system" of pedagogy that Paolo Freire identified. Freire contended that the banking system confirms the status quo: the prevailing canons of knowledge, the positions of those whose intellectual labor constitutes the canons, and the ways in which people are ranked in societies, students and teachers among them. The late twentieth century has seen major revisions of what counts as knowledge within the Euro-American university tradition, as evidenced by findings of feminist analysis, poststructuralist analysis, or the advent of chaos theory, to take just three areas. But shifts in how knowledge is produced and by whom has been much slower to change, as shown by the continued calls to increase the numbers of "the underrepresented" in university faculties and administrations. Against the banking model, Freire called for recognition that students as well as teachers possess knowledge, for them together to create new knowledge, and to liberate themselves. Applied to dance history pedagogy, I recommend fostering critical skills that will help students ask regarding the past and present what counts as knowledge in their societies, including what counts as dance; what structures locate or assign people relative position and power in society, including structures for movement practices; and what limits or facilitates their prospects and the possibilities for change, again including the barriers and latitudes dancing affords.

Many strategies are possible for implementing what I have called the querying stance; I call attention to four. First, insist on classrooms with movable desks or chairs, and get students to their feet at least once a week, if not once a class period, to embody some dimension of the movement practice under discussion on a given day. Three to five minutes of "trying on" a physical culture exercise, or assuming and then switching couples' gender assignments in ballroom "round dance" position, for example, can richly fuel students' engagement and provoke different ranges of questions.

Second, rotate responsibility, among students and between students and teachers, for pursuing and responding aloud to the lines of inquiry during class time, and for synthesizing and reflecting on the dialogue engendered. This may require a huge shift in courses given high enrollment ceilings that are expected to be taught as lectures, and it may be all the more difficult to achieve at typical "crunch" times in a term, such as midterm weeks.

Third, continue to assign writing as part of the course requirements, and consider devoting course time to "in-class" writings of, say, thirty minutes. Whereas term paper assignments have been valued for years, shorter and more frequent in-class writings may give students needed practice not just in writing but in framing for written communication the analytical gains made with a querying stance.

Fourth, include as a course requirement collaborative work by groups of students researching a project defined with the teacher. Cultivation of group collaboration counters the individualist basis on which many colleges evaluate students, and students can complain when group rather than individual grades are assigned. But group projects change the relative intimacy of the querying project. The different scale of interaction can further recognition of members' different class or race or sexuality locations and the insights they bring to bear from those positions regarding project questions, findings, and interpretations.

The research focus of this fourth strategy deserves additional mention, because dance history courses offer probably the best place to seed the interest of future dance historians. Advances in electronic technology and the Internet have actually created new possibilities for archival investigation by baccalaureate students, or perhaps it would be better termed the advent of "distance research," because more kinds of data can be accessed without requiring travel, and Web-crawling in search of sources is practically second-nature to students born since the 1970s. Databases available commercially and through library consortia make easier than ever identification and retrieval (increasingly online) of print sources such as newspaper accounts, book reviews, historical atlases, and business directories. While they have not replaced oral interviews, practitioner and artist-generated Web postings can give students up-to-the minute information and, sometimes, excerpts of video material that may not be available elsewhere. Equally exciting, some key repositories have used the Internet to open up access to photographs and rare or fragile treatises.[5] Students enjoy much greater possibilities for finding visual records and moving images to study without traveling during school terms.

Finally, when students work in groups to collaboratively research a question, the process reveals the range of activities requisite to current faculty research projects even as it allows them to divvy up the work. That includes the work of presenting findings. I recommend organizing oral presentation of findings, which is one more way to rotate the responsibility for forwarding the querying stance. Most students gain useful practice in verbalizing exegesis that they illustrate with visual materials. Another option is for students to create for part of their presentation a movement study that enacts principles or, say, choreographic strategies of the practice they have investigated. For dance majors, if not all dance history students, performance is a fact of life and a positive opportunity. Whether groups show visuals or present live enactments, the collaborators have the option to query class members about what they see, asking them to make connections on the spot — or identify puzzles still to be resolved. Group presentations can link more closely the plotting of research strategies, the pull and tug of interpretation, the articulating of findings. Especially when presentations incorporate new movement studies, students sometimes cross and sometimes fuse the analytical, the creative, the voiced, and the embodied, trying on and shifting between declamatory and querying stances, remaking dance history study in the millennium.

Bibliography

Appleby, Joyce, Lynn Hunt, and Margaret Jacob. *Telling the Truth about History*. New York: W. W. Norton, 1994.

Banes, Sally. "Breaking." In *Fresh: Hip Hop Don't Stop*, by Nelson George, et al. New York: Random House, 1985.

Barthes, Roland. *Mythologies*. Trans. Annette Lavers. 1957; New York: Hill and Wang, 1979.

Beard, Charles. *An Economic Interpretation of the Constitution of the United States*. 1935; New York: Macmillan, 1937.

Blassingame, John. *The Slave Community: Plantation Life in the Antebellum South*. New York: Oxford University Press, 1972.

Burt, Ramsay. *The Male Dancer: Bodies, Spectacle, Sexualities*. London: Routledge, 1995.

Butler, Judith. *Bodies That Matter: On the Discursive Limits of Sex*. New York: Routledge, 1993.

Cohen, Selma Jeanne. *Dance as a Theatre Art: Source Readings in Dance History from 1581 to the Present.* 2d ed. with additional material by Katy Matheson. Princeton: Princeton Book Company, 1992.

Davis, Martha. "Effort-Shape Analysis of Movement: An Evaluation of Its Logic and Consistency and its Systematic Use in Research." In *Four Adaptations of Effort Theory in Research and Teaching,* by Irmgard Bartenieff, Davis, and Forrestine Paulay. New York: Dance Notation Bureau, 1970.

DeFrantz, Thomas F. "African American Dance: A Complex History." In *Dancing Many Drums: Excavations in African American Dance,* edited by Thomas F. DeFrantz. Madison: University of Wisconsin Press, 2001.

Desmond, Jane. "Dancing out the Difference: Cultural Imperialism and Ruth St. Denis's 'Radha' of 1906." *Signs* 17 (Autumn 1991): 28–49.

DiMaggio, Paul and Michael Useem. "The Arts in Class Reproduction." In *Cultural and Economic Reproduction in Education: Essays on Class, Ideology, and the State,* edited by Michael Apple, 181–201. London: Routledge, 1982.

Elias, Norbert. *The Court Society.* Trans. Edmund Jephcott. 1969; New York: Pantheon Books, 1989.

Foster, Susan. *Dances That Describe Themselves: The Improvised Choreography of Richard Bull.* Middletown, Conn.: Wesleyan University Press, 2002.

Foster, Susan. *Reading Dancing: Bodies and Subjects in Contemporary American Choreography.* Berkeley: University of California Press, 1986.

Foucault, Michel. *Discipline & Punish; The Birth of the Prison.* Trans. Alan Sheridan. 1975; New York: Vintage Books, 1979.

Foucault, Michel. *The History of Sexuality, Volume 1: An Introduction.* Trans. Robert Hurley. 1978; New York: Vintage Books, 1990.

Foucault, Michel. *The Order of Things: An Archaeology of the Human Sciences.* 1966; New York: Vintage Books, 1973.

Franko, Mark. "Repeatability, Reconstruction, and Beyond." In *Dance as Text: Ideologies of the Baroque Body.* Cambridge, England: Cambridge University Press, 1993.

Freire, Paolo. *Pedagogy of the Oppressed.* Trans. Myra Bergman Ramos. 1970; New York: Continuum, 2000.

Giroux, Henry. *Border Crossings: Cultural Workers and the Politics of Education.* New York: Routledge, 1992.

Gitlin, Todd. "Television's Screens: Hegemony in Transition." In *Cultural and Economic Reproduction in Education: Essays on Class, Ideology, and the State,* edited by Michael Apple, 202–246. London: Routledge, 1982.

Gottschild, Brenda Dixon. *Digging the Africanist Presence in American Performance: Dance and Other Contexts.* Westport, Conn.: Greenwood Press, 1996.

Gramsci, Antonio. *Selections from the Prison Notebooks of Antonio Gramsci,* edited and translated by Quintin Hoare and Geoffrey Nowell Smith. 1971; New York: International Publishers, 1972.

Guest, Ann Hutchinson. *Labanotation.* 1970; New York: Theatre Arts Books, 1991.

Gutman, Herbert. *Work, Culture & Society in Industrializing America.* New York: Vintage Books, 1977.

Hartz, Louis. *The Liberal Tradition in America: An Interpretation of American Political Thought Since the Revolution.* New York: Harcourt Brace, 1955.

Haraway, Donna J. *Simians, Cyborgs, and Women; The Reinvention of Nature.* New York: Routledge, 1991.

Harris, Neil. "The Gilded Age Revisited: Boston and the Museum Movement." *American Quarterly* (Winter 1962): 545–566.

Hill, Constance Valis. *Brotherhood in Rhythm; The Jazz Tap Dancing of the Nicholas Brothers.* New York: Oxford University Press, 2000.

hooks, bell. *Teaching to Transgress: Education as the Practice of Freedom.* New York: Routledge, 1994.

Horst, Louis. *Pre-Classic Dance Forms.* 1937; New York: Dance Horizons, 1972.

Humphrey, Doris. "New Dance." In *Doris Humphrey: An Artist First,* edited by Selma Jeanne Cohen. Middletown, Conn.: Wesleyan University Press, 1977.

Humphrey, Doris. *The Art of Making Dances.* New York: Grove Press, 1959.

Jordan, John Bryce. "Light in the Heels: The Emergence of the Effeminate Male Dancer in Eighteenth-Century English History." Ph.D. diss., University of California, Riverside, 2001.

Kirstein, Lincoln. *Dance: A Short History of Classic Theatrical Dancing.* 1935; New York: Dance Horizons, 1977.

Laqueur, Thomas. *Making Sex: Body and Gender from the Greeks to Freud.* Cambridge, Mass.: Harvard University Press, 1990.

Leppert, Richard. "Music, Domestic Life and Cultural Chauvinism: Images of British Subjects at Home in India." In *Music and Society: the Politics of Composition, Performance, and Reception,* edited by Richard Leppert and Susan McClary. Cambridge, England: Cambridge University Press, 1987. 63—104.

Levine, Lawrence. *Highbrow/Lowbrow: The Emergence of Cultural Hierarchy in America.* Cambridge, Mass.: Harvard University Press, 1988.

Lott, Eric. *Love & Theft; Blackface Minstrelsy and the American Working Class.* New York: Oxford University Press, 1993.

McGee, Timothy J. "Dancing Masters and the Medici Court in the 15th Century." *Studi Musicali* 17 (1988): 201–224.

McMains, Juliet. "Brownface: Representations of Latin-ness in Dancesport." *Dance Research Journal* [U.S.] 33/2 (Winter 2001): 54–71.

Manning, Susan. *Modern Dance, Negro Dance: Race in Motion.* Minneapolis: University of Minnesota Press, 2004.

Moore, Carol-Lynne and Kaoru Yamamoto. *Beyond Words: Movement Observation and Analysis.* New York: Gordon and Breach, 1988.

Novack, Cynthia. *Sharing the Dance: Contact Improvisation and American Culture.* Madison: University of Wisconsin Press, 1990.

Perpener, John O. *African-American Concert Dance: The Harlem Renaissance and Beyond.* Urbana: University of Illinois Press, 2001.

Roach, Joseph. *The Player's Passion: Studies in the Science of Acting.* Ann Arbor: University of Michigan Press, 1993.

Ross, Janice. *Moving Lessons: Margaret H'Doubler and the Beginning of Dance in American Education.* Madison: University of Wisconsin Press, 2000.

Ruyter, Nancy Lee Chalfa. *Reformers and Visionaries: The Americanization of the Art of Dance.* New York: Dance Horizons, 1979.

Said, Edward W. *Orientalism.* New York: Vintage Press, 1979.

Schiebinger, Londa. *The Mind Has No Sex? Women in the Origins of Modern Science.* Cambridge, Mass.: Harvard University Press, 1989.

Shelton, Suzanne. *Divine Dancer: A Biography of Ruth St. Denis.* Garden City, New York: Doubleday, 1981.

Sklar, Kathryn Kish. *Catharine Beecher: A Study in American Domesticity.* New York: Norton, 1973.

Tomko, Linda J. *Dancing Class: Gender, Ethnicity, and Social Divides in American Dance, 1890–1920.* Bloomington: Indiana University Press, 1999.

White, Hayden. "The Value of Narrativity in the Representation of Reality." In *The Content of the Form: Narrative Discourse and Historical Representation.* Baltimore: Johns Hopkins University Press, 1987.

Williams, Raymond. *Culture & Society: 1780–1950.* New York: Columbia University Press, 1983.

Young, Iris Marion. "Lived Body vs. Gender: Reflections on Social Structure and Subjectivity." *Ratio,* new series, IV, no. 4 (December 2002): 410–28.

Notes

1. This passage draws on my familiarity at the end of the 1970s with undergraduate and graduate dance programs at UCLA, and through connection with colleagues teaching or matriculating at the time at the University of California, Riverside, Ohio University, Rutgers University, and Goucher College. Wendy Hilton's, Shirley Wynne's, Julia Sutton's, Emma Lewis Thomas's, and Angene Feves's teaching at several institutions were important nodes for dance reconstruction study.

2. My perspective has benefited from interaction with my UC Riverside colleague Fred Strickler, a founding member of the Jazz Tap Ensemble who helped spearhead the tap "renaissance," and I had the opportunity to view a number of JTE performances in Los Angeles during that period. See also Hill 2000.
3. Contact Improvisation and innovations by the troupe Pilobolus in their turn challenged definitions of dance, but no comprehensive account of challenges is intended or attempted here.
4. Written by distinguished academics from three historical fields, one response to such critiques is Joyce Appleby, Lynn Hunt, and Margaret Jacob, *Telling the Truth about History* (New York: W. W. Norton, 1994).
5. For photographs and dance treatises at the Library of Congress, see, <www.loc.gov>. For photographs at the Schlesinger Library on the History of Women in America, see <www.harvard.edu/libraries>, then choose "VIA — Visual Resource" under "Other Catalogs."

CHAPTER 7

On Teaching Dance Criticism

MINDY ALOFF

Everyone's a critic. Everyone has responses to and opinions about particular works of art. It is part of what makes us human to notice differences, to categorize those differences in order to function in the world, and to evaluate new experience in the context of past experience. For most people, these evaluations are personal and immediate — one thing is beautiful, another is boring, a third is ugly, a fourth is thrilling — and they let it go with that fundamental classification. A few of us, though, wonder why a work connects with our imaginations to make us feel the way we do, how it uses the human and technical resources at its disposal to produce its memorable passages or moments, or whether our responses are similar to those of other audiences in different locales or eras. We become interested in the work in its particulars, in the conditions that would have led its authors and fabricators to produce it, in its changes over time. If it is a work from the performing arts, we become fascinated with the way the theatrical effects and their significance may shift according to different performers and directors. Our motivation is still personal response; however, the more engrossed we become in the means whereby that response is provoked and in the different ways that others have responded, the less absorbed we are in ourselves and the more we focus instead on the provocateurs and their manipulation of their materials. We step away from our own lives, with its joys and turmoil, to give ourselves over to something other than ourselves. This is the secret garden of the arts: the bliss of forgetting oneself in order to learn about something else. If our interest primarily concerns the past, we become historians; if it is the present in relation to the past, we become critics.

In the case of theatrical dancing — whose effects depend on so many mutable elements, beginning with the condition of the dancers' bodies, that one is tempted to insist on the presence of chance and improvisation in even the most rigorously classical of repertories — it is almost impossible to separate the historians from the critics in real terms. Dance historians, for example, may confine themselves to researching the past. However, given the paradoxical situation in dance that films and videotapes of individual performances are only partial evidence of the choreographer's artistic intention (because the camera can't sort out the alterations owing to cast changes, mistakes in performance, and other local conditions) and that written notations for dances are only idealized blueprints for performance, rather than predictive texts in the sense that musical scores usually are (where composers can rely on comparatively standardized instruments), dances have no independent identity, no score, that can be universally accepted in place of performance.

In the case of nineteenth-century ballets, there is no certainty of authorship at all. For convenience, of course, everyone pretends that the titles *Giselle* or *Swan Lake* actually refer to specific ballets with choreography that, it is universally agreed, belongs to the work; in fact, what exists are the musical scores, the libretti, passages of choreography (some of which may have actually been fashioned by hands other than those of the original choreographer) that have become canonized with time, and familiar performance practices. The repertory of the Danish ballet master August Bournonville, sometimes cited outside Denmark as the most carefully preserved nineteenth-century ballet repertory in the world, has been a subject of contention for several decades. Some Danish scholars and dancers have espoused the view that the entire Bournonville repertory was given major overhauls by several ballet masters after Bournonville's death and that the importation of Russian training into the Danish school by revered teacher Vera Volkova also affected the identity of Bournonville's work (for the better, a number of those dancers and scholars would add). Even the copyrighted repertories of George Balanchine, Michel Fokine, and other twentieth-century giants, some of whose dancers are still alive, aren't fixed in the way that autographed scores, works of visual art, and literary texts are: in some cases, the choreographers themselves made alternate versions; in other cases, the original steps or — as, if not more, important — the original counts and accents became eroded in the passage of the ballets from generation to generation. Although historians attempt to draw up master lists of great dances, those canons do not usually survive their dancers and audiences to the next generation of historians. In dance, the reality is out of sight, out of mind: If the works aren't on the boards, they don't exist.

Even the canon of fifty Western masterworks that Lincoln Kirstein offered just thirty-five years ago in *Movement and Metaphor* is out of date: perhaps eight are available to be seen in the theater in a condition recognizably like their original productions and perhaps fifteen in something even remotely like their originals. The Kirov Ballet's effort, in the late 1990s, to restore *The Sleeping Beauty* to the condition of its 1890 premiere was fully successful in its music; however, the training of the dancers is so different from what it was in 1890 that the choreography, taken from post-1890 notations by the choreographer's régisseur, simply could not be performed by the Kirov as notated. Other concessions had to be made, such as the inclusion of a twentieth-century variation for the Prince, because there was none originally. Even the tutus had to be adjusted to contemporary expectations.

As for importance of influence, for the ballet masters of our time, no handed-down production of *Swan Lake* can compare in its impact on other choreographers with Matthew Bourne's 1990's version, in which all the swans were male and all the female characters were treacherous or stupid, and the Third Act, in which the hero is duped, replaced the Second as the ballet's theatrical and emotional center. Bourne's version is lively and provocative; I'm not against it in itself. To my sorrow, however, its gender reversals, rough manners, and suspicion of decorum and restraint speak to artistic directors and dancers of our moment as traditional productions do not. The tastes and theatrical mores of practicing dancers and their artistic leaders are crucial to an audience's experience. How one thinks of one's reason for being in the theater is transmitted onstage in the tiniest details of gesture and deportment: The stage magnifies "interior life" mercilessly. Bourne's iconoclasm, heartily welcomed by a new generation of dancers, has strongly affected many even more recent *Swan Lake*s that children and other audiences new to ballet encounter for the first time, without previous experience of a version in which the ballerina is paramount and the gentle lakeside scenes, with their monumental choreographic architecture for the ensemble — rather than the treacherous ballroom, governed by politics and cliques — constitute the heart of the ballet.

When we consider that these examples are drawn from some of the landmarks of Western dance, we begin to realize the issues facing both historians and critics. To compile or add to a canon, a dance historian must be a critic, too: sifting through various productions and making choices based on what seems most valuable by whatever standards the historian determines value in dancing.

As you can see, the interweaving of past and present is a fundamental process in dance, on both sides of the curtain. Without a historian's perspective, a dance critic's evaluations would also be partial in the extreme. This goes for new work as well as for older repertory, because it is impossible to recognize innovation unless one can put it in the context of the traditional. The most important aspect of this perspective cannot be learned from books and films alone, however: it requires quantity time in the theater, watching the stage closely and watching oneself watching the stage closely. And it requires quantity time at the keyboard, trying to report on all these observations over all these hours in a way that conveys them clearly and accurately yet also retains the magic or power or energy of the experience, even if it was a negative energy. I believe it was the critic Clive Barnes who suggested that, to be a dance critic — that is, to acquire the authority to evaluate theatrical dancing — one should have attended at least a thousand performances. Like Martha Graham's famous adage that it takes ten years to make a dancer, the point isn't the number itself but rather the idea that there are no short cuts.

For a teacher designing a one-semester course in dance criticism, and for a student signing up for it, these are daunting challenges indeed. Still, to deny or evade them renders the entire endeavor worthless. As the critic Arlene Croce once put it, you must write from where you are — that is, you must be truthful to your experience, background, and context. Books and films are indispensable supplements to theatergoing; however, they just can't replace it. Every time I teach dance criticism, at some point I relate Croce's recommendation to students, with her name attached, for no one has practiced it more honestly than she.

Teaching the Course: An Overview

My experience in teaching dance criticism on the college level has been primarily at Barnard College, where I am an associate professor (adjunct), and which has offered a course in the subject for many years, usually in the spring semester. However, I've also taught related courses at Sarah Lawrence College where I was a guest instructor in the graduate program during the spring 2004 semester; at Princeton University where I was a guest lecturer in 1996; and at Portland State University, in Portland, Oregon, where, in the 1970s, the department chair developed a one-semester course in dance aesthetics. On a short-term basis, I've run workshops for working critics in practical dance criticism, too, at annual conferences of the Dance Critics Association and, in 1985, at the Center for Arts Criticism, in Minneapolis, Minnesota.

At Sarah Lawrence, where the point of the seminar was to lead the students through dance history of the twentieth century (which I was able to do courtesy of *No Fixed Points*, the extraordinary new history by Nancy Reynolds and Malcolm McCormick) and help them to choose a topic for a twenty-page research paper, which they submitted at the end of the course, dance criticism and dance history were folded in together: the act of criticism was the choice of the topic. And at Portland State University and Princeton, I didn't assign the students to evaluate the dancing and choreography they saw on films and video or in live performance. It was sufficient to ask them to appreciate the works and/or performances in detail. That was difficult enough. At Princeton, too, I had a small budget for guest speakers, whose $100 honoraria I would supplement from my own pocket for lunches. So the class was able to hear Paul Taylor discussing how he felt and what he saw while watching his own dances as a member of the audience, Allegra Kent analyzing Balanchine's *Serenade*, Ze'eva Cohen (the department chair) recalling the circumstances of her performances in Anna Sokolow's *Rooms* and the choreographer's rehearsal procedures, Yuriko Kikuchi describing how she prepared to dance the lead in Martha Graham's *Primitive Mysteries*, and other distinguished guests who commented on landmark choreographers from a studio perspective. I modeled this particular course on a course in modern living poets given at the State University of New York at Buffalo by the poet and scholar Robert Hass, for whom, as a grad student in English, I served as a teaching assistant many years before he became Poet Laureate of the United States.

In contrast, a short-term workshop in dance criticism is essentially a course in writing and journalistic ethics, and its concerns tend to be practical ones. How does one render an evening's or a week's worth of complex perceptions and evaluations in the space of a paragraph? What is the value of description, and how is it possible to make movement and music vivid, in paragraphs no longer than one or two sentences, for a general reader who has no frame of reference for the languages of dancing? If dance companies are in financial difficulty in one's area, should one still try to critique them according to the highest standards? If backstage information about a dancer's or dance company's woes — information that directly affects the quality of a performance — is known, should one pretend, in reviewing, no special knowledge? How does one convince one's editor, who thinks that dance is frivolous, to allocate sufficient space for reviewing that will argue in favor of the seriousness of the art form? These questions are usually discussed in the context of writing exercises, in which the students write reviews of a live performance and then analyze them in a seminar the next day.

In a semester-long college course, however, which is typically geared to undergraduates who are not themselves reviewing professionally at the time, one wants to give a larger picture of the relationships between dance criticism and dance history, and between analysis of a choreographic work and a literary work or a work of music or painting. One wants to situate dance criticism for them within their general education in the humanities and to point them toward some of the largest issues and questions under-lying the field, because it is those larger issues and questions that, at best, they'll be able to take away. This will at least prepare them for the hard truths that:

1. Criticism, like poetry, can't be taught, really, in a how-to format, although aspiring critics can be encouraged and models from the recent and remote past provided.
2. A critic must know a tremendous amount about the field and about personal sensibility and predispositions and prejudices in order to contribute criticism of any value at all.
3. The necessary use of films, rather than live performance, as subjects of analysis and review is of limited value for a dance critic, however cost-efficient and expedient videocassettes and DVDs are. Writing based on film rather than live performance tends to be flatter, more distanced from personal response, than writing based on going to a theater and absorbing the energy of live dancers and musicians, which makes it a challenge to discover a tone of voice for the page.

The discovery of one's personal tone of voice is fundamental to all arts criticism, which is, ultimately, a literary endeavor, despite the fact that it is frequently subject to journalistic imperatives.

At the same time that one is trying to prompt the students to try setting down their observations and evaluations in writing, one is also trying to caution them about the readership for reviews: a readership that, inevitably, includes individuals who have no interest or background in dance, indi-viduals who have some background and also their own polemical views and agendas, and individuals who have deep background. And, finally, there is the writer himself or herself: the most important reader of all. Even if the review speaks to everyone else, if it does not also articulate the writer's actual perceptions and evaluations, it should not be published, regardless of how pleasing it might be to others or how well it serves a periodical's general editorial needs. Truly, if one keeps in mind Croce's recommendation to "write from where you are," it is possible for even a novice to produce interesting works of description and analysis. I've taught many students with no dance background who have written well on these terms about theatrical dancing by virtue of their ability to concentrate, to focus, to pay attention to their own responses, and to write in a way that doesn't arrogate unearned authority.

The most difficult lesson for any dance critic is to learn how to perceive what is actually transpiring in performance (what the dancers actually do, how the choreography is actually phrased, how the music is actually being played) and to distinguish those material and checkable facts from one's visceral response to the effects they create.

In my class, I ask that students account for both specific details of performance and the truth of their responses to it, with the understanding that in the first case they are accountable for getting the facts down accurately, just as any reporter on any subject is, while, in the second case they are accountable only to their own consciences.

This approach has evolved from my particular experience of publishing on dance and reading other critics over the past thirty years. It is very, very easy, especially for a powerful writer, to make up the facts of a performance or a work in order to justify a personal or an ideological response. The simplest effects in dance are often the result of extremely complex and arduous preparation that is meant to be invisible to the average audience; and although one is not writing reviews for the performers who are the subject, if the details of performance one cites cannot be validated by the performers and by connoisseurs in the audience who know what to look for in detail, then the criticism is suspect. One of the reasons I rely on Edwin Denby's criticism in teaching is that so many dancers whom he reviewed have spoken about his track record as a reporter of what actually transpired in the theater, even when his opinion of what he reports on differs radically from their own.

This emphasis on reporting stage detail, on documentation of some kind, as both a way to give the reader something of one's experience and as a calling card for one's honesty as an observer, is certainly not the only way to write substantial dance criticism or teach it. Stark Young's pre-World War II reviews of Martha Graham contain little description of what he actually saw her and her company do; however, they are visionary, essayistic appreciations of her general enterprise, and when one looks at the works he discussed in the theater today, one can readily see the effects with which he was enamored. I also think of certain essays by André Levinson, a dance critic of staggering brilliance in terms of his understanding of theatrical effects despite his narrowness of taste in responding to them.

In a class, however, especially a class for young writers, it seems to me a teacher's responsibility to accent approaches that will give the students the greatest intellectual and literary challenges and also the most protection in long-range terms. Young writers tend to be enthusiastic about making evaluations, and, if they're good writers, they do so with a charging vigor that can be very persuasive to readers who aren't very familiar with the subject. Newspaper and magazine editors, especially, respond to "the big picture" in arts writing and denigrate documentation as "minutiae"; they often encourage strong, even polemical opinion for its own sake, and young writers, anxious to please, provide it, or accede to an editor's rewriting to provide it. In the short run, the writer may get ahead in a career; however, over time, he or she will lose the respect not only of colleagues but also of the very editors who once demanded that the writing be skewed toward a statement that is more dramatic than the writer knew was actually warranted.

Alas, this situation obtains in nearly all areas of cultural coverage today, but it is especially pervasive in whatever coverage remains of the "high arts," which are deemed to be intrinsically elitist and boring for mass-market readerships. I have no hope whatsoever that the situation will change in my lifetime or that an emphasis on accountability of reporting in a college-level course in dance criticism is going to make much difference generally. Yet it may make a difference on some level to some of the individual students as writers or as readers. They need to develop the habit of reading skeptically and writing reflectively, and they may as well begin by analyzing the fare they encounter in the arts pages.

Although it may appear that I've arrived at a template for teaching and a fixed organization for the syllabus, the truth is quite otherwise. Each of the four times I've taught dance criticism at Barnard, I've designed the course differently, and I'm prepared for the possibility that it will take me years of teaching it heuristically, using many more approaches, to find the one that is most satisfactory for the greatest number of students. One should probably also factor into this my own personality, which is more of an editor's than a writer's: I'm happier listening than speaking in most situations, and I feel uncomfortable telling another person outright what to think or do. In editing, at least the way I apprenticed to it, one proceeds by query rather than fiat. It has been awkward bordering on the painful to learn how to lecture when that is necessary.

At Barnard, the dance criticism class is considered a seminar; however, the roster has varied from seven students to nineteen or twenty. (The optimum number, in my experience, is around twelve.) Furthermore, only once has the class been assigned a room with a seminar table, which encourages conversation; on the other three occasions, the room has been set up as a lecture situation, with a dominating table or a podium and the seats arranged in serried ranks. Even when we rearrange the chairs into something resembling a circle, the room is not transformed, and the ease of conversation is affected. The most probing and crackling discussions took place in the room with the seminar table, a small room built for seminars, where the videocassette player and monitor were sufficiently close to the table that everyone could easily see the images without having to shift.

I emphasize the conditions for discussion because, although many of my students at Barnard have demonstrated keen minds, and some have been dazzlingly brilliant, they do belong to a generation that seems to me comparatively quiescent in an intellectual setting. They are quite capable of complaining when they don't like something, but one must persist in provoking them to take strong positions over ideas. Again, part of the problem may be my own personality, which isn't very forceful; however, I'm not alone at the college in my concern about this phenomenon of student quiescence. In its wide-ranging First-Year Seminar (FYS) Program, where I also teach a writing and literature seminar in the personal essay called "The Art of Being Oneself," Barnard has developed a creative approach to try to habituate the freshmen to constructing strong, well-documented, organized positions on an issue. Called "Reacting to the Past: History as Hypothesis," this award-winning program, taught by a team of faculty and structured as a game, randomly assigns the student to adopt this or that position in a debate drawn from a key turning point in history: "Democracy at the Threshold: Athens in 403 B.C.," or "Confucianism and the Succession Crisis of the Wan-li Emperor, Set in the Forbidden City of Beijing, China, in 1587 A.D." How the student composes her argument is up to her, but she is expected to consult important historical texts for guidance. As a recent article about the program in *The New York Times* chronicles, "Reacting to the Past" has been extremely popular among students and faculty. Indeed, it has been so successful that, this year, a commercial series of games based on it is being issued for sale by Longman.

Criticism, or at least dance criticism, doesn't respond well to the institutionalization of this kind of lawyerly debating, because the crucial element of truthfulness to one's personal experience would be severed from the argument. Still, inspired by the program, I've tried out debating tactics in dance criticism from time to time on an ad hoc basis. During the spring 2003 semester, for instance, when the class read Arlene Croce's provocative essay "Discussing the Undiscussable" — her brief explanation of why she chose to publish a polemical column about "Still/Here" by Bill

T. Jones while refusing to see it in the theater — I devised an assignment that asked the students, first, to decide what their individual reactions were to the essay and, then, to write a short paper that argued a position diametrically opposed to what they actually felt. In doing this, I wanted them to have the experience of being distanced from their own responses yet also engaged by those responses as a point of reference. The result, surprising even to me, was that the quietest students in class discussion turned in the most fiery and engaged papers: They were stimulated and focused by that fillip of writing in opposition to their real feelings. I'd like to add that the subject of this short paper wasn't on the syllabus I'd prepared a month before classes began: I developed it midcourse, after hearing the students discuss the essay in one session and becoming concerned that they were relying on diffuse notions and on perspectives that they'd held before signing up for the course, rather than defending or arguing with the points being made in the essay itself.

Structure of the Course

Dance Criticism is a 300-level course at Barnard and so is open to students from Columbia as well. Columbia students who have enrolled in it have included choreographer Sydney Skybetter and dancers Alicia Graf of the Dance Theatre of Harlem, and Broadway gypsy and actor Jonathan Sandler — remarkable writers all. In the past couple of years, I've asked that enrollment be capped at 16, with permission required from the instructor, based on writing samples, usually.

There are, as I see it, two main approaches to the subject. One would be to make it a literary history course, reading dance critics chronologically from the nineteenth, twentieth, and twenty-first centuries with screenings of films that showed ballets and dances relevant to their criticism. One day I might try that approach; to date, though, I've pursued the other choice: to try to give a sense of the various components that go into dance criticism of all times and places — observation, analysis, evaluation, aesthetic principle, journalistic necessity, and personal preference — and, through this, to give a glimpse of how complex a matter it is to create a literary tone and to develop a sensibility that will keep one curious yet will also prove a reliable scale for evaluation. I try to introduce these various elements in as offhanded a way as I possibly can, rather than through systematized outlines and decrees. My hope is that students will leave the course with an affection for dancing that will continue beyond graduation, and I'd rather present the material in a way that gives them a chance to feel they've discovered something themselves and that I haven't discovered it for them.

And, of course, that's the truth: I haven't discovered everything. I learn from them as well.

Although I've emphasized that the course differs from semester to semester, there are some boilerplate elements to it. It always meets once a week for two hours; it always relies on videos and DVDs as well as on readings that always include large swaths of *Dance Writings and Poetry*, the only collection of reviews and essays by Edwin Denby in print. It nearly always asks for a midterm paper of five pages in which the student describes and analyzes a live performance. It always features at least one, and usually two, individual conferences of around a half hour with every student; and four or five in-class writing exercises are always assigned. And, up to now, it always has one session in which I interview Robert Greskovic, who writes on dancing for *The Wall Street Journal*. Although I could invite a number of colleagues quite happily for their literary brilliance, their ability to sum up their responses with a memorable flourish, their skill at documentation, and other admirable gifts, I rely on Robert to speak to undergraduates, because, in my opinion, he has the keenest eye and most judicious temperament of any dance critic working in America today, and he has graciously visited the class each year to discuss his way of seeing in the theater, his writing, and the profession in general. Other occasional visitors have included Barbara Newman, a dance critic in London, and Sunil Kothari, chief dance and drama critic for forty years for *The Times of India*, in New Delhi.

For the past three years, I've also assigned readings in Arlene Croce's selected criticism, *Writing in the Dark: Dancing at the New Yorker*, and, this past term, I've assigned readings in the selected criticism of Sally Banes, *Writing Dance in the Age of Postmodernism*, and in Lincoln Kirstein's blueprint for a canon of Western theatrical dancing, *Four Centuries of Ballet: Fifty Masterworks*. Denby and Croce are the dance critics with the best eyes and the most refined sensibilities. I know of in the history of dance criticism; their literary styles, while quite unlike one another, are also excellent models for aspiring writers. Sally Banes is a very good contemporary critic and historian, and I'll probably assign her collection again.

Lincoln Kirstein is sui generis, a giant of letters in the arts; however, before I ask students to read his book in another class, I'll have to give some deeper thought to ways in which it might be presented. His ornate prose style and uncompromising, even peremptory intellect offended the class this past spring, and they didn't give the book a chance to reveal the amazing treasures of wisdom and insight it contains. They don't yet have the maturity as readers to overlook the crustiness and arrogance of the tone in order to retrieve the thoughts it sheathes, and I don't yet have the maturity as an instructor to convince them of the value of suspending their initial reactions in the interest of more probing analysis. As I see it, then, the options are to leave out study of such writers; to simply insist that the students read them, regardless of how enraged they are that they have to do so; or to figure out some way to spoon-feed the prose in a context where the substance of it is vitally relevant to the readers in question. The last is my preference, but it's going to take me some time to realize it.

In terms of differences among the various semesters, a small one is that I sometimes assign a final, seven- to ten-page essay on one of several topics I construct (a review, a response to another essay, etc.) and sometimes choose to assign a final, open-book essay exam instead. It depends on what the median level of writing is in the class and how many of the students are working in English as a second language. I don't happen to believe that an excellent literary style inevitably demonstrates the best thinking, and I want the course to offer a level playing field to students who may not have had the good luck to study dance or to have attended many performances before arriving in college. Indeed, one of the most interesting students I've ever taught dance criticism was an undergraduate from Columbia whose native language was Japanese and whose major was, as I recall, philosophy. He had excellent observations; however, in order to articulate them, he had to use a translating machine. At the beginning of the term, he also mentioned that, in some of his other academic classes, he couldn't understand what people said, because they tended to speak at a rattling pace and to slur their words. I was actually glad to hear his concerns, because I'd also noticed that many students tended to lose clarity of pronunciation and of punctuation when they spoke in class, swallowing entire words and, often, thoughts. And so, on his behalf, I would often ask discussants to slow down when speaking. I also like to relate to them what Madeleine Ludwig — another Barnard student of dance criticism, who comes from Switzerland, whose native languages are French and German, and who also had trouble understanding some of the native American speakers — told a class that she had been drilled to do by her French teachers in elementary school during dictations: When reading aloud, count one beat of silence for a comma, two for a colon or semicolon, and three for a period. It is astonishing how this simple procedure produces clarity of articulation and, with it, clarity of thought.

A second difference from semester to semester is in the films we analyze and the way we analyze them. Dance Criticism has no lab fee for theater tickets, and because, even with student discounts, tickets to dancing can be expensive, everyone who has taught the course has had to rely primarily on films, rather than on live performance. In two of the years, when the class was made up of students more interested in and knowledgeable about modern dance than about ballet — their dance background is one of the things I learn immediately in a diagnostic writing assignment at the first class — I had very good luck with asking for analyses of Eiko and Koma's wonderful 10-minute film *Husk*. The students had to figure out which effects they thought were produced by the performer (Eiko) and which by the filmmaker (Koma). In one year, the film editor Miriam Arsham also came in to comment on some of the technical aspects of the filmmaking for *Husk*. I had good luck, too, with an in-class exercise in which I screened a film of a work by Paul Taylor up until the last five minutes, stopped the tape, and asked the students to write an in-class paragraph — in-class assignments are always no more than one side of one ruled page — about how they thought Taylor would end the dance, based on the logic of the choreography they had seen so far. It put them in the choreographer's shoes, of course; and it also reminded them that dances can unfold in time, as a literary work does, with linear as well as metaphorical logic.

On the other hand, in the class this past spring, where most of the students were either extremely interested in, or practitioners of, classical ballet, one of the most productive assignments was when I screened five film versions of a passage from the second act of *Giselle* with such artists as Mikhail Baryshnikov and Natalia Makarova, and Erik Bruhn and Carla Fracci, and then asked for an in-class paragraph about which version they found the most theatrically persuasive and powerful, and why. They had to choose at least one detail from the film and try to determine whether the power was a matter of the performances or of the filmmaking. Not all of my film choices have been popular. Contemporary students of my acquaintance have difficulty, for instance, relating to *The Red Shoes*, whose extreme either-or of love and art they find antiquated in a time when ballerinas routinely perform while they're several months pregnant and who routinely return to the stage for years after giving birth to several children.

I was also surprised to discover that the class this past spring found Bronislava Nijinska's landmark modernist masterpiece *Les Noces* both too elementary in its technique and too patriarchal to be of contemporary interest. Most surprising was the comment by one student, who sings in choruses and who has participated in a concert performance of Igor Stravinsky's score, that he didn't think the music had much popular appeal. At moments like this, the best thing to do, in my view, is to nod, ask why, sigh, and move on, perhaps after noting that one has been at per-formances of the ballet (to both live and taped music) in which the audience raised the roof with enthusiasm. That is, the best thing is to treat one's broken heart lightly, because sometimes it's the students who most earnestly reject a work of art or a working method in their teens and twenties who learn on their own to appreciate it deeply in their thirties and forties. I speak here from firsthand experience.

Finally, I'd like to mention an assignment that I tried one year and which was useful for a class made up of student dancers, working professionals, and aspiring choreographers, many of whom seemed to be suspicious that critics had some sort of axe to grind in critiques. For this class, in place of a midterm paper, I assigned each student to research the reviews and something of the career of a critic currently working in New York and to give an oral presentation to the class on that critic. The subjects of presentation included, in no particular order, Anna Kisselgoff, Jack Anderson, and Jennifer Dunning of *The New York Times*, Tobi Tobias of the online *ArtsJournal* (www.artsjournal.com/tobias), Joan Acocella of *The New Yorker*, Robert Gottlieb of *The New York Observer*, Doris Hering of *Dance Magazine*, Clive Barnes of *The New York Post*, and Deborah Jowitt and Elizabeth Zimmer of *The Village Voice*. What astonished me about the presentations as a group was how loving they were. Not a single presenter attempted to criticize the critic whose work he or she was curating, but rather they treated it with the care one might accord to a member of one's family. There's a lesson in here somewhere, and, perhaps, when I finally figure out how to teach dance criticism, I'll have learned it.

Dance Criticism

Required Readings for Barnard Course, Spring 2004

Banes, Sally. *Writing Dancing in the Age of Postmodernism* Wesleyan/New England, 1994.
Croce, Arlene. *Writing in the Dark, Dancing in* The New Yorker. Farrar, Straus & Giroux, 2000.
Denby, Edwin. *Dance Writings & Poetry*. Yale University Press, 1998.
Kirstein, Lincoln. *50 Ballet Masterworks: From the 16th to the 20th Century*. Dover, 1984.

Other Books of Dance Criticism and Aesthetics for the General Reader

Copeland, Roger, and Cohen, Marshall. *What Is Dance?: Readings in Theory and Criticism*. Oxford University Press, 1983.
Coton, A.V. *A Prejudice for Ballet*. Methuen & Co., 1938.
Croce, Arlene. *Afterimages*. Knopf, 1977.
Croce, Arlene. *Going to the Dance*. Knopf, 1982.
Croce, Arlene. *Sight Lines*. Knopf, 1987.
Croce, Arlene. *The Fred Astaire & Ginger Rogers Book*. Vintage, 1977.
Denby, Edwin. *Dance Writings*. Knopf, 1986.
Garis, Robert. *Following Balanchine*. Yale University Press, 1995.
Gautier, Théophile. *Gautier on Dance*. Edited and translated by Ivor Guest. Dance Books, 1986.
Haggin, B. H. *Discovering Balanchine*. Horizon Press, 1981.
Johnston, Jill. *Marmalade Me*. Dutton, 1971.
Jowitt, Deborah. *Dance Beat: Selected Views & Reviews 1967–1976*. Marcel Dekker, 1977.
Jowitt, Deborah. *The Dance in Mind: Profiles and Reviews 1976–1983*. David R. Godine, 1985.

Kirstein, Lincoln. *Ballet: Bias & Belief.* Dance Horizons, 1983.
Kirstein, Lincoln. *By With To & From: A Lincoln Kirstein Reader.* Edited by Nicholas Jenkins. Farrar, Straus, 1991.
Langer, Suzanne. *Feeling and Form.* Scribner's, 1953.
Levinson, André. *André Levinson on Dance: Writings from Paris in the Twenties.* Edited by Joan Acocella and Lynn Garafola. Wesleyan/New England, 1991.
Levinson, André. *Ballet Old and New.* Translated by Susan Cook Summer. Dance Horizons, 1982.
Lopukhov, Fedor. *Writings on Ballet and Music.* Edited by Stephanie Jordan. Translated by Dorinda Offord. University of Wisconsin Press, 2002.
Parker, H. T. *Motion Arrested: Dance Reviews of H. T. Parker.* Edited by Olive Holmes. Wesleyan University Press, 1982.
Reynolds, Nancy. *Repertory in Review: 40 Years of the New York City Ballet.* Dial Press, 1977.
Siegel, Marcia B. *At the Vanishing Point: A Critic Looks at Dance.* Saturday Review Press, 1972.
Siegel, Marcia B. *The Tail of the Dragon: New Dance 1976–1982.* Duke University Press, 1991.
Siegel, Marcia B. *Watching the Dance Go By.* Houghton Mifflin, 1977.
Steinberg, Cobbett, ed. *The Dance Anthology.* New American Library, 1980.

Useful Arts Criticism and Related Writings about Aesthetics

Art

Arnheim, Rudolf. *Art and Visual Perception: A Psychology of the Creative Eye.* University of California Press, 1974.
Arnheim, Rudolf. *Visual Thinking.* University of California Press, 1969.
Chipp, Herschell B. *Theories of Modern Art: A Source Book by Artists and Critics,* with contributions by Peter Selz and Joshua B. Taylor. University of California Press, 1968.
Danto, Arthur. *Brushes with History: Writing on Art from The Nation: 1865–2001.* Edited by Peter G. Meyer. Nation Books: 2001.
Delacroix, Eugène. *Journals of Delacroix.* Edited by Hubert Wellington. Translated by Lucy Norton. Phaidon Press, 1995.
Elkins, James. *Our Beautiful, Dry, and Distant Texts: Art History as Writing.* Routledge, 2000.
Gombrich, Ernst. *Art and Illusion.* Princeton University Press, 2000.
Singleton, Esther, ed. and trans. *Great Pictures as Seen and Described by Famous Writers.* Dodd, Mead, 1907.

Film

Agee, James. *Agee on Film: Criticism and Comment on the Movies.* Modern Library, 2000.
Kael, Pauline. *5001 Nights at the Movies.* Owl Books, 1991.
Sarris, Andrew. *The American Cinema: Directors and Directions 1929–1968.* Da Capo, 1996.

Literature

Aristotle/Horace/Longinus. *Classical Literary Criticism.* Translated by T. S. Dorsch. Penguin Books, 1965.
Barzun, Jacques. *An Essay on French Verse: For Readers of English Poetry.* New Directions, 1981.
Coleridge, Samuel Taylor. *Biographia Literaria.* Princeton University Press, 1985.
Eliot, T. S. *To Criticize the Critic and Other Writing.* University of Nebraska Press, 1992.
Jarrell, Randall. *Poetry and the Age.* Octagon Books, 1972.
Pound, Ezra. *The ABC of Reading.* New Directions, 1960.
Updike, John. *Hugging the Shore.* Knopf, 1987.

Music

Bernstein, Leonard. *The Unanswered Question: Six Talks at Harvard* (Charles Eliot Norton Lectures). Harvard University Press, 1981.

Schonberg, Harold C. *The Lives of the Great Composers*. W.W. Norton, 1970.
Shaw, George Bernard. *The Great Composers: Reviews and Bombardments*. Edited by Louis Crompton. University of California Press, 1978.
Thomson, Virgil. *The Art of Judging Music*. Greenwood Press, 1969.

Photography

Hartmann, Sadakichi. *The Valiant Knights of Daguerre: Selected Critical Essays on Photography and Profiles of Photographic Pioneers (1898–1913)*. University of California Press, 1978.

Theater

Benchley, Robert. *Benchley at the Theatre*. Edited by Charles Getchell. The Ipswich Press, 1985.
Shaw, George Bernard. *Shaw's Dramatic Criticism (1895–98)* Greenwood-Heinemann Publishing, 1989.
Young, Stark. *Immortal Shadows: A Book of Dramatic Criticism*. Octagon Books, 1973.
Young, Stark. *The Theatre*. Hill and Wang, 1954.

Some Recommended Dance Critics in Print Journalism

Ballet Review (Francis Mason, ed.).
Dance Magazine (Wendy Perron, ed.; reviews from the magazine and that may not be included in the magazine are also available online at www.dancemagazine.com.)
New York Magazine (Laura Shapiro).
New York Newsday (Sylviane Gold).
Pointe Magazine (ed. Virginia Johnson; the first 100 words of reviews are published in the hard copy of the magazine, and the full versions are available online at www.pointemaga zine.com).
The Boston Globe (Christine Temin).
The Boston Phoenix (Marcia B. Siegel).
The Los Angeles Times (Lewis Segal).
The New Criterion (Laura Jacobs).
The New Republic (Jennifer Homans).
The New York Observer (Robert A. Gottlieb; reviews are also available on line at www.newyorkobserver.com).
The New York Post (Clive Barnes).
The New York Times (John Rockwell, chief dance critic; Jack Anderson, Jennifer Dunning; Anna Kisselgoff, chief dance critic emerita).
The New Yorker (Joan Acocella).
The Orange County Register (Laura Bleiberg).
The Oregonian (Martha Ullman West).
The Star-Ledger (Robert Johnson).
The Village Voice (Deborah Jowitt; Elizabeth Zimmer, dance-page ed.; reviews from the paper and that may not be included in the paper are also available online at www.villagevoice.com).
The Wall Street Journal (Robert Greskovic).
The Washington Post (Sarah Kaufman)
Time Out New York (Gia Kourlas).

Recommended Dance Web Sites
Canada

www.maisonneuve.com (for the columns of Kena Herod)

Great Britain

www.ballet.co.uk

Germany

www.tanznetz.de

United States

www.danceviewtimes.com
www.danceinsider.com
www.artsjournal.com/tobias (for the columns of Tobi Tobias)
http://ballet.blogs.com/ (for the blog of Alexandra Tomalonis)
www.exploredance.com
www.voiceofdance.com

CHAPTER 8

The Anthropology of Dance: Textural, Theoretical, and Experiential Ways of Knowing

JILL D. SWEET

When I tell people that I teach undergraduate courses at Skidmore College that focus on the anthropology of dance, they frequently give me quizzical looks that ask, "What does anthropology have to do with dance and what does dance have to do with anthropology?" These are fair questions to ask, especially when the popular image of an anthropologist today is associated with Indiana Jones-types digging up past civilizations, or alternatively with Jane Goodall-types patiently observing the behavior of nonhuman primates in the wild. But for a cultural anthropologist like myself who studies the contemporary lifeways of "other" human groups, the relationship between anthropology and dance is a close one. It turns out, in fact, that dance is a near-universal human activity practiced in a variety of ways throughout the ages and around the world.

Groups of people everywhere repeatedly tell themselves about themselves through their social, ritual, and theatrical dance performances. Therefore, to study a people's dance is to study their view of their world: what they believe to be their purpose for being in the world, their origins and their destinies; what they consider to be beautiful, ugly, sacred, profane, good, evil, humorous, and serious. Seen in this light, dance is not the "frill" or "fluff" of life, but rather it is significant action that encodes and communicates and recreates some of the most basic and fundamental meanings at the core of a culture. That is what an anthropological study does.

This chapter is organized into three sections. The first part is a discussion of the personal journey I undertook to find and build connections between my two passions: anthropology and dance. The second section is a discussion of some very basic anthropological concepts that are applicable to dance studies. I also consider some central dimensions of dance studies that have the potential of further enhancing anthropology.[1] In the third and final section, I discuss one particular course I recently taught that brought together textual, theoretical, and experiential ways of knowing through anthropology and dance.

A Personal Journey

In 1971 at the age of twenty-one I experienced my first "episode" or "attack" of multiple sclerosis. It took seven years of additional episodes and many frustrating doctor visits, before I received a definitive diagnosis. Finally, in 1978 I was told it was MS. The confirmation of a debilitating neurological condition was a devastating blow, but at least I knew that I was not a hypochondriac with an overactive imagination. With a diagnosis I could begin to learn about the illness and to creatively rethink my life goals and priorities. I knew I wanted to stay involved in some aspect of dance, but in what form, I did not know.

Some of my first thoughts took me back to my MFA studies. Olga Maynard, my dance history professor at the University of California at Irvine, sparked my interest in dance as a product of a particular moment in time and as an expression of a particular cultural group. Particularly moving was a documentary film Professor Maynard showed us of a ritual dance event in a Greek village (Haramis 1966). I also remembered the dance ethnology courses I took from Allegra Fuller Snyder at the University of California at Los Angeles. Under Professor Snyder's guidance, I read what anthropologists had written about dance in non-Western settings. I also recalled traveling with Professor Synder and some of her graduate students to Tucson for the Yaqui Indian Easter celebrations. It was this Arizona trip, along with a previous visit to a New Mexico reservation to see a winter solstice/Christmas dance, that compelled me to think seriously about the anthropology of dance.[2]

The writings of cultural anthropologists gave me methodological and theoretical tools for making sense of the elaborate dance events I had witnessed in New Mexico and Arizona. While most anthropologists I read did not write specifically about dance, works by theorists such as Clifford Geertz (1973), Victor Turner (1974), Mary Douglas (1966), Edmund Leach (1976), and Claude Lévi-Strauss (1966) afforded me theoretical foundations from which I could begin to analyze and interpret dance events. I also read ethnographies more specifically tied to Native Americans in the Southwest. These included works by Edward Spicer (1967), Edward Dozier (1970/1983), Alfonso Ortiz (1969), Barbara Myerhoff (1974), and Keith Basso (1979). In Professor Synder's seminar we read other anthropological contributions with more direct references to dance, including the works of Judith Lynne Hanna (1979), Adrienne Kaeppler (1971, 1978), Joann Keali'inohomoku (1983), Gertrude Kurath (1970), Anya Peterson Royce (1977), and Drid Williams (1979).

Armed with the insights of these anthropologists and after completing the MFA in dance, I ventured back to New Mexico to see more Southwest Indian dance events and to apply for admission to the Ph.D. program in anthropology at the University of New Mexico. But unfortunately, the anthropology faculty at UNM were not eager to take a chance on a dancer from California, so as an alternative strategy I entered the UNM graduate school through the interdisciplinary American Studies Department. As an American Studies graduate student, I could take anthropology courses along with courses in American dance, American history, and American literature.

The first graduate course I took was an anthropology seminar on kinship taught by Louise Lamphere, who had conducted fieldwork among the Navajo. I did well in Lamphere's class, and with a new sense of confidence I applied again for admission to the anthropology graduate program. This time I was accepted, and I began studying with Philip K. Bock, who taught ethnomusicology; Alfonso Ortiz, who taught about Pueblo Indian cultures; and Marta Weigle, who taught folklore. Along with Allegra Fuller Snyder, these individuals became my mentors. With their help I finished my Ph.D. and found ways to explore dance through anthropology and anthropology through dance. Nevertheless, it was only during my subsequent postdoctoral teaching experiences that I began to appreciate the connections between anthropology and dance.

My first teaching appointment was a sabbatical replacement position in UCLA's dance department. From there I landed a tenure-track position at Skidmore College teaching in the anthropology program. Although I vowed that I would never take a job east of the Rocky Mountains, Skidmore turned out to be an ideal place for someone with my background and interests, because it was a liberal arts college with a growing anthropology program and a small but well-established dance program. Skidmore was also well suited for me because it had a tradition of interdisciplinary exploration and curricular experimentation. Furthermore, it was an institution that rewarded excellence in teaching as well as in professional scholarship. Best of all, I found that at Skidmore I had the freedom to create interdisciplinary courses with the potential of attracting both anthropology and dance students.

What Cultural Anthropology Can Bring to Dance Studies

When I introduce my beginning students to the anthropological perspective, I present it as an approach based on three "Cs" and three "Ms": Culture, Context, Comparison; and Method, Meaning, and Movement. While this may seem like a silly device for memorization, I find these six words can stimulate significant conversations between students with varying degrees of experience in anthropology and/or dance.

I begin the course with the three Cs, first by engaging students in conversation about what the term "culture" means to them and what they think anthropologists mean when they use the term. They soon discover that the culture concept, important to all four branches of anthropology — biological, cultural, archaeological, and linguistic — is a central notion that is constantly being defined and redefined by anthropologists. Nonetheless, for students embarking on an exploration of the anthropology of dance, I find that an ideational or knowledge-based definition of culture is most useful, particularly the notion of culture as *embodied knowledge.* This embodied knowledge is a system of learned and shared ideas that inform action. It is not something one group of people has more of than another. It is not tied to the idea that those who go to the opera have more "culture" than those who prefer to go to a baseball game. Furthermore, it is not a term used exclusively to describe colorful folk festivals performed by small ethnic minorities. Rather, all these situations are predicated on a learned and shared knowledge system. Opera, baseball, and ethnic festivals all involve shared and learned rules, meanings, and patterns that are *cultural constructions.*[3]

In anthropology, *context* refers to the idea that all actions must be viewed within a particular social and ideological environment. As my former professor Alfonso Ortiz repeatedly warned me, a student of anthropology and dance must not treat dance as something shorn from the culture and times within which it exists. Instead he urged me to explore the relationship between dance events and culture. I discovered how the dance of a group informs a particular view of the world and conversely how a particular view of the world informs a dance tradition.

Inherent in the culture concept and the contextualization process is the desire for *comparison.* The researcher cannot help but compare what he or she sees in an unfamiliar cultural setting with that which is familiar. Nevertheless, these comparisons should not be based on simple value judgments of "better" or "worse." Nor should they be based on a nineteenth-century idea of evolutionary stages of development. Both of these forms of comparison are driven by *ethnocentrism,* or the tendency to believe one's own cultural practices are superior and more evolved than are any others. Instead, a researcher working from an anthropological perspective strives to maintain a position of *cultural relativism.* After all, who is to say that a fire-walking dance event in Greece, where initiates enter a trance state and repeatedly run across a bed of burning coals is "better" than a dance event in West Virginia where worshipers welcome the Holy Ghost into their moving bodies as they prove their faith by handling poisonous snakes? And what about the Hopi Snake Dance, where the dancers carry poisonous snakes in their mouths as they slowly circle the plaza? Which of these activities is more or less meaningful, or more or less aesthetic, or more or less evolved? These types of questions may be significant for the dance critic, but for the dance anthropologist striving for cultural relativism, they are inappropriate.

Next, I teach on the three Ms of the anthropological perspective, beginning with *method.* Participant observation is the central method employed by cultural anthropologists. At dance events it is important that the researcher observes the dancers and all the activity around the dance event, such as preparatory practices, retreats, feasting or fasting, and the physical and mental transformation that the dancers experience as they don costumes and nonordinary postures and movements. When and where appropriate the researcher tries to execute and experience the dance in their bodies. They may also want to talk to the dancers about their performance experience, but of course this also needs to happen at an appropriate time and place.[4]

As the dance anthropologist collects data, he or she is interpreting that data in an effort to find *meaning* in the event. A good *interpretation* will take one to the heart of a culture. The more dance events researchers experience and the more they talk to the dancers, the deeper will be their understanding and interpretation. The result will be ethnographically rich with layer upon layer of meanings systematically observed within the context of the dance event.

Finally, the element of *movement* plays a part in the anthropological perspective in two ways. First, while the researcher would prefer to "hold a culture still" long enough to analyze it, the reality is that a culture is never static. The events produced by a culture are constantly being reinvented with new meanings reflecting changes in the entire lifeway of the group.

The second way movement is important in the anthropological perspective is that it is through moving bodies that a group of people make public the knowledge and meanings informing their particular culture. The research process in the anthropology of dance can illustrate how dance events are responsive to larger social changes. Again, the message is to view dance as part of a larger dynamic cultural system.

To summarize, some of the most basic anthropological concepts that have direct relevance for the study of dance are culture, context, and comparison; and method, meaning, and movement. Related to these six concepts are the notions of ethnocentrism, cultural relativism, participant observation, and interpretation. These are all central to an anthropological perspective. But what can dance studies bring to the mix?[5]

First, the student of dance studies typically develops a heightened *kinesthetic awareness*. They learn this awareness through experiencing motion in their own bodies as well as by observing others moving through time and space. They usually involve themselves considerably in one or more dance traditions. In U.S. colleges and universities, the most frequently offered studio courses include several levels of modern dance, ballet, and choreography classes. In larger programs the offerings might include martial arts, several types of ethnic folk dance, or classical dance of Asia, such as dance of Indonesia, India, or Japan. In addition to experiences in the studio with many kinds of dance, most dance studies students also learn about various dance forms by reading and writing about them. As a result, for a student of dance studies, there is less separation between linear knowing through the intellect and multidimensional knowing through the moving body. (See Novack 1990, 7, and Farnell 1995, ix–xi, on challenging the Cartesian bifurcation of mind and body.) [6]

Second, dance studies afford students opportunities to experience within themselves the process of *transformation*. By transformation I am referring to the temporary psychological and physical changes that can occur when a performer alters his or her appearance, postures, and gestures from the ordinary, utilitarian, and mundane to the extraordinary, powerful, and imaginary. These transformational experiences help the student of anthropology and dance understand something about altered states of consciousness, play, role reversal, trance, possession, or even simply an exhilarating "runner's high." Furthermore, after experiencing transformations, students of anthropology and dance learn about and appreciate the difficulty of describing the experience of transformation. They struggle with the question of how one can use linear verbal language to talk about a nonlinear and nonverbal experience.

Third, dance studies explore ways to describe and record human movement, which is complicated because dance fleetingly exists in time and space. In response to the challenge, dance studies programs typically introduce individuals to one or more *movement notation systems.* A notation system of dance translates three-dimensional movement into a one-dimensional score using a set of symbols. Nonetheless, movement notation systems can record a dancer's every action and, in the case of Labanotation, even the subtlest movements, such as the wink of an eye or a flattening of a palm. To learn all the intricacies of Labanotation, a student needs to devote considerable time to its study. Even brief exposure to the system can be very useful for a student of anthropology and dance, because it can sharpen the student's skills of observation and invest them with a movement vocabulary.

In order to produce a notation of a dance, the researcher must first learn to observe movement keenly. When I began to research Native American dance, I was determined to produce notations. Nonetheless, after I completed this process for a couple of dance sequences, I became concerned that some Girl Scout or Boy Scout troop might use my notations to recreate a dance devoid of its intended meaning and context. I knew that the Native people who shared their dances with me would be shocked to see them in the context of a Boy Scout jamboree. So for me, the product of notation was less important than the process, and as I tried to record detailed movements, I was learning to see as I had never seen before. Moreover I was learning a cross-cultural movement vocabulary. In my Southwest field situation, this was especially critical because I was never permitted to take notes or sketch dancers while I watched, and only rarely was I given permission to photograph them; these restrictions compelled me to notice and remember even the most understated movements, postures, and gestures. For a fieldworker trying to understand and describe an unfamiliar system of movement, the knowledge of a notation system is a skill from dance studies that can be highly beneficial to anthropological research.

An Example Course in the Anthropology of Dance

Over the years, I have taught many different versions of my course on anthropology and dance. In all cases, however, the course revolves around students: (1) critical reading and writing; (2) observing many forms of dance; and (3) individually or collectively experiencing within themselves aspects of the dance they have read about, written about, and observed. In the spring of 2004 I decided the course should emphasize the relationship between theory and practice, because over the years I found that too many undergraduate students dismiss theory as boring and/or irrelevant. I was determined to show them that theory could be exciting because it plays a critical role in the entire research process.

To enroll in this upper-division anthropology course the students needed to have successfully completed one introductory cultural anthropology course or they needed to convince me that they had performance background, motivation, and a willingness to independently read selections from an introductory anthropology text. For the 2004 spring term, twelve students enrolled. One was a chemistry major, another was an art history major, a third was a self-determined major with considerable dance experience, and the other nine were anthropology majors. Of those anthropology majors, three had taken classes in the dance department, one was a dance minor/anthropology major, and two had performed in one or more college dance productions. Four of the twelve students were seniors, and the others were in their third year at Skidmore. This was the mix of students with varying degrees of experience in anthropology and dance whose ways of thinking and knowing needed to be centered around issues of performance, most particularly sacred, social, and/or theatrical dance events.

In 2004 I began the course with a heavy dose of anthropological theory from "my era," or what I have always thought of as "symbolic anthropology of the late 1960s, '70s, and early '80s."[7] The students read, wrote about, and discussed several essays by Clifford Geertz (1973) and Victor Turner (1974). At first some of them complained bitterly about how "hard" or "dense" the readings were, forcing them to read each more than once! But I convinced most to see that these theoretical essays provided us with a vocabulary and ways of thinking, writing, and talking about performance situations. Furthermore, the works of Geertz and Turner offered ways to think about the performances that the students were experiencing in and out of class.

Throughout the course students were required to observe a minimum of ten performances, keeping a journal of their impressions along with indications of what they found useful from symbolic theory to aid them in their search for meaning and understandings. For this semester-long journal assignment, I specified that at least one entry should be of a sacred ritual performance, such as one they might see in a local temple or church service. Another should be a mundane informal performance, such as animated storytelling or joke sharing in the dorms. Yet another should be a social dance gathering, such as a hip-hop party. And, finally, one should be a theatrical performance. In all cases, they needed to pay attention to the body language, postures, and gestures used by the participants.

Next I had the students read Barbara Myerhoff's (1974) ethnography of the Huichol Indians and their sacred pilgrimage to collect peyote. I encouraged the students to look for evidence of Geertzian and Turnerian influences. What of Turner did Myerhoff find applicable to her Huichol study? What of Geertz did she build on? Could the students see how theory building works? Next I showed the class Peter Furst's (1969) documentary on the Huichol pilgrimage, "To Find Our Life: The Peyote Hunt of the Huichols of Mexico." When they watched this documentary, they glimpsed Myerhoff herself working in the field with the Huichol pilgrims. They also viewed Ramon, the shaman who taught Myerhoff about the deer, the maize, and the peyote as the key symbolic trio of the event. Throughout it all they saw the pilgrims dancing and making music in the desert.

After further reading in symbolic anthropology including writings by Edmund Leach (1976), Mary Douglas (1966), Keith Basso (1979), and McKim Marriott (1966), the class began to discuss some of the limitations of the symbolic approach. To get the group talking critically, I assigned an essay by William Roseberry (1989), entitled "Balinese Cockfights and the Seduction of Anthropology." Roseberry convincingly argues that Geertz and other symbolic anthropologists write as if blind to postcolonial issues of political economy and feminism. The Roseberry critique paved the way for the second half of the course, where we turned to more recent interpretive ethnographies that focus on dance and build on, but go beyond, Geertz, Turner, and the symbolic anthropology of the 1970s.

In the second half of the course, I used Jane Cowan's (1990) *Dance and the Body Politic in Northern Greece*, Cynthia Novack's (1990) *Sharing the Dance: Contact Improvisation and American Culture*, and Zoila Mendoza's (2000) *Shaping Society Through Dance*. For all three of these ethnographies, students discussed the theoretical approach as it compares to the perspectives of earlier symbolic anthropology; they saw film footage of the dance, and they participated in an experiential workshop on an aspect of the dance presented in the ethnography.

Before turning to these three contemporary ethnographies, the students and I paused to consider the key issues we had been talking and writing about during the first half of the course. Some of the central topics that dominated the first seven weeks included:

Role of theory and theory building in anthropology and dance.
Humanistic and scientific dimensions of anthropology and dance.

Basic assumptions and vocabulary of symbolic anthropology with direct relevance for the anthropological study of dance.

Active and passive sides of symbols and symbolic action in dance events.

Liminality, rites of passage, rites of intensification, and rites of affliction as situations for dance.

Geertz's notions of thick description and layers of interpretation particularly related to dance.

Turner's notions of multivocality, communitas, and social drama as they apply to dance events.

To begin the second half of the course, students read Cowan's (1990) ethnography of contemporary dance in a northern Greek community. This ethnography illustrates well the issues of gender display in dance events and also demonstrates how dance can inspire conflict as much as it can promote social solidarity (see, for example, Cowan, Chapter 8). Furthermore, Cowan's analysis of *kefi*, or a heightened sense of joy and abandonment, is an excellent example of a dancer's transformation from an ordinary to the nonordinary state.

For a visual complement to the Cowan ethnography, I showed a series of Greek dance videos. These tapes were obtained from the film distributor, dancer, and leader of the Greek Orthodox Folk Dance Festival, Charlie Kyriacou. From studying the tapes, students attempted to emulate the repetitive movements performed in unison and the ease with which people joined in or dropped out of the circling dance line. Several said they could feel the power of the group moving, as well as the power of the leader at the front of the line waving a white handkerchief overhead.

Next we turned to Novack's ethnography of American Contact Improvisation. This ethnography illustrates the application of interpretive theory to a more familiar, "closer to home" dance form. Like Cowan, Novack's study deals with issues of gender, collectivity, individuality, spontaneity, equality, and power in dance. Novack convincingly shows how the contact improvisation movement developed from the 1960s American counterculture. But she does not stop there. Rather than simply seeing the dance as a pale reflection of an American counterculture, she also shows the active side of contact improvisation. In other words, Novack reveals that a dance form can reflect the values and embodied knowledge of a group, but it can also simultaneously and actively create those values and knowledge.[8]

After reading the Novack ethnography and watching several videotapes of contact improvisation, the students and I went to the dance studio where the Skidmore Professor of Dance, Mary DiSanto Rose, took us through simple to more complex improvisational exercises. After the session, students talked about the sensations they felt as they interacted with and moved about other members of the class.

The students also talked about how important it was for them to "try it out" in their moving bodies and about the different ways a dance can be experienced: through reading a descriptive empirical text, through applying a theoretical perspective, and by actually physically doing it. Interestingly, it was not until the students moved from the seminar room to the studios that they came to realize what I meant by multiple ways of knowing.

The final ethnography for the course was Mendoza's analysis of mestizo ritual performance in Peru. Like the other two ethnographies, Mendoza focuses on power, domination, and resistance. Unlike the other two, however, the students were confronted with the lasting impact of colonialism on local populations. To see a visual counterpart to Mendoza's ethnography, the book includes a CD-ROM.

After reading and discussing Mendoza, the students discovered that one important aspect of the Peruvian dance events involves masking. For the experiential component to our exploration of Mendoza and masking, we engaged in a simple but effective masking workshop. I requested that members of the class bring to campus homemade percussive instruments, such as pennies in a can, car keys hanging from a belt, or scrapers from a cheese grater. All the students sat on the floor in a circle and collectively played repetitive rhythms on their homemade instruments. Then two students at a time left their place in the "orchestra" to select from an array of nondescript white, striped, or halved masks. They returned to the circle but sat in front of a mirror set up at opposite sides of the circle. Sitting on the floor again, they studied their faces in the mirror, put on the mask, and again studied themselves. When I felt they had taken a good look at their altered identity, I instructed them to face one another.

Following verbal directions from me, the two students approached one another, circled one another, reached out to one another, touched one another, withdrew from one another, and interacted playfully, aggressively, and tentatively. To control the action, students were told to stay close to the floor, never rising above their knees. After these interactions, the masked students returned to the mirror and studied themselves again. Students then removed their masks and the orchestra stopped playing. The pair then spoke about the experience, as did the members of the orchestra who had watched and played throughout. The other pairs of students took their turns until all had a chance to experience the masking interactions.[9] Through this experiment, the students learned about the different ways of knowing text, theory, and movement.

Some key issues we considered in the second seven weeks of the course included:

Political economy of dance events.
Power, domination, and resistance displays in dance.
The impact of colonialism and globalization on dance events.
Gender and the influence of feminist theory in dance.
Ethnicity and identity in the dance arena.
Reflexivity in anthropological and dance research.
Hegemonic dimensions of dance events.

The three dance-centered ethnographies I used for the second half of the course were not the only ones I have used in the past or plan to use in the future. Another selection I used with considerable success was *Body, Movement, and Culture: Kinesthetic and Visual Symbolism in a Philippine Community* by Sally Ness (1992). This work raises interesting questions about dance within an urban, multicultural, postcolonial environment. It also raises questions about authenticity, religious devotion, and changing ethnic identities. For a visual component, Ness was kind enough to send me a copy of some video footage she had taken during her fieldwork.

Another ethnography that could prove useful in the course is by Sylvia Rodriguez, entitled *The Matachines Dance: Ritual Symbolism and Interethnic Relations in the Upper Rio Grande Valley.* This is a study of a dance that speaks to interethnic relations and competition for water, land, and political survival in the Southwest. For footage of the Matachines dance, I use a documentary on this Hispanic and Indian dance form that is still very much alive in the Southwest (Shipley 1988).

Brenda Farnell's (1995) ethnography, *Do You See What I Mean? Plains Indian Sign Talk and the Embodiment of Action,* offers still other possibilities for the course. This study of Assiniboine Plains Indian Sign Talk (PST) is an action-centered semiotic analysis of communication through movement. The text has an accompanying CD-ROM that permits students to experience the Nakota language in its unified verbal and gestured forms. Through an interactive format, students can see and hear the storyteller on video, study the words in the Assiniboine language, refer to an English translation, and view the Labanotation script.[10]

Another ethnography that could be used in the course is Deidre Sklar's (2001) *Dancing with the Virgin: Body and Faith in the Fiesta of Tortugas, New Mexico.* This self-reflective ethnography raises many interesting questions concerning the role of the researcher in the research process. It also develops her idea of "experiential somatic knowing" and the relationship between believing, feeling, and doing through dance. [11]

In summation, the course became a site for collective learning through critical reading, writing, discussing and physical participation. What began as a class of unconnected students with different backgrounds and experiences in anthropology and dance developed into a tight group sharing concerns of movement and meaning. By the end of the course, most students could see connections between theory, data, and practice. They were able to reflect on how theory shapes the kinds of questions one asks of data and the answers one develops. Last but not least, they began to see themselves as a tight group of neophytes intimately experiencing the course as an exciting rite of passage. Particularly after participating in the contact improvisation and masking workshops a bond had formed between them. They frequently described this bond as similar to Turner's notions of "communitas" and "liminality."

As the semester came to a close, I heard in the student's discussions and saw in their writing that most understood that there are different, but often equally compelling, ways of knowing. I heard them express that the course enabled them to see theory in a new light and that they understood more about the social world around them.[12]

References

Basso, Keith. *Portraits of 'the Whiteman': Linguistic Play and Cultural Symbols Among the Western Apache.* Cambridge, Mass.: Cambridge University Press, 1979.

Cowan, Jane K. *Dance and the Body Politic in Northern Greece.* Princeton: Princeton University Press, 1990.

Daly, Ann. "Unlimited Partnership: Dance and Feminist Analysis." *Dance Research Journal* 23 (1): 2–5, 1991.

Douglas, Mary. *Purity and Danger: An Analysis of the Concepts of Pollution and Taboo.* New York: Routledge, 1966.

Dozier, Edward. *Pueblo Indians of North America.* Long Grove, Ill.: Waveland Press, 1970 (reprinted 1983).

Farnell, Brenda. "Moving Bodies, Acting Selves." *Annual Review of Anthropology* 28 (1999): 341–373.

———*Do You See What I Mean?: Plains Indian Sign Talk and the Embodiment of Action.* Austin: University of Texas Press, 1995.

Furst, Peter. *To find Our Life: The Peyote Hunt of the Huichols of Mexico* Film. 1969.

Geertz, Clifford. *The Interpretation of Cultures.* New York: Basic Books, 1973.

Hanna, Judith Lynne. *To Dance Is Human: A Theory of Nonverbal Communication.* Austin: University of Texas Press, 1979.

Haramis, Peter. *Anastesaria* Film. 1966.

Kaeppler, Adrienne. "Dance in Anthropological Perspective." *Annual Review of Anthropology* 7 (1978): 31–39.

———. "Aesthetics of Tongon Dance." *Ethnomusicology* 15(2) (1971): 175–185.

Keali'inohomoku, Joann. "An Anthropologist Looks at Ballet as a Form of Ethnic Dance." *Journal of Anthropological Study in Human Movement* 1(2) (1980): 83–97.

Kendon, A. "Gesture." *Annual Review of Anthropology* 26 (1997): 109–128.

Kurath, Gertrude. *Music and Dance of the Tewa Pueblos.* Santa Fe: Museum of New Mexico, 1970.

———. "Panorama of Dance Ethnology." *Current Anthropology* 1 (3): 233–254.

Leach, Edmund. *Culture and Communication.* Chicago: University of Chicago Press, 1976.

Lévi-Strauss, Claude. *The Savage Mind.* Chicago: University of Chicago Press, 1966.

Marriott, McKim. "The Feast of Love." *Krishna: Myths, Rites and Attitudes.* Honolulu: East West Center Press, 1966.

Mendoza, Zoila. *Shaping Society Through Dance: Mestizo Ritual Performance in the Peruvian Andes.* Chicago: University of Chicago Press, 2000.

Myerhoff, Barbara. *Peyote Hunt: The Sacred Journey of the Huichol Indians.* Ithaca: Cornell University Press, 1974.

Ness, Sally. *Body, Movement and Culture: Kinesthetic and Visual Symbolism in a Philippine Community.* Philadelphia: University of Pennsylvania Press, 1992.

Novack, Cynthia. *Sharing the Dance: Contact Improvisation and American Culture.* Madison: University of Wisconsin Press, 1990.

Ortiz, Alfonso. *The Tewa World: Space, Time, Being and Becoming in a Pueblo Society.* Chicago: University of Chicago Press, 1969.

Quigly, C. "Methodologies in the Study of Dance." *International Encyclopedia of Dance* 4:368–372. Oxford: Oxford University Press, 1998.

Reed, Susan. "The Politics and Poetics of Dance." *Annual Review of Anthropology* 27 (1998):503–532.

Rodriguez, Sylvia. *The Matachines Dance: Ritual Symbolism and Interethnic Relations in the Upper Rio Grande Valley.* Albuquerque: University of New Mexico Press, 1996.

Roseberry, William. "Balinese Cockfights and the Seduction of Anthropology." In *Anthropologies and Histories: Essays in Culture, History and Political Economy.* Piscataway, N.J.: Rutgers University Press, 1989, 17–29.

Royce, Anya Peterson. *The Anthropology of Dance.* Bloomington: Indiana University Press, 1977.

Shipley, Charles. *The Matachines Dance.* Film. New Mexico Geographic, 1988.

Sklar, Deidre. *Dancing with the Virgin: Body and Faith in the Fiesta of Tortugas, New Mexico.* Berkeley, California: University of California Press, 2001.

——— "In memoriam: Cynthia Jean Cohen Bull." *Dance Research Journal* 29 (1) (1997): 111–115.

———"On Dance Ethnography." *Dance Research Journal* 23 (1) (1991): 6–10.

Spicer, Edward. *Cycles of Conquest: The Impact of Spain, Mexico, and the United States on the Indians of the Southwest, 1533–1960.* Tucson, Arizona: University of Arizona Press, 1967.

Sweet, Jill. *Dances of the Tewa Pueblo Indians: Expressions of New Life,* 2nd edition. Santa Fe, N.M.: School of American Research Press, 2004.

———"The Beauty, Humor and Power of Tewa Pueblo Dance," *Native American Dance.* Edited by Charlotte Heth, 83–103. Washington, D.C.: National Museum of the American Indian, Smithsonian Institution, with Starwood Publishing, Inc., 1992.

———"'Let 'Em Loose': Pueblo Indian Management of Tourists," *American Indian Culture and Research Journal* 15 (4) (1991): 59–74.

———"Burlesquing 'The Other' in Pueblo Performance," *Annals of Tourism Research* (special edition: Semiotics of Tourism), edited by Dean MacCannell, 16(1): 62–75, 1989.

Turner, Victor. *Dramas, Fields, and Metaphors: Symbolic Action in Human Society.* Ithaca: Cornell University Press, 1974.

Williams, Drid. "The Human Action Sign and Semasiology." *Dance Research Annual* 10 (1979): 39–64.

Youngerman, Suzanne. "Methodologies in the Study of Dance: Anthropology." In *International Encyclopedia of Dance,* 4:368–372. Oxford: University of Oxford Press, 1998.

Notes

1. For extensive and thoughtful scholarly reviews of the literature relevant to anthropology and dance studies see Farnell 1999, Reed 1998, Youngerman 1998, Quigly 1998, Kendon 1997, Kaeppler 1978, and Kurath 1960. See also Sklar (1991) for an insightful discussion of dance ethnography and Daly (1991) for a discussion of feminist theory and dance research.
2. Other terms for this subfield of study include "dance ethnology," "ethnochoreology," and the broader designation of the "Anthropology of Human Movement." Further, in some cases the topic is viewed within the larger category of "performance studies." I prefer "the anthropology of dance" because it is parallel to the widely accepted categories such as "the anthropology of food" or "the anthropology of tourism." Nevertheless, I appreciate the

desire of some dance researchers to avoid the term "dance" because what is considered to be dance in one culture may not be considered dance in another. For example, are martial arts dance or sport?

3. In recent years, cultural anthropologists have begun to question the "shared" aspect of the culture concept because they argue that not everyone in the society sees the world from the same vantage point. Gender and age, for example, can influence one's status and one's beliefs, so it may be an illusion to assume that everyone in a group shares a cultural system. While these are interesting debates that challenge a key anthropological concept, at the beginning levels students first need to grasp the difference between genetically inherited characteristics and socially learned characteristics. In addition, they need to differentiate between individual idiosyncratic ideas and beliefs and those notions more widely accepted by most members of the group. Critics of the culture concept as shared knowledge prefer to write of "hegemony," emphasizing the political and economic realities of uniquely positioned subjects (see Cowan 1990, 11–14).

4. In many cultures determining what constitutes an appropriate time and place may not be obvious to someone from outside the group. For this reason, a researcher cannot be in any great rush to "get the data," but rather he or she must be prepared to spend considerable time getting to know the cultural rules or etiquette for polite observation. (For discussions on researcher/subject or host/guest relationships in the field see Sweet 2004, 1992, 1991, 1989.)

5. Following Daly (1991), Reed (1998: 504) describes dance studies as "an interdisciplinary field focusing on the social, cultural, political and aesthetic aspects of dance."

6. Kinesthetic awareness became particularly important to me in recent years as I worked with physical therapists on the many movement issues I now face with MS. Invariably the therapists will comment on how easy it is to work with me because I have a "highly developed kinesthetic awareness." In other words, my years of dance enable me to kinesthetically visualize, remember, and feel what the therapist asks of me. This awareness is also important in the field as I observe moving bodies.

7. Although the phrase "symbolic anthropology" at the time was associated with Geertz, Turner, and others, Geertz eventually rejected the term because it suggested too limiting a focus on symbols. Geertz came to prefer the phrase "interpretive anthropology" to characterize his work. At the time of this writing, "interpretive anthropology" is generally favored over "symbolic anthropology."

8. The career of Cynthia Novack, who was also known as Cynthia Jean Cohen Bull, was cut short in 1996. Near the end of her life, she and I shared our individual health struggles. We laughed and cried about the state of the medical profession and crossing back and forth between the world of the healthy and the world of the ill. She encouraged me to experiment with dance from my wheelchair, which I did in 1997 at an American Anthropological Association posthumous session in her honor. Cynthia is missed by many of us in the worlds of dance and anthropology (see Sklar 1997).

9. This masking workshop idea was inspired by New York City actor/teacher/coach, Shelley Wyant.

10. It could be interesting for the students to compare the path that I followed from symbolic anthropology to interpretive anthropology with the path Farnell followed from kinesics, proxemics, semasiology, linguistic, and cognitive anthropology to the anthropology of human movement (Farnell 1999).

11. In recent years it has become more acceptable for an ethnographer to include himself or herself in the ethnography. This trend is a reaction against the years of denial that the researcher will influence the actions they wish to observe and describe. It is also a reaction against the illusion that the researcher can be an objective scientific researcher without bias. Dance scholars in particular have been eager to prove that their work can stand up to scientific scrutiny and rigor. Nonetheless, as I have tried to show in this chapter, dance research as well as other forms of investigations of human action, calls for both humanistic and social scientific inquiry.

12. The title of the course has periodically changed to reflect changing notions in the field and in my particular interests. These titles have included "Expressive Culture: the Anthropology of Dance, Drama, and Music," "Performance and the Search for Order," "Dance and the Human Search for Meaning," and "Symbolic Theory and Performance." Regardless of the course emphasis and title, I am indebted to the many the Skidmore students who have taken AN 346 over my twenty-three years of teaching at Skidmore. These students bring something new to the course each time it is offered and in this way they have helped shape the experience. After the semester ended this spring, we got together for food and drink and reflected back on the semester. Knowing how much I admire Geertz, several of them presented me with a T-shirt they had made up that said on the front, "Clifford is more than a big red dog" and on the back it read, "Got Geertz?"

CHAPTER 9

Standing Aside and Making Space: Mentoring Student Choreographers

LARRY LAVENDER AND JENNIFER PREDOCK-LINNELL

Perhaps the most exciting aspect of teaching dance at the college and university level is the opportunity to mentor student choreographers. In their role as mentors, dance teachers continually renew the art of dance by helping tomorrow's dance artists to discover their own creative sensibilities. Moreover, mentoring students is an especially important part of a teacher's job because it is in making dances that students have the opportunity — indeed, the responsibility — to draw on and integrate all of the knowledge and insight they have gained through their academic and studio-based dance courses, and their life experiences. Being guided by a sensitive and skilled mentor enriches the student's experience both educationally and artistically.

For dance students to gain the maximum benefit from their choreographic experiences, it is important for faculty not to let the mentoring process become one of dictating, rather than facilitating, the students' artistic development. This means that while mentors must, literally and figuratively, remain close at hand — ready to step in and offer assistance and advice — they must always be willing, at the same time, to stand aside and make space for students to exercise their own artistic will. For genuine mentoring to take place, the teacher's artistic agenda must take a back seat to the student's.

What Is Mentoring?

The term "mentor" comes to us from the Greeks. In Homer's *Odyssey* (c. 800 B.C.), Mentor, the companion of King Odysseus, was instructed by the King as he departed for battle to remain behind and raise the King's son, Telemachus, to become fit to take over the throne at a suitable time. As John Carruthers (1993, 9) explains, "this meant that Mentor had to be a father figure, a teacher, a role model, an approachable counselor, a trusted advisor, a challenger, and an encourager, among other things, to the young Telemachus in order that he could become, in time, a wise and good ruler." The role played by Mentor in overseeing the safe and proper development of Telemachus has given rise to the term "protégé" (from the French verb *protéger*: to protect) for the one who is being mentored. Carruthers writes that protection and development "make up the core of what has been meant by mentoring down through the centuries" (9). Our principles for mentoring student choreographers have been developed in accordance with this conception of the term.

By including the idea of protection in this process, we do not mean that the mentor should shield the protégé from authentic encounters with the myriad challenges that can make the art-making process seem difficult or frustrating. On the contrary, the mentor should encourage and help the protégé to identify and confront these challenges head on, to persevere in spite of occasional setbacks or feelings of confusion. Only in this way can the mentor help the protégé become a self-confident and autonomous artist, which is the fundamental objective of mentoring.

We use the term "protection" to emphasize that part of the mentor's job is to help the protégé avoid becoming stalled by common barriers to artistic creativity. The barriers most often blocking the efforts of new choreographers are a trio of common misleading assumptions about art and art-making: the "idealist notion"; that works of art should "say something"; and that popular success is equivalent to artistic success.

A brief analysis of these barriers to creativity paves the way for concrete suggestions for faculty mentors working with student choreographers.

Misleading Assumptions about Art and Art-Making

The Idealist Notion

There are three assumptions about art and art-making that new choreographers often bring with them to their dance-making experiences. The first assumption suggests that a dance exists (or should exist) in complete or nearly complete form in the choreographer's mind before he or she begins to work. Under this assumption, the creative activity of the choreographer is assumed simply to be a matter of molding the physical materials of the art form — that is, movements — into the shape and form dictated by the preexisting idea or meaning intended in the artist's mind. This assumption is called the "idealist notion," although students usually have never heard this term.[1]

It is common for choreography students, particularly at the beginning level, to approach dance-making with the idealist notion in mind. They tend to spend a great deal of time imagining what their dances will eventually be like, and can usually articulate elaborate ideas for their works. For example, they can describe the organization the dance will have, the costumes, and the lighting and sound accompaniment. Unfortunately, reality generally intercedes and these students often have great difficulty in actually choreographing the dance they have envisioned in such intricate detail. More important, the dances they do create are often loaded with movement clichés, simple pantomime, or very literal quasi-dramatic action among dancers who function more as characters in a wordless "skit" than as movers. Because the students have devoted so much energy to developing an idealized mental image of their dances, they have few creative resources left for the actual invention, development, or exploration of movement material.[2] These students are often very discouraged when they discover the difference between how their movement ideas look on actual dancers' bodies and the way in which they had imagined that the movement would look.

Students holding the idealist notion do not understand that it is neither required nor necessarily advantageous for artists to begin with a clear or highly developed conception of the complete work. Regardless of how the project begins, the process of making dances, like any creative process, is essentially a revisions process. Each dance inevitably evolves through a series of stages on its way to completion. During each stage of the work's development, the choreographer's job is to explore and manipulate the movements, movement structures and patterns, temporal and spatial possibilities, energy dynamics, and the expressive properties of the work-in-progress in order to select, shape, and form the particular combinations of these artistic elements that will become "set" in the finished work. The painter Ben Shahn (1957) referred to this process when he wrote that while the artist may, at one point, "mold the material according to an intention," at other times "he may yield intention — perhaps his whole concept — to emerging forms, to new implications (49)" within the work-in-progress.

Discovering and understanding the "revisions process" concept of art-making helps students recognize that choreographic ideas and meanings emerge naturally as one experiments with movement, and that these emergent ideas and meanings often are quite different from those with which the choreographer may have begun — if indeed he or she began with any predetermined image at all. Once students come to see that art-making is a process of discovering ideas and meanings inherent to movement rather than merely one of transposing fixed images inside one's head into movements on dancers' bodies, their way of working with movement and dancers becomes more reflective, and the dances they create gain sophistication.

Works of Art Should Say Something

The second assumption posing an obstacle to new choreographers is that works of art do, or should, communicate a literal message; that to make a dance is to "say" something. This view holds that a dance, like a poem or an essay, is a "text" that can be "read." Accordingly, an observer viewing a particular dance is supposed to be able to "understand" what the choreographer is "trying to say." When this understanding does not occur, the work is considered flawed because "communication" has failed.

The idea that dances do and should "say" things has long been espoused in much of the standard literature on modern dance and choreography. For example, Doris Humphrey (1959), in what is probably the most widely used text on choreography, declares in a discussion of the necessary characteristics of the choreographer that "our choreographer had better have something to say" (21). Esther Pease (1966) writes that dance "is meant to be looked at in terms of its communication — if its meaning is unclear or its purpose does not come across, then the creator tries harder next time" (24). Later, Pease advises her readers to "bear in mind the unalterable fact that dance cannot change its basic purpose: Art is communication" (65).

More recently, Blom and Chaplin (1982) write, "Let's face it, we should know what we are trying to say with movement" (8). Paulette Shafranski (1985) writes, "To reach out and communicate with each other is the aim. That is what the creative impulse, within us, is all about." Finally, Smith-Autard (1992) writes that "it should be clear that movement is a vast communicating language and that varieties of combinations of its elements constitute many thousands of movement 'words'" (23).

Some of these writers do go on to imply that dance may be only metaphorically construed as "communication"; that the movements in dances are not literally to be considered as analogous to words, and that the ways in which dances communicate are not exactly the same as written texts. But none of these authors actually spells out what they imply, nor addresses the complexity of the concept of communication, or its limitations when applied to dance. One exception is Lois Ellfeldt (1967), who writes that "it is important to evade the trap of invariably associating certain movements with certain meanings. For example, 'vertical movement implies heights and depths,' 'curved movement is always smooth and legato,' 'jagged movement is nervous and uncertain.' When movement is so codified it loses its potential as a subtly expressive medium. Such responses are oversimplified and are usually passed on by conditioning the young" (26).

These remarks notwithstanding, it is difficult to know precisely where even Ellfeldt stands on the question of whether or not, and to what degree, dances are to be considered as analogous to texts. In her preface she writes that her book identifies "the alphabet and the rules of grammar and spelling of dance." She also writes that "making a dance is very much like writing a composition: first find something to say, then say it as well as you can" (78). Later she declares that success in dance-making "is always a question if the meaning intended by the choreographer is the same as that perceived by the audience. Obviously a dance is more successful when audience reaction bears a close resemblance to the choreographer's intent" (86).

Because most college and university choreography teachers were themselves trained in accordance with these ideas, it is likely that, as Ellfeldt suggests, they pass on to their students, through ordinary dance talk, the assumptions and values contained in that literature.[3] Yet in passing these assumptions on to the next generation of dance artists, an important — and basic — distinction between denotative and connotative communication tends to be overlooked, as does the critical but little-discussed distinction between linguistic and perceptual communication.[4] (See Best 1978; Metheny 1968)

The pedagogical problem with all assumptions dealing with the "meaning" or "purpose" of art is that they are assumptions: that is, they are ideas that are taken for granted as being correct. To be "assumed," then, means that an idea is not being extensively analyzed by whoever is assuming it. Instead, the ideas embedded in assumptions tend uncritically to be taken as facts. Furthermore, their status as assumptions actually protects them from genuine scrutiny.[5]

A powerful way that ordinary dance talk at every pedagogical level tends to instill in students the assumption that dances do and should "say" things — that is, that dances are, literally, texts — is by employing linguistic terms to refer to movement. For example, it has been our experience that teachers consistently refer to the movements in particular dances and of particular styles of dance as "vocabulary." Similarly, in technique classes, combinations of movements are nearly always referred to as "phrases" of movement analogous to verbal sentences. Finally, there is a nearly universal tendency among dance educators to speak of dance as being a "language," to speak of the development of students' choreographic "voices," and explicitly to state that dance simply is "communication." These examples have elevated to the status of "fact" in the minds of many students the idea that dances are appropriately conceived of as nonlinguistic analogues to specific linguistic meanings or messages that choreographers seek to communicate to their audiences. But this is actually a very questionable idea.[6] Thus in expressing the view that "dance is communication," or in asking a teacher following the presentation of their works-in-progress, "Do you see what I'm trying to say?" students are assuming (without fully understanding the ideas embedded within the assumption) that dance is a mode of denotative linguistic communication.

Though the consensus for the view of dance as denotative communication is strong, the arguments for it are virtually nonexistent. For in suggesting that to create a dance is to "say" something, and in speaking of dance as "communication," dance writers and educators (and, ultimately, their students) mistakenly assimilate such ambiguous and multifaceted notions as "artistic intention," "expression," and "conveyance" of meaning to the single concept of "communication." Moreover, they tend to conflate the multiple distinct senses of that term to the single sense of denotative linguistic communication[7] (see Best 1978; Metheny 1968; Crusius 1989). Thus, rather than coming to be seen as one of many choices or possibilities available to an artist, the notion that choreographers simply do or should try to "say" something in and through their works is passed off as a fact.

The ubiquitous writing about defining and discussing dance in terms of "communication" not only misleads students, but actually deters many from experimenting with movement. Rather than working uninhibitedly with such choreographic concepts as energy, space, and flow, many students shy away from what would amount to genuine artistic investigation. Some students even edit out of their works-in-progress any trace of abstraction or ambiguity for fear that their works will send the "wrong message" or — even worse — no "message" at all.

The responsibility of mentors is threefold. First, the mentor must seek to foster in the protégé an understanding of the ways in which abstraction and ambiguity add richness, intensity, and meaning to dance works. Second, using the protégé's work-in-progress as the point of reference, the mentor must teach the protégé how to recognize and develop the work's intrinsic expressive properties so that these may be fully realized.[8] Finally, the mentor should help the protégé understand how a conception of the term "communication" that is too narrow or too literal can thwart the creative process before it even begins.

One effective way to accomplish these aims is through an exercise called interpretive projection. This involves inviting a group of students to observe one of their colleague's dances early in its development. Then the observers are asked to make brief notes in which they identify specific aspects of the work that they found particularly expressive or meaningful, and to describe the meaning or significance they perceived in those aspects and from the work as a whole. Next, the observers describe to the choreographer the meanings and expressive properties they found to be operating in the work. The ensuing discussion gives the choreographer a great deal of insight into the ways a work, or a work-in-progress, is perceived by different viewers and about how ideas and meanings can be expressed through a dance even though the choreographer may not have deliberately "put" these ideas and meanings into the work. Instead of addressing predetermined "intentions" the choreographer may have had for the work, interpretive projection engages the meanings that viewers actually experience from seeing the work. It often turns out that the latter have greater interest for the choreographer than the former.

It is important to note that in arguing against the assumption that dances do and should "say" things, and in recommending the use of interpretive projection, we do not mean to suggest that dances cannot or should not be created with specific linguistic ideas, or "content," at their core.[9] We recognize both that to work with movement so as to deliver a specific message to an audience is one of many options at a choreographer's disposal, and that sometimes this effort can succeed. But the fact that it is possible to "say" things through dances does not mean that it is necessary to do so, or that dance is inherently discursive. Thus our argument is not against the possibility of saying something through a dance. Rather, it is against the presentation to students of that possibility either as a defining characteristic of dance, or as a creative imperative — as if to say something were the only or the best reason to choreograph.

Popular Success Is Equivalent to Artistic Success

We have seen how the first two common and misleading assumptions about art and art-making can hinder students' creative work. The third assumption that mentors need to help their students to overcome is that popular "success" — that is, producing a work that viewers "like" or "enjoy" — is the equivalent of artistic success.[10] It is common for students who labor under this assumption to develop dances consisting primarily of clever or startling images, or eye-catching movements and patterns they have seen in other (often commercial) dances. Other students create safe dances that deal with conventional themes in relatively unimaginative ways, using movements drawn mostly from technique classes and arranged in predictable patterns. For both kinds of students, presenting a dance that audiences will find uncontroversial and likable is felt to be more important than engaging in a more authentic creative process that carries with it the risk of generating something new that audiences may neither understand nor enjoy.

This third assumption is more difficult for mentors to dispel than either of the other two. While students' attitudes toward art and art-making tend to be relatively recently acquired, flexible, and subject to change through creative experiences and critical discussions, their desire to gain the approval of others is far more deeply rooted and often driven by the fear (or by the past experience) of being laughed at, ignored, misunderstood, or condemned by others. Making sure that students have nothing to fear from exercising the full range of their creative energies is an important responsibility of all faculty members in a dance program.

On the other hand, mentors should guard against a presumption that every student who shies away from taking creative risks and from artistic experimentation does so out of fear of engaging fully in the creative process. For many students have no such fear; they just happen to be interested in making more traditional, conventional, or commercial kinds of dances. It is important for mentors to keep this in mind and resist the urge to psychoanalyze. To suggest or to insist to students that they are "blocked" or have a "problem" with being creative is miseducational and intrusive, and can undermine students' trust in their teachers. As Richard S. Kay (1990) reminds us, "Mentoring is not an activity in which the mentor imposes change on an unsuspecting protégé." (27) This means that while mentors should help students find ways to expand their creative horizons, they also have to avoid denigrating the student's current artistic preferences. Some healthy ways for mentors to foster their students' artistic growth include showing videotapes of interesting and unusual dance works students may never have seen, promoting discussion among groups of students about the rich variety of dance in the world, and exposing students to a variety of improvisations, choreographic exercises, and approaches to dance-making.

The Common Thread: Premature Closure

A common thread runs among all three of these misleading assumptions about art-making: students holding any of these assumptions (and some students hold all of them) often seek "premature closure" in their dance-making experiences. Students seeking premature closure declare their dances finished at what is actually an early point in the creative process, either because they do not know how to continue developing or refining their works, or because they lack the self-confidence to wrestle further with the artistic problems they are encountering in their works.

A student under the influence of the "idealist notion," for example, will often declare the dance-in-progress finished as soon as it expresses the rudiments of the predetermined ideas the student had about the work before beginning to create it, or when the inevitable difficulties that accompany the attempt to force movement material into the mold of such fixed ideas or images (which by now may have lost their luster) become obvious and overwhelming. Similarly, a student laboring under either the "to dance is to say something" or the "popular success is artistic success" assumption will often declare a dance complete either when it seems to express, more or less clearly, an idea he or she is willing to own, or when it has gained sufficient form or character to be accepted by the student's peers as "a pretty good dance." In each of these cases, premature closure can abort the creative process before the student has reflectively investigated and explored alternative possibilities for shaping and forming the work. Indeed, the willingness of many students to declare closure too readily — to settle for the first, or the easiest, artistic solution they find, without knowing it is premature — is one reason student artists need the guidance of mentors in the first place.

It is often possible to stimulate students heading for premature closure to think further about their work simply by asking, "Why do you think the dance is finished at this point? What is it that satisfies and dissatisfies you about the work as it is?" In their responses to these questions, many students discover that they are unsatisfied but just do not know how to proceed further in developing the work. For these students, mentors should suggest specific aspects of the work that might benefit from revision and provide specific pointers on how the student might proceed in this next stage of the work's development.

Students who report that they are genuinely satisfied with the dance as it is need a different approach. While the mentor's job is still to identify aspects of the work that might benefit from further development, extra care is required to make sure that this is done without implying disrespect for the student's judgment that the work is already complete. It is useful in these situations to say, "You have done a lot of good work here, but there is the potential to do even better. I'll bet if you did some more thinking about … and played around a little more with … you might discover some new ideas you'd want to use." Such comments initiate discussion in which suggested revisions can be made clear without bruising the student's ego. As all successful teachers know, the tone with which critical remarks are delivered is just as important as their content.

Insensitive or Vague Critical Feedback

For any mentor/protégé relationship in the arts to succeed, there must be an open and frank dialogue between the participants. This dialogue naturally includes the evaluation by the mentor of the protégé's work.[11]

As already discussed, in working with student choreographers, mentors must exercise caution in delivering critical feedback. The creative efforts of even the most skilled and self-confident students are easily derailed by criticism that is perceived as disrespectful or insensitive, or by criticism that fails adequately to address the visible properties of the protégé's work-in-progress.

We categorize as "insensitive" any critical remark that summarily rejects or dismisses—directly or indirectly—the artistic values and principles that seem to be operating within the work, or that seeks to impose upon the artist implicitly or explicitly the aesthetic values and assumptions of the critic. Examples of insensitive critical responses include: "Well, if you want to make that entrance like that you are certainly free to do so"; "Everybody knows that it is a mistake to …"; "I'd get rid of that ending if I were you and put in something more …"; "Why would you want to place the solo figure there?" Comments like these, which deliver unfavorable and unsupported judgments of the work, tend either to silence completely, or to provoke defensive reactions from, the artists to whom they are delivered. Rather than fostering mutual trust and respect, these remarks reflect an attitude of superiority on the part of the mentor, as if he or she expects to be regarded as a critical authority whose views are to be adopted by the protégé without question.

Some mentors may inadvertently deliver insensitive critical feedback in an effort to protect the protégé from one or another of the assumptions that function as barriers to creativity. In an effort to help their students grow as artists, these teachers may try to steer them away from working in what seems to the mentor to be a naive or unsophisticated manner. But to protect a student from the pitfalls of a particular artistic path does not mean preventing the student from exploring that path; mentors should be careful not to effectively stop students in their creative tracks and forcibly shift their direction. This is tantamount to telling the student, "Stop, you don't need to learn this lesson because I learned it for you years ago. Trust me and do as I say." Attempts to influence students in this way, which amount to a kind of coercion, ultimately alienate students from their mentors and impede future healthy interaction. Shula Newick (1982) speaks to this point when she writes:

> What most students, at all levels of education, find intolerable in their quest for autonomy as artists is the teacher who enforces changes in or inhibits the direction of their work and who by implication interferes with the discovery of that which is truly their own. These actions, far from manifesting belief in the potential of students to find themselves as artists, intrude with a deadening and impoverishing effect. (69)

It is not the mentor's job to enable the protégé to skip phases of development; rather, it is to develop the protégé's fullest awareness of the artistic and philosophical implications of each creative choice. If, for example, a student incorporates into a dance some movement material learned in a technique class without any further development of that material, the mentor should not condemn the effort or instruct the student not to continue doing so. Instead, the mentor should engage the student in a discussion about the importance of learning how to invent and manipulate one's own movement. The mentor might suggest some ways for the student to work with the movements from the technique class to make them her own and recommend some ways of improvising and developing entirely new material. In this way the mentor protects the student from developing the habit of merely copying others' movements by providing the tools to generate her own movements for her dance.

In addition to misunderstanding the appropriate role of protectiveness in mentoring, there are two common assumptions that would appear to justify teachers' positioning themselves as critical authorities whose job is to decide for students what is "good" and "poor" dance:

1. Students' artistic taste tends inevitably to reflect oversimplified conceptions of art and dance.
2. Students lack the analytical skills necessary to formulate substantive critical responses to their own and others' dances.

Following the logic of these assumptions, setting up the teacher as the sole critical authority in a class or mentoring situation seems to be the only way to provide students with an acceptable level of critical response to their work so they will learn how to respond critically to works of art themselves. The fallacy in this approach, however, is that if the critical standards and assumptions of the teacher are left unexamined, students have no choice but to supplement, and eventually to replace, their own unexamined critical assumptions with those conveyed by the teacher. In other words, this approach both erroneously elevates the teacher's judgments to the status of factual propositions and ignores the educational value of actual critical dialogue.[12]

Successful mentoring cannot be accomplished by a teacher who takes the stance of infallible critical authority, because the mentor's proper role is to instruct rather than to indoctrinate the protégé (see Green 1971, 27–32). Indoctrination makes the student adopt what the teacher considers to be the "correct" position or belief, or take the action prescribed by the teacher, regardless of whether that position or action is justified by solid evidence or grounds. On the other hand, instruction places a value on discussion of the reasons and principles underlying the particular recommendations or conclusions being delivered. It allows students to safely question the critical assumptions of the teacher.

The difference between the aims of indoctrination and instruction can be discerned in the language teachers use in talking with students about their dances.[13] Those whose tendency, conscious or not, is to indoctrinate use language that is directive in tone and/or content. Directive language simply tells the student what to do. For example, "Change the ending," "Edit that middle section," and "Make that transition faster" are directive statements. Moreover, these remarks are insensitive insofar as they seek to impose on the artist the aesthetic values and assumptions of the critic.

In contrast, the language of instruction is informative and thus empowering to students. It provides information about the dance and invites further discussion rather than to deliver a command. For example, the comments, "The suddenness of the ending doesn't seem to fit with the rest of the dance," "There may be too much repetition in the middle section," and "A faster tempo for that transition might be interesting" address the same concerns as these directive comments. But a student hearing the latter comments is far more likely to feel safe in asking questions or in seeking elaboration from the teacher than a student hearing the first set of comments.

While insensitive criticism stalls the dialogue between mentor and protégé, vague criticism derails discussion by providing the protégé with too little information. For example, such comments as, "I like what you've done so far" and "That is really interesting" leave the choreographer without any specific information about how the dance has been perceived. While both comments seem to contain favorable judgments, neither addresses any actual properties of the work. For any useful discussion to take place following one of these remarks, the choreographer would have to press for more information by asking, "What exactly is it you like?"

or "What part did you find interesting?" Many students hesitate to ask follow-up questions, particularly if the mentor's comments seem to them to imply unfavorable judgments.

Critical comments work best when they contain what David Perkins (1981) terms "where reasons," pinpointing a particular part of the work; "what reasons," describing precisely some aspect or quality of the pinpointed part of the work; and "why reasons," justifying the evaluative conclusions one draws from "where" and "what" reasons by referring to one's critical standards (106). Some examples that illustrate the use of "where," "what," and "why" reasons include: "The last section of the dance could be trimmed" pinpoints *where* in the dance the comment is directed; "the gestures of the soloist are very clear" indicates *what* particular aspect of the dance is being addressed; "the work's originality makes it very strong" provides a *why* reason for judging the work favorably. (It is important to note that the criterion of "originality" underlying the judgment that the work is strong should also be discussed; different viewers may disagree both on the meaning of the term and on whether it is an important quality in a dance.) Some critical remarks, such as, "The opening image of the dance is very powerful because it is symmetrical and placed at center stage," include where, what, and why reasons. Critical remarks like these are clear and informative. They provide the artist whose work is being discussed a clear indication of what the viewer has noticed about, and found aesthetically rich within, the work. These comments pave the way for open and productive dialogue between the student and the teacher.

Students need (and deserve) reflective dialogue with their mentors, not directives from them. As Allan Walker and Kenneth Stott (1993) explain, the most effective mentors are those "who are willing to spend the time necessary to transfer skills and knowledge, and who are open enough to take risks, willing to share experience, and desire to help" (80). To engage in reflective dialogue with the protégé signals that the mentor is less interested in "fixing" the protégé's dance, or in thinking of the completed dance as a reflection of the mentor's expertise, and more interested in the development of the artistic vision and autonomy of the protégé.

Effective mentors know that criticism is useful only when it stimulates the protégé to reflect anew on the work-in-progress; to see it in a new way; to recognize more clearly both how its parts fit together to form the whole; and to consider how the work may be improved through continued effort. Students are most receptive to specific recommendations for revision if these are made after they have had a chance to hear, and to reflect on, substantive comments about the dance as it is. Until an artist clearly understands others' reasons for suggesting a particular revision, proposals likely will fall on deaf ears. As one of our students remarked, "I need to know what someone sees in my work before I hear how they think I should change it." This means that a mentor wanting to make a recommendation for revising, say, the ending of a student's dance, should share his or her observations about the current ending of the dance, invite the student to discuss how that particular ending was developed, and carefully consider both the student's replies to the observations and the student's artistic objectives before suggesting a change to the ending.

Questions for Reflective Dialogue

Asking is very often a better teaching choice than telling. Indeed, it is widely recognized that one of the best ways to promote the growth of student artists is through the use of "open-ended" and "clarifying" questions[14] (see Clements 1964, 1965; Armstrong and Armstrong 1977; Johansen 1982; Taunton 1983; Hamblen 1984; Sadker and Sadker 1990). Open-ended questions, also called "process" questions, encourage the student to think aloud in a stream-of-consciousness manner. Such questions as, "How did you come up with that idea?" and "What is your next step in developing this work going to be?" can lead students to important self-discoveries. Posing clarifying questions such as, "What else can you tell me about that?" in response to students' remarks about their work, helps to elicit even deeper thinking and further discovery on their part. Even though their mentors often could simply tell students the same things the students are now "discovering," the self-discovery process empowers student artists more than receiving the same information or advice from their mentors.

The use of open-ended process questions and clarifying follow-up questions is especially helpful in situations when:

1. Students appear to be dissatisfied with their work.
2. Students are having difficulty in articulating ideas about their work.
3. Students make the same artistic choices in every dance they create.
4. Students resist the efforts of mentors.
5. Students try to transfer responsibility for their work onto their mentors.

It is important for mentors to recognize that at some points during the creative process students need to talk about their work without being told what anyone else thinks about it. This is usually the case when students express dissatisfaction with their work, or apologize in some way for part or all of it, either before or after showing it. In these cases, the mentor should ask the student, "What have you been working on in the dance since last time we met?" or, "What do you think about the work at this point?" to encourage the student to sort out his or her thoughts about the work.

Some students have very little to say, and answer even the most open-ended questions with brief noncommittal responses, such as, "Oh, I guess it's going okay," or "I'm not really sure what I need to do next." There are several reasons for students to respond this way. First, many students have never had the opportunity to develop skills in talking about their own work. Second, many students are afraid of sounding stupid or of saying the "wrong" thing to teachers. It feels safer for these students to remain silent rather than to risk being "corrected" by teachers. Third, many students, assuming a dance "speaks for itself," have never even tried to think systematically about discussing their work. Finally, some students are literally stuck and do not know what to do next in developing their dances.

In these cases it is tempting for mentors to jump in and supply the "answer." But to do so cuts off the student's thinking process before it has begun and replaces it with the mentor's. We recommend asking students who have little to say about their dances to do several minutes of free writing in response to such nonthreatening writing prompts as, "What matters to you in this dance?" or "What was good about that last run through?" Free writing is informal stream-of-consciousness expression that is not meant to be seen by others, and need not consist of complete sentences or use correct grammar or syntax. It is a way of writing that generates ideas rather than recording ideas already in mind. Keeping a free-writing journal is an effective way for students to reflect on their works-in-progress and to develop new ideas between sessions with their mentors (see Lavender and Oliver 1993).

While a student is writing, the mentor should move to some other place in the room or step outside for a few minutes so that the student senses no pressure to hurry and finish. When he or she is done, the mentor need only ask, "What did you come up with?" or "What do you think?" The vast majority of students will find this free-writing process very helpful in focusing on one or two ideas, and will be able to articulate these to the mentor.

With students who make the same artistic choices in dance after dance, a special kind of process "game" is useful. We call this the "What if?" game. Instead of criticizing the student for repeatedly using the same narrow palette of artistic choices, we make such suggestions as, "What if that unison section were broken up with some out-of-unison movements?"; "What if some material were created with rhythmic counterpoint to the music?"; "What if the patterns of accents were varied a bit to avoid predictability?"

Introducing possibilities to students in this way helps stimulate them to think about — and usually to select — new creative options without losing any artistic autonomy. Videotaping "What if?" experiments and watching/ discussing them with students is an effective way to help them to see and evaluate possibilities for revision.

There are some students who, no matter how sincere the mentor's efforts to create an open, student-centered learning environment, resist mentoring and insist on working completely alone. We have discovered several reasons for this. First, some students believe that art-making is so personal a process that no one should "tell them what to do." These students misunderstand the nature of mentoring, often associating it with coercive kinds of teacher/student relationships they have experienced else-where. Many of these students have been wounded by insensitive criticism from teachers and assume that all criticism will come in the form of put-downs or directive commands. Second, some students lack the self-esteem necessary to be able to ask for or accommodate help. These students tend to think that accepting help is a sign of weakness or inadequacy. Finally, some students fear losing "control" over their work, believing that if they get too many suggestions from others they may become overwhelmed by choices, or that adopting the others' suggestions means that the completed work will not truly be their own creation.

These students need extra assurances that the purpose of the mentoring relationship is to facilitate rather than to hinder their creativity, and that the mentor has no intention of taking over the work. It is also important to remind students that while feedback from other artists can certainly be very valuable, receiving suggestions from others does not obligate the artist to employ those suggestions. Each artist must decide independently what changes to make in the work.

In working with students who resist mentoring, asking such casual questions as, "How did you think of that?" or "What are you working on?" gives students confidence that discussions of their work will be on their terms, not the mentor's. Once a positive dialogue with the student has been estab-lished, it is not difficult to progress to slightly more specific questions, such as, "What else could you do there?" and "Have you ever thought of ...?" By not calling attention to any specific weaknesses in the work, and by not making specific recommendations unless they are solicited by the student, the mentor continues to develop the student's trust. Once a genuine level of trust has been established, the student usually will begin to ask such ques-tions as, "Can you help me with ...?" and "What do you think about ...?" Even when this occurs, however, the mentor should continue to exercise caution, using such responses as, "Sure, I'll help you — what is it you are tying to do here?" Responses like these keep the student engaged in thinking about and controlling the development of the work while receiving guidance.[15]

In sharp contrast to students who resist mentoring, there are some students who only want the mentor to tell them what to do to improve their work. Instead of doing their own thinking, these students continually pose such questions to their mentors as, "What do you think I should do next?" or "What would you do to improve the piece?"

Students who try to coax their mentors into doing their thinking for them should be reminded that in serving as an adviser, guide, and role model to the protégé the mentor must at the same time strive to empower the protégé to become an autonomous decision-maker so that, eventually, the protégé will no longer need the mentor. As Kay (1990) writes, "Mentoring should never involve doing something for a person that the person can benefit most by doing for him/herself. Mentoring is helping not substituting for the protégé. Efforts toward helping another develop self-reliance should not build dependency" (34). The best response to students who invite mentors to control their creative process is to suggest a number of options and encourage the student to take some time to reflect on which one seems the most appropriate. This response provides the necessary guidance while maintaining the responsibility for making decisions about the dance with the student, where it belongs.

Conclusion

Mentoring student choreographers is an active and a reflective process. In working with student choreographers, mentor-teachers constantly encounter new educational, artistic, and personal challenges. They must continually decide when, how, and to what degree to involve themselves in their students' creative efforts. They must stand ready to provide substantive advice for handling myriad and complex artistic problems but at the same time be alert to situations where, as Theresa M. Bey (1990) puts it, "too much help is overpowering or is causing the protégé to feel burdened by the relationship" (62). At this point, the mentor must be willing to step back a little and give the student some space.

A mentoring relationship acquires its greatest significance when it leads to the protégé's eventual independence from the mentor. To become independent artists, students must first become self-reliant in their creative efforts. This means they must be able to make artistic choices for themselves, to recognize when these choices need rethinking and revising, and they must know how to revise their works. Above all, they must know that only in becoming a lifelong student of dance and of the choreographic process can one become a true dance artist. Those teachers who possess skill in listening and effective questioning will, by exercising these abilities, impart the necessary knowledge to students with the greatest efficacy. Moreover, by seriously focusing on helping their students to become the best choreographers they can be, teachers will discover more about their own teaching and art-making processes. Through the practice of mentoring student choreographers, teachers' own identities as dance artists will be nourished and sustained.

References

Armstrong, Carmen L., and Nolan A. Armstrong. "Art Teacher Questioning Strategy." *Studies in Art Education* 18 (3) (1977): 53–64.

Bandman, Bertram. *The Place of Reason in Education.* Columbus: Ohio State University Press, 1967.

Best, David.. *Philosophy and Human Movement.* London: George Allen and Unwin, 1978.

Bey, Theresa M., and C. Thomas Holmes, eds. *Mentoring: Developing Successful New Teachers.* Reston, Va.: Association of Teacher Educators, 1990.

Blom, Lynne Anne, and L. Tarin Chaplin. *The Intimate Act of Choreography.* Pittsburgh: University of Pittsburgh Press, 1982.

Caldwell, Brian J., and Earl M. A. Carter, eds. *The Return of the Mentor: Strategies for Workplace Learning.* London: The Falmer Press, 1993.

Carruthers, John. "The Principles and Practice of Mentoring." In *The Return of the Mentor: Strategies for Workplace Learning,* edited by Brian J. Caldwell and Earl M. A. Carter, 9–24. London: The Falmer Press, 1993.

Clements, R.D. "Art Student-Teacher Questioning." *Studies in Art Education* 6 (1) (1964): 14–19.

_____. (1965). "Art Teacher Classroom Questioning." " *Art Education* 18 (4): 16–18.

Collingwood, R.G. *The Principles of Art.* New York: Oxford University Press, 1958.

Croce, Benedetto. *Aesthetic.* New York: The Noonday Press, 1909.

Crusius, Timothy W. *Discourse: A Critique and Synthesis of Major Theories.* New York: The Modern Language Association of America, 1989.

Ellfeldt, Lois. *A Primer for Choreographers.* Prospect Heights: Waveland Press, 1967.

Field, Barbara, and Terry Field. *Teachers as Mentors: A Practical Guide.* London: Falmer Press, 1994.

Gablik, Suzi. *Has Modernism Failed?* New York: Thames and Hudson, 1984.

Green, Thomas F. *The Activities of Teaching.* New York: McGraw-Hill Book Company, 1971.

Hamblen, Karen A. "An Art Criticism Questioning Strategy Within the Framework of Bloom's Taxonomy." *Studies in Art Education* (26) 1 (1984): 41–50.

Hawkins, Alma. *Moving from Within.* Chicago: a capella books, inc., 1991.

_____. *Creating Through Dance.* Princeton: Princeton Book Co., 1988.

Heller, Mel, and Nancy W. Sindelar. *Developing an Effective Mentor Teacher Program.* Bloomington: Phi Delta Kappa Educational Foundation, 1991.

Humphrey, Doris. *The Art of Making Dances.* New York: Grove Press, Inc., 1959.

Johansen, Per. "Teaching Aesthetic Discerning Through Dialog." *Studies in Art Education* 23 (2) (1982): 6–13.

Kay, Richard S. "A Definition for Developing Self-Reliance." In *Mentoring: Developing Sucessful New Teachers,* edited by Theresa M. Bey and C. Thomas Holmes 25–38. Reston, Va.: Association of Teacher Educators, 1990.

Lavender, Larry, and Wendy Oliver. "Learning to 'See' Dance: The Role of Critical Writing in Developing Students' Aesthetic Awareness." *Impulse* 1(1) (1993), 10–20.

Martin, John. *The Dance in Theory.* Princeton: Princeton Book Co., 1965.

Metheny, Eleanor. *Movement and Meaning.* New York: McGraw-Hill Book Company, 1968.

Minton, Sandra Cerney. *Choreography.* Champaign: Human Kinetics, Inc., 1986.

Newick, Shula. "The Experience of Aloneness in Making Art." *Journal of Aesthetic Education* 16 (2) (1982): 65–74.

Odell, Sandra J. "Support for New Teachers." In *Mentoring: Developing Successful New Teachers,* edited by Theresa M. Bey and C. Thomas Holmes, 3–24. Reston, Va.: Association of Teacher Educators, 1990.

Pease, Esther E. *Modern Dance.* Dubuque: William C. Brown, 1966.

Perkins, David. *The Mind's Best Work.* Cambridge: Harvard University Press, 1981.

Ryle, Gilbert. *The Concept of Mind.* New York: Barnes and Noble Books, 1949.

Sadker, Myra, and David Sadker. *"Questioning Skills" in Classroom Teaching Skills.* Edited by James Michael Cooper and Sandra Sokolove Garrett. Lexington, Mass.: D. C. Heath and Company, 1990.

Shafranski, Paulette. *Modern Dance: Twelve Creative Problem-Solving Experiments.* Glenview, Ill.: Scott, Foresman and Company, 1985.

Shahn, Ben. *The Shape of Content.* Cambridge, Mass.: Harvard University Press, 1957.

Smith-Autard, Jacqueline M. *Dance Composition: A Practical Guide for Teachers.* London: A & C Black, 1992.

Taunton, Martha. "Questioning Strategies to Encourage Young Children to Talk About Art." *Art Education* 36 (4) (1983): 40–43.

Timmons, Christine, and Frank Gibney, eds. *Britannica Book of English Usage.* New York: Doubleday/Britannica Books, 1980.

Tomkins, Calvin. *The Bride and the Bachelors.* New York: Penguin Books, 1962.

van Manen, Max. *The Tact of Teaching: The Meaning of Pedagogical Thoughtfulness.* New York: State University of New York Press, 1991.

Walker, Allan, and Kenneth Stott. "Preparing for Leadership in the Schools: The Mentoring Contribution." In *The Return of the Mentor: Strategies for Workplace Learning,* edited by Brian J. Caldwell and Earl M. A. Carter, 77–90. London: The Falmer Press, 1993.

Weitz, Morris. "The Role of Theory in Aesthetics." *The Journal of Aesthetics and Art Criticism* 14(1) (1956): 27–35.

Notes

1. In the philosophy of art the idealist notion is represented most influentially by R. G. Collingwood's (1958) development of Benedetto Croce's (1909) theory of art as " "intuitive expression."

2. We are not suggesting here that students should be discouraged from engaging in preliminary reflections on their dances. We would only remind teachers and students alike that intellectual and imaginative planning processes are not, in and of themselves, the choreographic process. Making a dance is, in the final analysis, a physical process during which both previously imagined and newly discovered ideas must be tested on the body. It is these ideas-made-physical on which we think students should primarily focus in learning how to choreograph.

3. We are aware that much serious theoretical writing construes dance as a form of "discourse" or attempts to link dance with semiotics. Our concern here, however, is solely with the chilling effect that the unexamined notion that "dance is communication" tends to exert on the creative efforts of fledgling choreographers, most of whom have not yet been exposed to much of the dance-theoretical literature, nor begun to think critically about the relationship to choreographic practice of the issues with which that literature attempts to deal.

4. David Best (1978) explains in detail this latter distinction and the fallacy of using the term "communication" to define dance (pp. 138–161). The *Britannica Book of English Usage* (1980) describes the distinction between denotation and connotation as follows: ... while the denotation of a word provides its strict definition, the connotation of that word provides the additional ideas that have come to be associated with it. For example, childhood denotes the period during which a child grows up. To some it may connote a pleasant period of innocence and few responsibilities, while to others it may connote a period of fear, frustration, and general discomfort (p. 292). Eleanor Metheny (1968) discusses denotative and connotative communication, and the relevance of these concepts to movement.

5. See Morris Weitz (1956) for a rigorous explanation of the idea of art as an "open concept." Following Wittgenstein, Weitz shows how all attempts to provide a fixed or "real" definition for art inevitably fail, for each theory "purports to be a complete statement about the defining features of all works of art and yet each of them leaves out something which the others take to be central" (p. 29). We concur with Weitz, and argue that it is profoundly miseducational to take one or another theory, definition, or purpose of dance as an assumption about its essential character.

6. This notion is, of course, key to traditional "author-centered" approaches to critical interpretation. Merce Cunningham (in Tomkins, 1962) rejects the semantic paradigm upon which this notion is based when he writes, "I don't ever want a dancer to start thinking that a movement means something. That was what I didn't really like about working with Martha Graham — the idea that was always being given to you that a movement meant something specific. I thought that was nonsense" (p. 246).

7. In Discourse: A Critique and Synthesis of Major Theories (1989), Timothy W. Crusius examines the differences among four major theories that "have helped us to envision the universe of discourse" (p. 2). His analysis is helpful in understanding how and why it is a fallacy — even with regard to written and oral speech — to speak and write of "communication" as if the term has a single, or simple, meaning.

8. Our approach to mentoring is informed here by Gilbert Ryle's (1949) distinction between knowing "that" and knowing "how" (pp. 25–61). Mentors must not only teach students that abstraction and ambiguity exist as artistic concepts, they must teach (show) students how they might apply these concepts in creating and revising their dances.

9. We use the term "content" only to mark a conceptual, not an ontological, distinction between the idea, theme, or subject matter of a work — what it is "about" — and the visible structural features of the work.

10. The commercialization and commoditization of art in the twentieth century is no doubt largely responsible for the prevalence of this assumption among today's students. See Suzi Gablik (1984) for a thorough discussion of this art-historical development and what steps might counteract it.

11. It is important to encourage the protégé to evaluate the mentor as well. We often ask students to tell us how we are doing in helping them to develop their dances. Students take seriously and appreciate the opportunity to theorize with their teachers on teaching/learning issues. We believe that the teacher's own contribution should always be an open topic for discussion in any educational setting.

12. See Part I of Bertram Bandman's The Place of Reason in Education (1967, pp. 9–92) for a thorough discussion of the differences between various kinds of formal arguments. Following Bandman we deduce that while evaluative arguments — e.g., aesthetic judgments — look and sound like formal analytic arguments they are, in fact, not the same. It is thus a fallacy for teachers, or anyone else, to deliver judgments about a work as if these were facts about the work. See Thomas F. Green (1971, pp. 173–192) for an analysis of the concept of judgment showing the manner in which judgments differ from facts, hunches, guesses, and feelings.

13. See Max van Manen's The Tact of Teaching (1991) for an excellent discussion of the pedagogical importance of reflective and thoughtful language.

14. It is important to note that questioning is as much a learning tool as it is a teaching tool; students should be encouraged to ask questions of their mentors about any aspect of the creative process.

15. Allan Walker and Kenneth Stott (1993, pp. 82–83) provide a discussion of five stages of mentoring relationships, pointing out that if trust is not established or fails to move "past a fairly superficial plane," interaction between mentor and protégé remains routine and directed largely by the mentor."

CHAPTER **10**

Kinesiology and Injury Prevention

MARY VIRGINIA WILMERDING

Introduction

Kinesiology is the study of human motion. College-level courses for the dancer in the science of kinesiology and injury prevention should be at least a year in length and should include the most recent research in the field of dance science and medicine. Traditionally, courses such as kinesiology have been found in the physical education departments of colleges and universities. It is important, however, that specialists in dance as an art form be available to instruct preprofessional performers and future teachers in the science of human movement and safe performance.

Dancers need to be aware of the physical demands of their art form and the potential problems that can arise from maladaptive technique, overuse, fatigue, and poor training and poorly executed choreography. No two humans are alike; furthermore, no one human body is perfectly symmetrical. Basic training in human mechanics and an understanding of how to put theory into practice are essential to the longevity of every dancer. The college or university community is an excellent place to create a solid knowledge base in the science of dancing. Prerequisites for an undergraduate degree should be tailored to suit the specific needs of the developing artist. Courses within a fine arts curriculum should be augmented with human biology, exercise physiology, research methodology, and statistics. This will encourage independent thought and develop an aptitude in the performer to read and comprehend current literature published on injury issues, training methodologies, nutrition, and the psychological aspect of the performer.

There are a number of books written on kinesiology and related subjects (found in the bibliography at the end of this chapter). It is important that students of dance become as familiar with these as possible. No one text provides the full scope of education for dancers. Students must also be aware of sources of current research and information on the physical aspect of dancing. *The Journal of Dance Medicine & Science* and *Medical Problems of Performing Artists* are but two of the publications that focus on the problems and issues of the physical performance.

Theory

The Formal Kinesiology for Dancers Class

It is essential that the dance student become knowledgeable about human anatomy. Kinesiology for Dancers should begin as most anatomy and physiology classes do, with an understanding of the planes of motion (sagittal, frontal, and horizontal) and the basic movement choices (flexion and extension, abduction and adduction, inward and outward rotation, and circumduction; see Figures 10.1 and 10.2, 10.3, 10.4). The integration of planes and types of movements take time to learn. Students should be

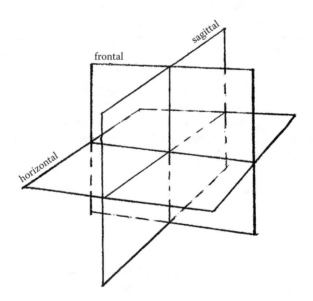

Fig. 10.1 Three planes of motion.

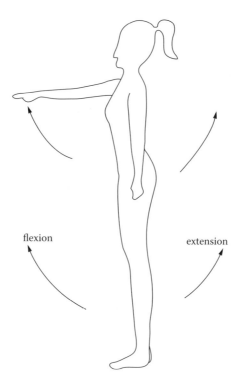

flexion

extension

Fig. 10.2 Sagittal plane movements.

encouraged to understand that learning kinesiology is not unlike learning a new language; repetition is a key component to success in this unit of class.

A review of the bones of the body and their surface landmarks, which serve as sites for muscular attachment, comprise the next segment of class. Types of bones (long, short, flat, irregular, sesamoid) should be introduced. The dancer should be expected to classify all moving bones in the body by their type.

The student should be expected to maintain an awareness of the three major classifications of joints within the body: (1) synarthrodial, or immovable, found, for example, in the sutures of the skull; (2) amphiarthrodial, or slightly movable, found, for example, at the acromio-clavicular joint; and (3) diarthrodial, or fully moveable joints. Greater attention should be paid to the six subcategories of diarthrodial joints (gliding, hinge, pivot, condyloid, saddle, and ball and socket). Once again, the dancer should be expected to be able to identify all diarthrodial joints by their subcategory.

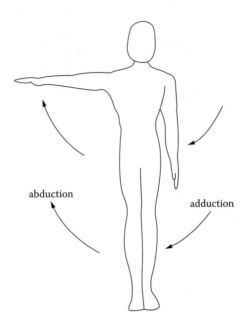

Fig. 10.3 Frontal plane movements.

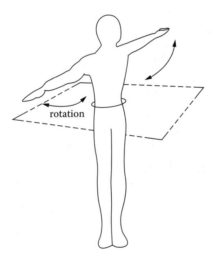

Fig. 10.4 Horizontal plane movements.

An awareness of muscle components and characteristics must precede study of specific muscle action at specific joint sites. Concepts of contractility, extensibility, elasticity, and excitability should be introduced. The notion of origin and insertion should be addressed, as well as Wolff's Law. Muscle actions should be covered (agonist, antagonist, stabilizer, synergist) in a generalized format. Greatest attention should be paid to the theories of muscle action (isometric, isotonic, isokinetic). The condition of concentric loading (shortening a muscle to move against the pull of gravity) and eccentric loading (lengthening a muscle to move toward the pull of gravity) tends to be a particularly challenging segment of kinesiology class. It is expected that this series of ideas will take the longest to integrate and be understood by the professional mover and teacher of dance, so this is discussed again under "Movement Analysis."

Basic physiology of muscular contraction is included as an essential part of a complete dance science course. Dancers should be expected to know the components of a muscle, including the proteins found in a muscle cell and the process by which muscles contract and relax. Many colleges and universities offer classes in exercise physiology, where this subject is treated in depth. In addition, the hypotheses concerning neurological stimulation of muscle, while not formally part of the domain of kinesiology, are essential for a thorough understanding of the subject: the dancer's body and movement capacity. Again, if it is not a component of the college curriculum, it should be a component of a dancer's kinesiology class.

Biomechanics is the final component of the didactic segment of this lecture series. Basic information on Newton's Three Laws of Motion (inertia, acceleration, action-reaction) need to be presented with relevant examples for the dancer's consideration. Likewise, the model of the first-, second-, and third-class levers as they exist in and out of the body should be presented in the most relevant format available. This has special value for dancers in understanding the mechanics of all technical movements — that is, leaping, turning, and especially partnering.

Once the theories of these kinesiological models have been addressed, a focus on every joint system should follow in sequential order, integrating all previously presented materials. This should take up the majority of the lecture class format. Thus a full lecture series for the first half of a curriculum in Kinesiology for Dancers should progress through these topics:

Planes
Types of Movement
Bone
Muscle
Nerves
Biomechanics
Shoulder

Elbow
Wrist and Hand
Hip
Knee
Foot and Ankle
Trunk

Movement Analysis

Movement analysis requires a special integration of the components of anatomy and kinesiology into actual dance movement. This part of a dancer's science training is crucial. Analysis of actual movement executed in dance technique class should be scrutinized closely. Focus should be on the plane, the type of movement, the type of muscle contraction (concentric or eccentric), and the prime muscle mover and its antagonist. It should begin as early on in the class as possible, shortly after planes, types of movements, and types of muscle contraction have been introduced. As each joint system is discussed, the teacher should integrate new knowledge of the function of specific muscle groups.

The dancer needs to understand the role of gravity in the creation of movement and muscle contraction. In a concentric contraction, the muscle belly shortens; in an eccentric contraction, the muscle belly lengthens. Thus, in a singular movement, the same muscle group is responsible for moving a body part and bringing it back to neutral. For instance, in a plié in parallel position, the quadriceps muscle at the front of the thigh eccentrically lengthens to control the downward descent of the body (to flex the knee joint); the muscle belly lengthens (see Figure 10.5). To return to upright from the plié, the same quadriceps muscle at the front of the thigh concentrically shortens to create the upward movement of the body (to extend the knee joint); the muscle belly shortens (see Figure 10.6).

Table 10.1 presents movement analysis grids for Figures 10.5 and 10.6.

Likewise, in a plié in first position, the quadriceps muscle at the front of the thigh eccentrically lengthens to control the downward descent of the body (to flex the knee joint). The muscle belly lengthens (see Figure 10.7). To return to upright from the plié, the same quadriceps muscle at the front of the thigh concentrically shortens to create the upward movement of the body (to extend the knee joint). The muscle belly shortens (see Figure 10.8). The plane, however, has changed from sagittal to frontal.

Table 10.2 presents movement analysis grids for Figures 10.7 and 10.8.

Eccentric contraction does not occur in the horizontal plane. Physical therapists refer to this plane as "gravity eliminated," because it is understood that knee flexion in a side-lying position requires concentric contraction

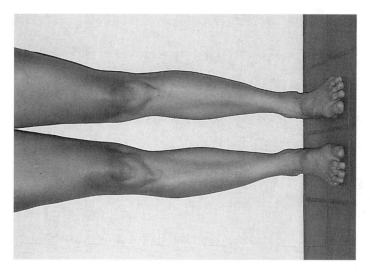

Fig. 10.6   Concentric loading of a parallel plié.

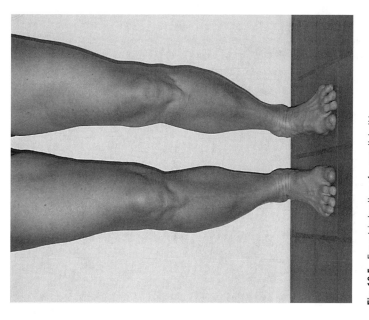

Fig. 10.5   Eccentric loading of a parallel plié.

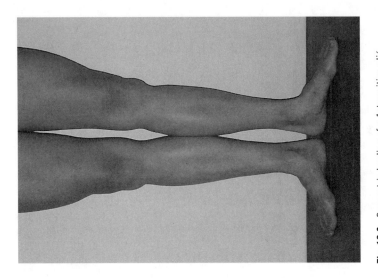

Fig. 10.8 Concentric loading of a 1st position plié.

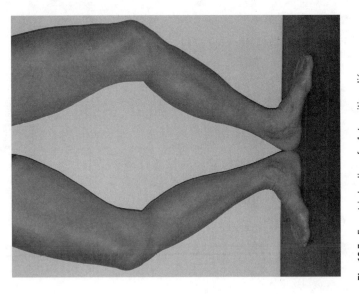

Fig. 10.7 Eccentric loading of a 1st position plié.

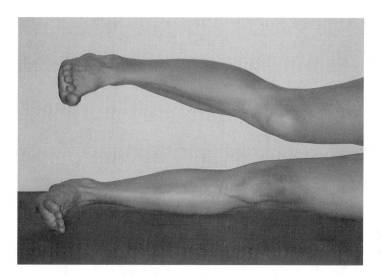

Fig. 10.9 Flexion of knee in horizontal plane.

Fig. 10.10 Extension of knee in horizontal plane.

of the hamstring muscle group, and knee extension requires concentric contraction of the quadriceps muscle group (see Figures 10.9 and 10.10).

Table 10.3 presents movement analysis grids for Figures 10.9 and 10.10.

TABLE 10.1.a Movement analysis grid for Figure 10.5

Joint	Movement	Plane	Contraction Type	Agonist	Antagonist
Knee	Flexion	Sagittal	Eccentric	Quadriceps	Hamstrings

TABLE 10.1.b Movement analysis grid for Figure 10.6

Joint	Movement	Plane	Contraction Type	Agonist	Antagonist
Knee	Extension	Sagittal	Concentric	Quadriceps	Hamstrings

TABLE 10.2.a Movement analysis grid for Figure 10.7

Joint	Movement	Plane	Contraction Type	Agonist	Antagonist
Knee	Flexion	Frontal	Eccentric	Quadriceps	Hamstrings

TABLE 10.2.b Movement analysis grid for Figure 10.8

Joint	Movement	Plane	Contraction Type	Agonist	Antagonist
Knee	Extension	Frontal	Concentric	Quadriceps	Hamstrings

TABLE 10.3.a Movement analysis grid for Figure 10.9

Joint	Movement	Plane	Contraction Type	Agonist	Antagonist
Knee	Flexion	Horizontal	Concentric	Hamstrings	Quadriceps

TABLE 10.3.b Movement analysis grid for Figure 10.10

Joint	Movement	Plane	Contraction Type	Agonist	Antagonist
Knee	Extension	Horizontal	Concentric	Quadriceps	Hamstrings

Practice

Once the dancer has gained facility with the language and point of view of kinesiology, putting the knowledge gained into practical application should be enjoyable and rewarding. There are a number of ways in which dance students can gain a practical understanding of their science. The most personal is an understanding of one's own body and its strengths and weaknesses.

Screening for Dancers

The well-being of the dancer is an essential component of a college curriculum, including "readiness" to dance. Physical screening involves a process of the evaluation of a dancer for asymmetries, preexisting physical limitations, or potential conditions that may lead to injury and limit his or her career. In the best-case scenario, screening should be undertaken by a medical professional. If such support is not available, dancers can come to understand some basic issues about their own bodies, learn to make some basic assessments, and learn how they might help themselves prepare for their craft more effectively and efficiently. This can be an essential part of the practical application of a college kinesiology class.

Components of any screening begin with a prescreening health history questionnaire. The form should be brief but should include general demographics such as height, weight, age, history of conditions or illnesses, and family history. It is important to know if the dance student is taking a prescription medication that might affect his or her ability to dance. It is also important for the female dancer to be queried as to the onset of menses and the relative condition of eumenorrhea or amenorrhea. Specific questions on this topic will shed light on the potential problems of eating disorders, condition of the dancer's bone density, and other potentially harmful physical conditions. It is essential to know if the dancer is a smoker. The health history questionnaire should also ask about the number of years that the student has trained, and the type and level of technique that the dancer claims. Identifying the number of hours the dancer usually spends in technique and rehearsal is also essential.

The actual screening can be done by a teacher or by groups of Kinesiology for Dancers students working in teams. Measurements of functional capacity in the form of flexibility of major joints (shoulders, hips, ankles, etc.) should be taken with a goniometer (Figure 10.11). Posture and symmetry should be assessed with the dancer standing in front of a grid. Symmetry of the shoulders and hips can be assessed in this manner, as well as spinal flexibility and low back position. If possible, some measures of strength and muscular endurance should be assessed. This might require special equipment or simply requesting that the dancer execute a simple dance move, such as temps lévé or rélévé, until fatigued. Again, symmetry between right and left sides is most important. Special consideration should be given to the feet. Most published dance screening assessments place particular importance on the look of the feet, noting possible deformities like *hallux valgus* (bunions), and the range of motion of the metatarsophalangeal and ankle joints that could affect one's ability to dance.

If possible, body composition (percent body fat) should be measured with skinfold calipers or a bioelectrical impedance analyzer (BIA). I do not recommend an assessment of one's body composition by height and weight alone, known as Body Mass Index or BMI. Also if available, dancers should be tested for aerobic capacity in the form of a graded exercise test on a bike or treadmill. Anaerobic testing to assess power and muscle

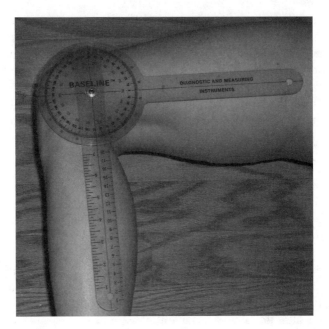

Fig. 10.11 Goniometer.

fatigue is also a valuable tool. (For more extensive screening possibilities, the reader is referred to the Screening Special Issue edition of the *Journal of Dance Medicine & Science*, Volume 1, Number 3, 1997.)

Following a screening process, recommendations should be made to the individual dancer by a teacher or medical professional so that each may have a preventive "prescription" pointing out areas of weakness or points of potential injury. This personal knowledge of kinesiology as it is reflected in the dancer's own body is a valuable tool for understanding and for good health.

Injury Prevention

The most powerful tool available to the dancer to prevent injury is education. Once dancers have gained a basic education of kinesiology and an awareness of personal strengths and weaknesses, they can begin to understand the most common causes of injuries.

The most common cause of injury for dancers is overuse, which may account for two-thirds to three-quarters of all dance injuries. The educated dancer is given the tools for self-care: an understanding of the need for sufficient rest, adequate nutrition, establishing a healthy body weight, special conditioning exercises for personal weaknesses, and an awareness of the warning signals of fatigue. Overuse injuries tend to create chronic conditions; they recur over time and are often due to maladaptive technique, poor training habits, and some sort of personal compensation for performance errors. For example, most dancers do not have the same degree of turnout of both legs. An uneducated dancer will tend to force the less flexible hip to externally rotate as much as the more flexible hip. The educated dancer will know that the limits of one's turnout should be determined by the less flexible hip. A common overuse injury in dancers is Achilles tendinitis. The condition rarely goes away by itself, nor can it be "worked out" by continuing normal dance class.

An awareness of the types of injuries that can happen to dancers and when it is appropriate to seek medical attention is paramount in a dancer's education. An overview of traumatic injuries, such as bone fractures, muscle strains, joint sprains, soft tissue bruises and contusions, and dislocations and subluxations should comprise the injury prevention segment of Kinesiology for Dancers.

Injury management is also an important component of a dancer's health. The educated dancer has the tools to understand the basic first-aid principles of R.I.C.E. (rest, ice, compression, and elevation), commonly employed at the onset of a traumatic injury. Again, a multidisciplinary approach to education, utilizing athletic training staff, medical staff and facilities, and any other types of health care resources will best serve the needs of the college or university dancer.

Special Considerations

There are a number of special considerations that should be factored into the college dance curriculum. One of these is the psychology of the dancer. A growing amount of research is being undertaken to understand the psychological readiness to dance, what separates the successful from the unsuccessful dancer, the role of the teacher in creating a supportive environment for learning, and the psychological impact of injury on the dancer. If students have completed sufficient prerequisite courses in research design and statistics, Kinesiology for Dancers students will be capable of comprehending original research articles published in refereed journals on the psychological aspects of the training and preparedness of dancers.

Another special consideration that should be factored into the curriculum is a unit on nutrition. Dancers are a special "breed," having an inordinate amount of pressure placed on them to be thinner than the average college student. How this thinness is to be attained is often left out of a dancer's education. Most research identifies that dancers are woefully uneducated on the topic of nutrition and often subject to odd and unfortunate "diets" designed for fast weight loss. This leaves the dancer in a physically vulnerable state.

This unit of study should begin with an overview of how body composition is assessed, what the errors can be in such measurement, and what is "normal" for the average population versus what is "normal" for dancers of differing disciplines. This material should be followed with a general overview of nutritional needs of the active and nonactive person. Finally, an assessment of a dancer's daily nutritional intake should be matched against the dancer's actual caloric needs. It cannot be stressed enough that most colleges and universities have nutrition classes as an independent discipline or as a component of exercise physiology programs. Whenever possible, students should be exposed to as many professionals from as many different disciplines as possible. It is not all that unusual for college-age dancers to succumb to disordered eating or clinical eating disorders. In such a circumstance, a licensed therapist should be contacted for intervention.

A final special consideration in Kinesiology for Dancers should be the differing needs of the various disciplines of dance that may be offered in a college or university setting. Ballet, particularly pointe work, places significant and unusual stresses on the foot and ankle complex. Modern dancers tend to have differing needs relative to preparedness for dance, because the use of the torso is so uniquely different when compared to that which is required of ballet dancers. The same holds true for African dance, jazz dance, and many other forms. Any dance form that requires a heeled shoe will require that a dancer pay special attention to the change in alignment at the ankle, knee, hip, and spine. The teacher of kinesiology, if not familiar with all of these disciplines, should invite the technique teachers of each dance program into the classroom for a discussion of the various requirements of each idiom.

Conditioning

Most colleges and universities have support or conditioning classes for dancers. The overall intent is to provide a time and place where strength and flexibility can be the focus of attention, in an effort to augment the existing technique class. These classes should not be devised to substitute for technique. The student of kinesiology for dancers should be assigned to experience and assess the conditioning class. The movement-analysis grids provided earlier offer a gateway to understanding how any given conditioning class is devised and what it should accomplish. Various methods will have differing objectives, and the lessons learned will be invaluable for students to understand which methods serve them best and which least. If the student has enough facility with this task, undertaking the assisting and teaching of a conditioning class should be the next step.

Teaching

Many dancers support themselves financially and/or emotionally by teaching dance class. Following the observance of conditioning class, the student of kinesiology for dancers should also be assigned the task of observing classes in and outside of his or her discipline. Again, the movement-analysis grid is a starting point. Any given exercise should be assessed for its purpose, factoring not only which muscle groups are used for what type of muscular contraction, but also how the warm-up supports the exercises of actual dancing in the center or across the floor. This type of assessment will begin to give the student of dance a deeper sense of how to understand their art form. Thus, when they begin to devise a technique class to teach themselves, they may approach their art form with both an understanding of the nature of technique and the physical demands and limitations of their students. This understanding will make the student a better teacher.

Research

Research now abounds in the field of dance science and medicine, but not all of it is of good quality. It is important for the faculty to educate under-graduate and graduate students in dance on how to read and assess the value of a research paper. As previously stated, this requires prerequisite training in research methods and statistics, and may be beyond the scope of a given college curriculum. It is important, however, that the preprofessional and professional dancer become an "educated consumer" of dance research. Educated dancers can make better choices with regards to their own personal health and training if they are capable of reading and understanding current research.

Technology

Finally, it should be understood that there are many ways to teach kinesiology for dancers and many different types of technology that may be employed to support this endeavor. For the didactic lecture, there is no substitute for the immediacy of writing on a blackboard. Overheads and slides provide commanding visual aids, as well. Computer-generated slides, animated and displayed on a digital projector, are a powerful method of disseminating information. The use of drawings and photographs of the bones and muscles of the human body is encouraged. There are a number of animated programs on the market that provide a strong visual representation of the theories of human muscular contraction. Video programs of anatomical dissections are also very evocative visual aids for the teacher of kinesiology for dancers.

Above all, it must be remembered that dancers are experiential learners. All the technical devices available as teaching aids cannot take the place of creating an environment where dancers learn by doing. Time and space must be made available for the student to move, in order to understand concepts such as concentric and eccentric, and to feel which muscles contract under which conditions. The greater the opportunity to experience the physical manifestations of a kinesiological concept, the more likely it is that dancers will have this knowledge available to them while they actually dance.

Conclusion

Clearly, there is no one "correct" way to teach the science of kinesiology to artists who are dancers. What can be universally embraced is that dancers need a strong intellectual as well as physical understanding of the mechanism by which the body functions. The immediate goal is the development of more effective artists that can sustain the greatest professional longevity of their physical art form with the fewest number of traumatic and chronic injuries. In addition to a strong base of prerequisite education to support this endeavor, dancers must be educated by as many exercise, nutrition, and medical specialists as possible throughout this time of study. Exposure to these health care specialists creates an atmosphere of open dialogue that serves both populations well.

Acknowledgments

The author thanks Jake Pett for the illustrations and Molly McKinnon for the photographs in this chapter.

Selected Readings or Class Texts and Support Publications

Calais-Germain, Blandine. *Anatomy of Movement*. Seattle: Eastland Press, 1993.

Dowd, Irene. *Taking Root to Fly*. New York: Irene Dowd, 1995.

Golding, Lawrence and Scott. *Musculoskeletal Anatomy and Human Movement*. Monterey: Healthy Learning, 2003.

Hammill, Joseph and Kathleen Knutzen. *Biomechanical Basis of Human Movement*. Philadelphia: Williams & Wilkins, 1995.

Huwyler, Josef. *The Dancer's Body: A Medical Perspective on Dance and Dance Training*. Germantown: International Medical Publishing, 1999.

Oatis, Carol A. *Kinesiology: The Mechanics & Pathomechanics of Human Movement*. Philadelphia: Lippincott, Williams & Wilkins, 2004.

Rasch, Philip. *Kinesiology and Applied Anatomy*. Philadelphia: Lea & Febinger, 1989.

Sevey Fitt, Sally. *Dance Kinesiology*. New York: Schirmer, 1988.

Shell, Caroline ed. *The Dancer as Athlete.* Champaign: Human Kinetics, 1984.

Sparger, Celia. *Anatomy and Ballet.* Tonbridge: Whitefriars Press, 1970.

Thomasen, Eivind and Rachel-Ann Rist. *Anatomy and Kinesiology for Ballet Teachers.* London: Dance Books, 1996.

Selected Reading for Screening

Solomon, Ruth, Sandra Minton, and John Solomon, eds. *Preventing Dance Injuries: An Interdisciplinary Perspective.* Reston: AAHPERD, 1990.

Selected Readings for Injury Prevention

Allan J. Ryan, and R. E. Stevens, ed. *Dance Medicine: A Comprehensive Guide.* Chicago: Pluribus Press, 1987.

Solomon, Ruth, Sandra Minton, and John Solomon, eds. *Preventing Dance Injuries: An Interdisciplinary Perspective.* Reston: AAHPERD, 1990.

Selected Readings for Special Considerations

Laws, Kenneth, and Cynthia Harvey. *Physics, Dance and the Pas de Deux.* New York: Schirmer, 1994.

Selected Readings for Conditioning

Spector-Flock, Noa. *Get Stronger by Stretching.* Hightstown, N.J.: Princeton, 2002.

Selected Readings for Teaching

Clarkson, Priscilla, and Margaret Skriner, ed. *Science of Dance Training.* Champaign: Human Kinetics, 1988.

Gray, Judith A. *Dance Instruction: Science Applied to the Art of Movement.* Champaign: Human Kinetics, 1989.

Kimmerle, Marliese, and Paulette Cote-Laurence. *Teaching Dance Skills.* Andover, N.J.: J. Michael Ryan, 2003.

Research Articles

For a listing of dance research articles, organized by subject as well as author, I recommend that you access this source:

Solomon, Ruth, and John Solomon. *Dance Medicine & Science Bibliography.* Andover: J Michael Ryan Publishers, 2001.

Organizations

International Association for Dance Medicine & Science: www.iadms.org

Performing Arts Medical Association: www.artsmed.org

CHAPTER 11

Labanotation

ILENE FOX AND DAWN LILLE

Labanotation (LN) is not just for writing and reading dances. The system, with its identifying, defining, and naming of movement concepts, allows us to organize our thoughts and to understand what we are seeing. It offers us names for different movement concepts that clarify aspects of dance such as time and space, and it gives us a vocabulary that allows for improved communication between teacher and student, choreographer and dancer, dancer and dancer. A better understanding of movement can only improve performance.

Notation is not about symbols; it is about ideas. It is about learning to understand, recognize, and perform different movement concepts. Students learn to really see what is taking place and are able to reproduce it more accurately. They learn to analyze their own performance, making self-corrections as they more accurately analyze the movement. Using the LN vocabulary also allows the teacher/choreographer to make corrections in a way that is understood. When everyone has the same understanding of what the vocabulary means, it facilitates communication. Notation provides a tool that can enrich the entire dance curriculum.

Notation symbols are used in two related ways: Structured Description and Motif Description. Both use most of the same symbols and terminology, have a similar format, and record fundamental components, such as direction, action, dynamic, and timing. Structured Labanotation gives a literal, all-inclusive, detailed description of movement so it can be exactly reproduced. Motif Description depicts core elements and leitmotifs, and it highlights and records what stands out as most important about the movement. Which type of description is used depends on what needs to be communicated.

Using motif for movement exploration in an improvisation class forces students to move out of their comfort range and explore ways of moving that they do not ordinarily use, extending their range and introducing them to new ways of thinking about and organizing movement. Students learn from master choreographers, analyzing classic works, identifying the main movement ideas, and creating a motif score. They may then use the motif score to create their own works.

In repertory class and dance history class, the archive of notated works provides materials that introduce students to works from their dance heritage. Use of notated dances or excerpts broadens the access of students to more than just the work of the faculty or one guest artist. No longer do the great choreographers need to be remembered solely as a name in a book. Students learn about masterworks in the best way possible, by dancing them.

History

Dance notation, or the writing of movement in order to record and then reconstruct it, dates to the second half of the fifteenth century, which produced the Cervera dance manuscripts in Spain. Throughout the centuries, different forms of movement notation developed as dance became more complicated and subtle. The first book to record dance steps was Thoinot Arbeau's *Orchésographie* (1589), in which the Jesuit monk used illustrations to convey both the steps and the proper social behavior. The first real system of notation was invented by the seventeenth-century dancer, choreographer, and ballet master Pierre Beauchamp. Trained in both music and dance, he was director of the Royal Academy of Dance. He was so busy that he never had time to complete his work, which finally appeared in Raoul-Auger Feuillet's book *Choreographie ou l'Art d' Ecrire la Danse* (1700) and has since been known as Feuillet notation. We don't really know how much was Beauchamp's and how much was Feuillet's, but the notation is still a source of much reconstruction of Baroque dance.

Among the dozens of movement notation methods, a few stand out. Arthur St. Leon devised a system using abstracted stick figures under a musical staff (*Sténochorégraphie*, 1852) and Vladimir Stepanov in *L'Alphabet des Mouvements de Corps Humain* (1892) recorded movement in anatomical terms through musical notes. Scores in his system (not all done by him), smuggled out of Russia and now in the Harvard Theatre Collection, were the source for several restagings in the West of the late nineteenth-century

Russian classics. Margaret Morris, in England, published *Notation of Movement* in 1928, which is also anatomically based.

Rudolf von Laban, the German teacher, theorist, and director of the Allied State Theaters in Berlin, had an initial interest in how the body moves through the surrounding space, which resulted in the development of modern dance in Central Europe. He invented his system of notation in order to indicate the spatial location of a body part. His notation system was published in 1928 under the title *Schrifttanz*. Later, more highly developed, it came to be known in the United States as Labanotation, which is taught in many colleges and universities. The Dance Notation Bureau (DNB), located in New York City, is the center for these activities, with an extension at The Ohio State University.

Two other currently used notation systems are Eshkol/Wachman, invented in 1956 in Israel, and Benesh, devised by Joan and Rudolf Benesh in 1955. Noa Eshkol, trained in dance, and Avraham Wachman, an architect and mathematician, based their system, which has been used to explore the nature of movement for scientific and choreographic purposes, on the circular movements anatomically possible in the body and meeting at certain specific points. Benesh Notation, which has been adapted by the Royal Ballet of England, with which Joan Benesh danced, indicates positions on the five-line musical staff and has been used for recording many ballets.

Laban's system is inherently logical; within it each concept builds on the previous one. He created a set of abstract symbols that serve as an alphabet of movement. Different combinations of symbols are capable of recording any type of human movement, akin to the capability of letters. Labanotation employs a three-line vertical staff, which represents the human body, with the center line dividing the movements of the right from those of the left. Nine basic directional symbols are the foundation of the system, and each symbol conveys four pieces of information. The shape describes the direction of movement; the length shows how long it takes to perform the movement; the shading tells whether the movement is in low, middle, or high level; and the placement on the staff indicates which part of the body is in motion. The staff is read upward from the bottom, with lines across the entire staff indicating measures that correspond to the musical accompaniment and short strokes across the center line marking off the counts in each measure.

The quality of movement — the different aspects of flow, weight, time, and space that were also explored by Laban — is described by another set of symbols that clarify the dynamics of a particular movement sequence. Using Labanotation to provide the quantitative aspects and the dynamic symbols the qualitative ones, the full range of movement is recorded.

Labanotation Basics

Each Labanotation symbol gives four pieces of information:

Direction of the movement is indicated by the shape of the symbol.

The level of a movement is shown by the shading of the symbol; diagonal strokes for high, a dot for middle, and blackened for low.

Forward high.   Place middle.   Right side low.

The part of the body that is moving is indicated by the column on the staff in which the symbol is placed. A Labanotation staff represents the human body; the center line of the staff divides the left side of the body from the right. Symbols to the left of the center line refer to the left-hand side of the body, symbols to the right of the center line to the right-hand side of the body.

Some body parts must be identified by a symbol, for example:

 C = the head,   = the face,   = the hands,   = the front of the left shoulder

Duration of the movement is shown by the length of the symbol. The staff is read from the bottom up, moving ahead in time. The tick marks on the center line divide the time into counts and the horizontal lines correspond with the bar lines in the music. Movements written on the same horizontal line occur simultaneously; movements written one above another occur sequentially. Measure numbers and dancers' counts appear to the left of the staff.

Direction Symbols   The Staff

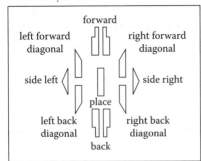

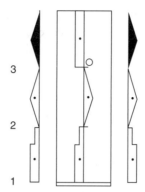

Count 3, the left foot steps next to the right foot; weight is on both feet. The arms stay to the sides but lower to a 45-degree angle.

On count 2, step to the right side with the right foot. Release the weight from the left foot. The arms open to the side, still parallel with the floor.

Count 1, on one beat, step forward on the left foot. The knee is straight. At the same time, raise the arms forward, level with the shoulders. The arms finish parallel to the floor.

Applications

Seeing

Learning the basics of any movement notation system forces a student to really observe and understand what is taking place or what they are asked to perform, as opposed to just looking at the movement. There is a difference between looking and really seeing. If you wish to perform even the simplest movement, you must be sure of exactly what is happening and how it is accomplished. This is immediately transferred to absorbing what is being taught in a technique class, at an audition, or learning a work from a choreographer or restager. Where is that arm moving in space, how long does it really take to get there, and what is its relationship to the torso? How does the timing of the arm differ from the timing of other parts of the body that are moving? At exactly what count does the head turn? Does the torso tilt or twist, or both?

Using the notation vocabulary in technique class, with short explanations of what is meant by the term, provides a tool for the dancer and educator that allows more accurate communication. As a student turns away from his or her arm, leaving it where it is in space, he or she is told to put a space hold on the arm. Even without notation training, this term clearly conveys what is intended: that is, the arm remains where it is in space. Notation gives a tool for naming differences such as that between a twist, where the free end turns more than the fixed end, and a rotation, where the whole limb turns an equal amount.

Improvisation

Notation is a perfect tool with which to explore improvisation and, eventually, dance composition. Ann Hutchinson Guest, the doyenne of contemporary Labanotation and an expert on historical systems, was one of the first to suggest Motif Writing, which she called a method for recording movement concepts rather than specific steps. She identified prime actions and ideas of movement, such as stillness, rotation, traveling, direction, or an aerial step. She now teaches a Language of Dance® course that codifies this material. These actions are given to students in a written form, which they then expand on, initially in an improvisatory manner and eventually in creating a full-scale work.

Motif Description

In a Motif Description, the notation indicates the important components of a dance sequence; other aspects of the movement are left to the discretion of the performer. For instance, the notation states that the first part of the sequence is about turning. The manner of turning is open to interpretation. It might be done on one foot or while sitting on the floor, using a free or controlled quality, finishing with the body facing the front or the back of the room, or with some other variable. All of these interpretations would be valid, as long as turning is the movement's focus.

The notation, as shown on the opposite page, is written going up the page — that is, first there is turning, then flexing, then extending, and so forth. The length of the symbols indicates the timing of the movement; longer indications have a greater time value than shorter indications.

Another way to use notation for improvisation is to take a phrase of movement from a notated work or sequence and use it as a starting point for additional development. What is the main concept in the notation? How can this be changed or how can the same principles be used to create different movement?

Dance Composition

In training choreographers, it helps if they are able read a score. Talking about a theme and variations is not as good as being able to see how Doris Humphrey treated this important element of dance composition

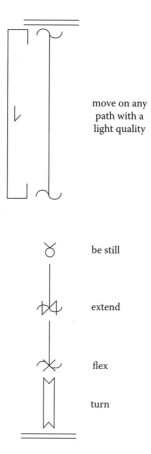

move on any
path with a
light quality

be still

extend

flex

turn

and then trying to follow her example with different movements based on the same variation concept. It is also possible to see the basic form in her dances — where she repeats certain themes or shapes — by studying the score. Canons are easily identified in notation scores. Looking at how Balanchine used canonic forms is an excellent learning experience for young choreographers.

Manipulating movement symbols on paper is another method for creating unforeseen results. This is also a good way to break the tendency of many student choreographers to repeat the same patterns of movement or to use the space in identical patterns.

Motif is also used to help students identify choices that they make. By creating a motif score of their own compositions, they soon begin to recognize when there are movement choices that they use repeatedly.

History

Using notated material — full scores, short dances, movement sequences, or a notated description of style — allows a student with even limited reading ability to understand more fully a particular period, country, or artist. He or she will actually perform a Renaissance dance or read Arbeau's steps or study Romantic ballet, all from the notation. There are excerpts from *Coppelia, Swan Lake,* and *Carnaval,* among hundreds of other dances from cultures all over the world and examples of many contemporary choreographers. It is possible to study the concept of a turn through different centuries, styles, and countries. There are specific examples of Asian and African dance techniques that the entire class can perform from a score or an instructor can teach to the class.

One dance history class called it "The Revenge of Doris Humphrey"; because she had the vision to get her work notated, today she is more than just a name in a book. Dance history classes are able to dance examples from her work, learning about her distinctive style and choreographic techniques. They are not able to know many of her contemporaries in the same way.

Criticism

A knowledge of dance history is helpful to the many students who study dance criticism. Here it is possible to read the score of a particular ballet in order to familiarize oneself with the main movement themes and to be able to notice any changes or new variations. Reading notated material in unfamiliar dance styles gives the student or potential critic a sense of the elements inherent in this style.

A critic is able to go to the blueprint of the dance, without artistic interpretation and mistakes. Just as a music critic studies the score before reviewing a particular performance, a dance critic is able to study the choreographer's intent prior to evaluating a specific performance.

Education

The question of how to teach teachers to teach is an old one, but it begins with an understanding of their material, their students, and the easiest way to connect the two. Teaching is sharing, and the dance student who wishes to teach dance, particularly to young children, must have a clear and consistent movement vocabulary that can be imparted to other students. Notation, motifs, and the dynamic symbols are easily taught and incorporated into technique and improvisation classes, giving all a comfortably shared vocabulary and a foundation on which to build. The young teacher then bases an entire class on one or two symbols, which children absorb without realizing they are being "taught."

Other Applications

Other ways of using notation include: as a tool for actors to indicate block-ing and entrances and exits; for stage managers to record movement cues for lighting and other production changes; to record movement patterns as a diagnostic tool for physical therapists and physicians; and for dance ethnologists to record movements and dances of the cultures they study.

How to Teach Notation

Labanotation is taught as a separate class or introduced in other parts of the curriculum so that the material is used to enhance the content of a particular course.

Teaching Labanotation as a Separate Class

The most important thing to remember is that notation is about move-ment, not about symbols. When teaching a notation class, the focus should be on movement and it should be taught in a studio, like any other movement class. For the most part, students find notation more interesting when the focus is on reading and dancing rather than on writing. They discover that it reveals an exciting look at the work of choreographers whose names are legendary. It also provides access to dances of other cultures. Any student who expresses an interest in writing scores should be encouraged and referred to the Dance Notation Bureau for further training.

Many educators like to begin introducing notation by first working with motif. Students start by learning and experiencing the various movement concepts, each with a symbol to clearly represent it. Later, as they move into structured notation, it is easy to take the symbols they already know and use them in a very specific manner on a Labanotation staff.

It is recommended that classes begin with a movement exploration so the students can experience and understand the concept and its varia-tions. The movement exploration can take many forms. The important element is that it stresses the movement concept, such as turning. Once the students have a physical understanding of the movement idea, symbols are introduced.

In a motif class, the student adds the new ideas and symbols to his or her movement vocabulary and uses them in a creative experience. He or she might take a prepared motif and create his or her own composition or create a motif to exchange with another student. They may start by cho-reographing a phrase and then notating it. The possibilities are endless. In looking at the compositions and talking about them, both choreographic and performance aspects are stressed. The students learn not only about movement ideas but also choreographic structures and techniques and about developing performance qualities needed for a professional dancer.

After the movement experience, a structured notation course might proceed with short readings designed to reinforce the movement idea. They then go on to longer readings, taken from repertory. In addition to learning the work, students learn about the artist and the historical context. They talk about the choreographer's choices in the use of space and time and other choreographic elements. They see graphically the rhythmic structure and talk about it. Readings are selected to complement what they are learning in other areas of the curriculum.

Students should be assisted in developing their analytical skills. Notation classes provide many opportunities to build the ability to see, understand, and realize movement ideas. In a motif class, they are asked to watch each other perform a composition they created from a motif and compare it with the score. Are the concepts specified in the score the most important movement ideas of the composition? They might be asked to create a motif score of choreography by another student. How do the motifs compare with the intention of the choreography? How do they compare with each other? Is the dancer indeed stressing the intended concept? If not, what can they do to achieve the notated ideas?

In a structured notation class, the students coach each other, helping to achieve the desired performance. What do they see that needs to be changed or refined? How do they express what they want the dancer to do for an accurate and artistic performance? Or they might each be assigned a different section of a dance to learn and then perform for their fellow students. What do they need to tell the dancers so they understand the work?

Introducing Labanotation in Other Parts of the Curriculum

Improvisation. As previously stated, motif can be introduced in improvisation classes to help students explore the many movement possibilities and develop their range. Movement concepts are introduced and explored, as in the motif class already described, and then the symbols are introduced. Motifs are prepared and distributed to students as a basis for improvisation. As the phrases develop and change, they become longer and acquire more form, all of which may be indicated in a more structured motif and, eventually, a score.

Composition. In composition class, young dancers need to learn how to move from being an imitator to a creator. They need to develop into an artist who makes conscious decisions about what he or she sees and produces. In order to do this, they must develop cognitive tools that support their creativity. Labanotation is a proven method for synthesizing the cognitive and creative processes. Symbolic representation of movement plays a key role in effective movement expression and observation. The symbols then provide a conceptual framework for understanding the principles of movement and thus become a choreographic tool. It is not a substitute for creativity, but rather a tool for stimulating and enhancing that creativity. It serves to broaden movement vocabulary, thus providing resource material for choreographic exploration.

A certain Labanotation teacher uses Motif in her Composition class to get to the root of abstraction. She asks her students to choose an everyday event and then analyze the elements present in each movement of the event. They notate these elements in Motif and then use the symbols as the outline for their abstraction of the event. Basically, Motif Writing has allowed them to deconstruct the event and then provided them with movement ideas to reconstruct it in an abstracted form.

Other ideas for the use of motif and structured notation have already been given. These ideas include starting from a prepared motif and building a composition using the stated movement concepts, creating a motif score from an excerpt of choreography by a master choreographer and then using it to develop student work, and looking at scores of master works to analyze techniques used by the choreographers.

Music for Dancers. Motif and structured notation is used to provide a visual representation of musical timing, enhancing the understanding of young students. A continuous vertical line, which serves as a timeline, is added to the center of a Motif staff or can be found within a full Labanotation staff. The line has small horizontal tick marks across the center to delineate beats of music and longer horizontal lines across the staff to denote the end of a measure. The number of beats in a measure is determined by the time signature. In 4/4 time you would have space for four beats; in 3/4 time, you would have three beats. The length of a symbol indicates how long it takes to do the movement, providing a visualization of the rhythm. Dancers are able to freely translate music into dance notation and into movement in any order. This method, which is basically a bilingual approach to time, allows the student to create a fluid perception of time as a concept of choreography — one that can be endlessly manipulated.

Movement for Theater. Motif is used in many ways to enhance the training of theater students. It explores movement possibilities, opening the range of actors and directors. This expands their ideas of what movement implies and ultimately gives them the information they need to understand more fully how they can move as individuals and relate to other actors.

Students apply the same basic process discussed above in abstracting an everyday event to abstracting a scene. They break the scene down into dramatic beats (steps in the dramatic progression of the scene), identify the emotions present in those dramatic beats, and then select symbols that relate to those emotions. Again, they end up with an outline for a movement abstraction.

Dance History. In studying dance history, think how much richer and immediate it is for the students to be able to experience and perform excerpts from the periods and choreographers they are studying. With notation, this becomes a reality, bringing our dance heritage alive. As periods are introduced and choreographers are studied, a key component of the class is the experience of the work from a score. Background is set, giving students context and information needed to understand the dances. Then scores are used to enhance their understanding, allowing them to intimately know the work. When studying Antony Tudor's works, for example, his use of dramatic gesture becomes evident.

Dance Ethnology. Notation is used to get at the essential movement elements and qualities of the dances from a particular culture. Layering is used to deconstruct and reconstruct elements of the dance. First directions and timing might be shown, then details added. Notation can bring simplicity to movement vocabulary rather than intricacy. It can allow the dance ethnologist to study the movement without the constraints of temporal time.

Notation and Technology

The notation field is breaking new ground in technology. There are three programs for writing notation, Calaban (developed in England), LabanWriter (developed at The Ohio State University), and Labanatory (in development in Hungary). All three programs function similarly to word processing applications, allowing the user to create clear, easy-to-read notation scores.

The Dance Notation Bureau is developing a program called LabanDancer, which translates the notation created in LabanWriter to computer animation. The user sees the animated dancer perform the movement on the computer screen at any angle. On the left of the screen is a window that shows the notation score. The stage window is in the center. On the right of the screen are buttons for preset viewing angles, although, using the mouse, the viewer can turn the stage to look from anywhere. The user can zoom in and out, and move the stage up, down, or side to side in the window. At the bottom of the screen are controls to play the animation and a time line that shows the time in seconds.

The user can also select from various models, turn a metronome on to hear the beat, select the tempo at which the notation should be played, show the dancer's footsteps on the floor to see the path of the movement, and select the "follow" button that operates as though a camera is following the dancer, keeping her in the center of the window.

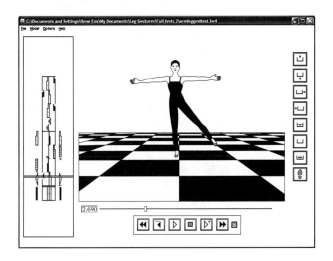

A highlight bar scrolls up the notation, synchronized with the movements of the dancer. The bar can be dragged to anywhere in the notation, and the dancer will move to that part of the phrase. The DNB is also designing distance-learning modules to introduce notation in the context of the dance curriculum. The modules are intended for use in dance history, pedagogy, and composition classes. They will be used over a two- or three-week period, highlighting a part of the course curriculum, using notation to enhance the material, and will provide a tutorial to help the student learn to read the included notation. They are conceived for use in settings where there is no notation faculty on staff.

Dance Notation opens up new opportunities for dancers and students to enrich their art and it provides a resource for all areas of the dance curriculum, creative and academic. It allows us to read the vast collections of choreographers and dancers from different cultures, past and present. And even if we have not come to the point where we cuddle up at night with a good dance score, it is comforting to know that we could.

Bibliography

Dell, Cecily. *A Primer for Movement Description Using Effort Shape and Supplementary Concepts.* New York: The Dance Notation Bureau, 1970.

Edelson, Jane, et al., eds. *Readings in Modern Dance, vol.1.* New York: The Dance Notation Bureau, 1974.

Guest, Ann Hutchinson. *Your Move.* New York: Gordon and Breach, 1983.

———. *Dance Notation: The Process of Recording Movement on Paper.* London: Dance Books, 1984.

———. *Labanotation: The System of Analyzing and Recording Movement.* 4th rev. ed. New York and London: Routledge, 2005.

Laban, Rudolf. *The Language of Movement.* Boston: Plays, Inc., 1974.

Topaz, Muriel. *Elemementary Labanotation: A Study Guide.* New York: Dance Notation Bureau Press, 1996.

———. *Study Guide for Intermediate Labanotation.* 2nd ed., rev. by Topaz and Jane Marriet. New York: Dance Notation Bureau Press, 1986.

Varon, Michelle, ed. *Readings in Modern Dance, vol. 2.* New York: The Dance Notation Bureau, 1977.

Warner, Mary Jane with Frederick E. Warner. *Laban Notation Scores: An International Bibliography. vol. 1* (1984), *vol. 2* (1988), *vol. 3* (1995), *vol. 4* (1999). The International Council of Kinetography Laban.

CHAPTER 12

Documentation, Preservation, and Access: Ensuring a Future for Dance's Legacy

ELIZABETH ALDRICH

It is often mistakenly assumed that the keystones of America's dance heritage — dance documentation and preservation as well as the often politically charged concept of access to materials — are activities of concern only to archivists and librarians. Indeed, librarians and archivists can and do provide leadership for establishing and encouraging best practices required for the survival of the artifacts that make up our dance heritage. They need support, however, in sustaining the stewardship of this legacy from a wide variety of people and institutions: dancers, choreographers, presenting organizations, experts in emerging technologies, filmmakers, scholars and writers, festivals, and members of the diverse communities found in all corners of this country.

Dance heritage is found in two primary forms. First, there are the artifacts, which might include programs, reviews and articles, photographs, videotapes, costumes and sets, contracts, music scores, correspondence, notation or choreographic notes, and so forth. Second, there is the dance itself, an ephemeral, multidimensional, and far less tangible entity. To record and preserve a dance in perpetuity, using methods that all can access, is a difficult challenge. The steps can be notated in a score or recorded on film or videotape but, in many cases, dances are preserved only in the memories of the creators or performers who pass them along to others by direct interpersonal contact.

In an era that has lost and continues to lose pioneers of dance to old age and young artists to AIDS, as well as the critical deterioration of paper and analog media, the issues of preserving and ensuring access to America's dance heritage have taken on a new and very real urgency. This chapter will begin with a brief definition and function of an archive and will then focus on dance documentation, preservation, and access to materials as activities of concern for the entire dance field. It is axiomatic that the heritage of dance is intrinsic to its future development. It is also imperative that we continue to document and make this legacy accessible to future generations.

What Is an Archive?

Most public and academic libraries include dance books, dance-related magazines, and commercially available dance videos. Archives and research libraries collect unpublished, original material, although most also hold some published resources, such as newspaper and magazine articles, reviews, and programs.

Archival collections range in size from a few pieces of correspondence or even a single sheet of choreographic notes to collections that contain thousands of videotapes. (Known as *primary sources*, archival collections can include materials in all the formats mentioned throughout this chapter.) Archival collections — when compared with the dance books held in a local public library — are different in that they are unique, original materials; thus, they must be handled with care to ensure long-term survivability. These materials are stored in environmentally appropriate locations and are brought to a researcher upon request. To locate items within an archival collection, a researcher will use a finding aid.

Taming Your Personnel or Company Archive

Archivists and library catalogers are professionally trained, so this technical work is best left to them. However, there are several basic responsibilities, which can and should be undertaken by any dancer, choreographer, dance company, dance scholar — in fact, anyone who is accumulating archival materials and who wishes to preserve the history of what he or she has created.

First, it is important to appraise the materials to determine their value for purposes of preservation. Standard elements of this appraisal involve the evaluation of the *general characteristics* of the materials, such as age, quantity, physical form, and value for general research. *Administrative values* provide information about the administrative, financial, and legal uses of documents. *Research values* include the exceptionality of the information: a document's probable intellectual value and potential frequency of future use. For this phase, one simply determines what materials should be retained as "archival." The next phase is to create a plan, known as a *retention schedule*, which identifies the materials that should be maintained, and for how long. For dance companies and choreographers, artistic and production records should be retained in perpetuity; however, duplicates can be discarded. At-risk materials, such as original newspaper reviews and articles and videotapes more than ten years old, should be scheduled for reformatting.

After determining the physical and intellectual importance of your documents, the next step is to *process* the materials by arranging and grouping them in order to easily retrieve the information. The basic divisions are called *record groups* and *record series*. For example, a dance company would create *record groups* for artistic, administrative, legal, financial, and educational documents. All documents of a similar nature would be further divided into *record series,* and an *item level* description might include the description of a single letter or photograph within a record series (Kopp 1995).

Finding aids are documents that provide contextual information about an archival collection and generally consist of an inventory or description of the contents of the collection. Finding aids may also be called inventories, collection registers, lists, or surveys and can be used via electronic databases or card catalogs. Typically, a finding aid will consist of the following information:

Title of the collection.
Descriptive summary, which is an overview of the collection.
Administrative information, such as access restrictions, publication rights, and provenance.
Biography of the subject, or history, if the subject is an organization.
Scope and content of the collection.
Container list of the collection, including box and folder numbers and their contents.

A finding aid will, most often, describe a collection at broad levels. Usually, the researcher will be referred to a box location of a *record group* or *record series,* rather than *item level* descriptions (Kopp 1995, 8).

A Brief History of the Field of Dance Documentation and Preservation

In 1990 the Andrew W. Mellon Foundation and the Dance Program of the National Endowment for the Arts funded a study to investigate the existing system of dance documentation and preservation, how transactions were conducted within the system, and to what extent the needs of the dance community were met. The report, *Images of American Dance: Documenting and Preserving a Cultural Heritage* (1991), concluded that (1) vast historical, geographic, cultural, and artistic chasms exist in the record of dance in the United States; (2) video technology profoundly changed the way dance is documented, what is recorded, and how the field thinks about preservation; (3) although there were small, informal networks, there was not a fully functioning, institutionalized dance documentation and preservation network; (4) access was often impeded by a vast array of problems, including union and copyright restrictions as well as a lack of uniform cataloging standards and guidelines for dance materials; and (5) educational initiatives would be required to train artists and administrators in basic documentation and preservation techniques. The report recommended that greater financial support be made available; that the field support a larger and more diverse array of documentation and preservation projects; that improved technical assistance be made available; and that a "formal association among the major repositories" be formed (Keens et al. 1991).

In response to the report, a Coalition Planning Group — consisting of representatives from the Harvard Theatre Collection, the Library of Congress, the New York Public Library, Dance Collection, San Francisco Performing Arts Library and Museum, and an adviser from the Research Libraries Group — was organized to seek collaborative solutions. The group systematically set about to address issues in the report as well as to tackle serious backlogs in processing and cataloging (some of which were estimated to be up to three years). The group concluded that:

> Cataloging efforts should be aimed at creating a single union catalog, which would be integrated into the national bibliographic utilities. Thus, dance materials would be located with research materials in other disciplines.
> Guidelines for cataloging performing arts materials should be created.
> Cooperative work on name authorities and coordinated subject heading development should commence (Snyder and Johnson 1999, 20).

It was important for the Planning Group to establish standards for the cataloging of dance materials. Traditionally, library-cataloging systems focused their attention on book materials. Information on dance is often found in documents other than books, however, including programs; press releases; reviews; contracts; touring records; correspondence; film, video- and audiotape; notation and choreographic notes; field notes; and photographs. Thus, as noted by librarian and author Catherine Johnson, "The book-centered systems of library catalogs were inadequate for in-depth dance research" (Snyder and Johnson 1999, 17). The issues were further complicated by the Library of Congress's classification system, which defined dance within the spheres of sports and recreation. Headings for dance subjects were located under the term "dancing," an active verb, rather than "dance," a noun, which would describe an art form. This might well be due to the fact that early books on Western dance concentrated on instructional how-to books, with a smaller number of books on dance theory and history. At this time, many college and university dance programs were located within departments of physical education. In short, dance was considered a recreational activity.

As a result of this early collaboration among institutions, in 1992, the Planning Group developed into the Dance Heritage Coalition (DHC), a national alliance of major dance collections and archives that focuses on strengthening the national dance documentation and preservation network.[1] The newly formed DHC undertook a cooperative project called the *Access to Resources for the History of Dance in Seven Repositories Project*. Funded by the National Endowment for the Humanities, with additional support from other foundations, the project, which began in 1994, successfully completed many of the recommendations made in *Images of American Dance*.

The project involved the cataloging and processing of archival materials and other primary resources, located at the Dance Collection, New York Public Library for the Performing Arts; Harvard Theatre Collection; and the Library of Congress along with four smaller repositories: San Francisco Performing Arts Library and Museum; Lawrence and Lee Theatre Research Institute, Ohio State University; the University of Minnesota; and the American Dance Festival.

At the conclusion of this project in 1997, the participating institutions had processed over 2,000 linear feet of archival material and added 6,500 catalog records and 60,000 authority records to the national library databases (RILN and OCLC). Thus, the dance holdings of each participant became available through a number of avenues, including the online catalogs of each institution, the national bibliographic networks, and finding aids. A *Processing Procedures Manual for Dance and Other Performing Arts Collections* was created along with guidelines for applying national cataloging standards for dance-related materials (Dance Heritage Coalition 1996, 1997, n.d. [a], n.d. [b]).

Phase II was a one-year project designed to make accessible online, full-text finding aids to primary research resources in dance history, including manuscript and archival materials, audio- and videotape, printed materials, and visual collections that were created during Phase I. Mark-up of the manuscript finding aids was done by using the standard generalized markup language (SGML) document type definition (DTD) for finding aids for encoded archival description (EAD). The project also assisted in testing and further developing EAD as it moved toward becoming a standard. After encoding, the finding aids were mounted on the DHC Web site. The site was also linked to national library catalogs and to the catalogs of DHC member institutions.

As well as providing a model for communication among the participating institutions and establishing standards, the project provided the basis for national cooperative collecting policies and documentation strategies in the field of dance, guaranteeing that dance would be incorporated into the larger universe of knowledge and ensuring that it was adequately represented as our nation's libraries looked to the future.

Documentation, Preservation, and Access to Dance Materials

Documenting and preserving allows us to pass along the history and stories of dance to be experienced by others. If a dance has not been documented, or if the record has not been preserved and has deteriorated, it is lost forever.

Documentation

Prior to the commissioning of *Images of American Dance,* dance scholarship lurked just outside the boundaries of scholarly debate, consigned to be the neglected stepchild of other art forms. Few books of dance scholarship had been published, no major reference work yet existed, and the subject was absent from other discourses, including those on aesthetics and philosophy. (Notable exceptions included *Dance Index,* which began publication in 1942; *Dance Perspectives,* which was started in 1959 and edited by Selma Jeanne Cohen and Al Pischl; and Dance Horizons Books, which in the 1960s started to publish republications of dance books, notably those from the eighteenth century.) It was ignored by most American universities — at that point, hardly any offered courses in dance history and graduate programs were embryonic. Consequently, "dance as a discipline [was] largely relegated to the margins of serious intellectual interchange in this country" (Keens et al. 1991, 10). This was due, in part, to the fact that the field had no easy methods of documenting itself: "Poetry and fiction can be affixed on the printed page; visual art can be set on canvas or in stone; drama can be passed on through scripts; music has a widely understood notational system" (Keens et al. 1991, 10). The ability to create concrete records of its history, which can be readily accessed, is a relatively recent development for dance. Regrettably, this lack of documentation led to what critic John Martin once called a "limbo of illiteracy" (cited in Keens et al. 1991, 10). The noted dance historian Allegra Fuller Snyder, eloquently summed up the problem: "[The] shortage of recorded dance gives the impression that dance itself does not have a history, which creates a particular stigma in a culture where the past gives credence to the present" (Snyder and Johnson 1999, 1).

What Is Documentation?

The documentation of dance involves creating comprehensive and stable records that will provide access to the experience over time. Historically, this has been far from ideal in practice, fragmented at best. Retaining our dance heritage for the future requires answering questions, such as: What types of records most accurately document dance? Are current dance-documentation efforts adequate? How can we better document dance and fill the gaps in the current record?

Documenting dance must reflect all aspects, including the creative process, the funding, the performance, and audience response. It should tell the who, what, when, where, and how of a production. Thorough documentation will illustrate what was good and not so good about a production.

Early dance documentation includes visual representations of dance through paintings, drawings, and on artifacts, such as pottery. Written evidence for Western dance goes back, at least, to the writings of the early Greeks. The ability to dance well, which went hand-in-hand with deportment and courtly social standing, is documented in the Renaissance and Baroque eras by dancing masters who verbally described and recorded their work.

Efforts at notation, including that of Thoinot Arbeau in his 1588 *Orchesographie* and, later, Raoul-Auger Feuillet's notation, published in 1700, help to bring alive those dances for contemporary audiences. Later notation innovators include Rudolf Laban, who published his abstract-symbol notation in 1928 and Rudolf Benesh, whose system was published in 1956. The last decades of the twentieth century saw the evolution of software for the creation of choreography, such as Life Forms and experimentations in the use of motion capture, ushering in a new era of technology-based methods of dance documentation.

Dance companies and organizations are slowly becoming increasingly aware of the importance of documentation. Without documentation, companies would be unable to revive works out of repertory, study past publicity, provide information for grant proposals, or create press kits. These are also the key materials that are examined and analyzed by dance scholars, who contextualize the materials to provide greater understanding and appreciation for dance.

Dance documentation can include the following formats:

Videotape and film
Photography
Set, costume, lighting designs
Oral history and video history interviews
Documents on paper, which fall into two subcategories:
  Artistic Records, which include programs and playbills, souvenir programs, news clippings and reviews, scrapbooks, publicity materials, notation scores, and choreographic notes
  Business Records, which include correspondence, minutes of the board of directors, annual reports, grant proposals and reports, contracts, performance logs, touring records, financial and tax records, biographical and personnel files, and school records

Keens et al. (1991) noted that "ballet and modern dance have been favored over other forms; European-based traditions are more present in the records than non-European; finished work tends to be documented more than the creative process; and most of the personal stories of people who have contributed to the making of dance history are missing altogether" (4).

As we look forward to the early decades of the millennium, libraries are facing critical funding cutbacks. This means fewer catalogers and archivists to process the materials, bringing about a radical change in the types of collections libraries can and will accept. Some of the larger repositories will only accept a collection if it is fully organized, preferably with a container list and housed in archival-quality folders and boxes. On the other hand, if a collection arrives with a subvention that will cover the costs of processing, it is more apt to be accepted. While libraries certainly cannot be faulted for these policies — too many collections are already languishing in the storage facilities of institutions — it raises serious questions about the types of collections that will be processed and made available in the future. To compound the problem, few institutions have funds to seek out unusual or unconventional dance archival collections.

Documentation tools must be provided to the nonmainstream dance communities, such as folk, traditional, and ethnic, which customarily do not have access to such information. Traditions that prefer to rely on oral transmissions of their dances must also be respected and encouraged to keep their traditions alive. Preservation and archiving information should be distributed and those that have nontraditional collections encouraged to provide access to qualified researchers.

There will always be gaps in documentation as well as access; however, these will become less significant when all the stakeholders — from dance companies to individual dance scholars, from dance administrators to choreographers, and the funding community — take the responsibility to become aware of the importance of the issues, take advantage of emerging technologies, embrace the need to better document the world of dance, and preserve that documentation with systematic, safe, and secure methods.

Improving Your Documentation. There are many documentation tools available: videotape, oral histories (recorded on either audio or video), notation (formal systems, such as Labanotation, Benesh notation, or choreographic notes), photographs, programs, and costume and set design sketches, just to name a few. These suggestions can be considered starting points:

Evaluate the documentation you now create by identifying and analyzing the accuracy of these materials.

Determine how you can improve the accuracy or extent of present efforts. This might include the assurance that photographs are fully identified; by securing signed consent agreements from all those involved in any performance videotape; and by consistently and routinely labeling in detail each videotape created.

Obtain information on resources, for example, from the Dance Heritage Coalition, or create partnerships with organizations, such as public libraries.

Videotape as a Documentation Tool There is no question that videotape has become the documentation tool of choice. Choreographers use videotape to document rehearsals and the creative process; dance companies and festivals use videotape to document performances and for auditioning dancers and companies; and dance administrators use videotape documentation as supporting material for grant applications and for publicity: "No other single technological invention has had as great an impact on the field of dance documentation as video" (Kopp 1995, 1). It is of paramount importance, however, for those in the dance field to remember that a videotape is a record of a single performance and should be supported by dance notation, extensive choreographic and performance notes, and the other formats already mentioned.

Preservation is the physical safeguarding of documentation — materials and objects — that hold the information about a dance or dance tradition. The challenges of preserving our physical dance legacy are substantial, however. The myriad formats used to document dance include magnetic tape, manuscripts and other paper-based materials, photographs, costumes and sets, and digital materials, just to name a few. Not only do all these items have diverse preservation requirements, they all have differing long-term stability. It is important to remember that without proper attention, *all* these materials will eventually deteriorate.

Preserving these materials is expensive. Throughout history, many creators of dance have faced economic hardships in simply trying to pay for dancers and rehearsal space and to put their work on the stage, with few remaining resources for high-quality documentation or for safeguarding that documentation. Contracts, photographs, programs, and choreographic notes are often stuffed into boxes — sent into exile under a bed, into a closet, or into a damp barn. Videotapes are stacked without regard to humidity control and are often exposed to dust, dirt, food, and tobacco smoke.

Unfortunately, too, many dance collections are located in large institutions that suffer from budget constraints, and the costs of maintaining controlled environments in libraries and museums are enormous. Likewise, institutions often must literally fight for access to the centralized preservation services, and those services usually concentrate on print and paper materials. For smaller dance companies and organizations that wish to maintain their own archives, the costs can be prohibitive.

Archivists integrate preservation with documentation and, ultimately, with access, and they have long encouraged the dance community to think about preservation at the time of documenting a work. For example, printing programs and copying newspaper clippings on acid-free paper and using high-quality tape, such as Betacam SP, when videotaping a performance, are two examples of how to increase the life span of archival materials.

Some Preservation Tips. These recommended practices can, and should, be incorporated into a personal archive:

Store archival materials in acid-free folders or envelopes, and place them in acid-free, dust-tight boxes.

Do not use staples, paperclips, rubber bands, or tape on any of your documentation.

Remove photographs from glassine envelopes and place them in archival-quality, nonacid and adhesive-free folders. All identification should be made with a soft pencil on the back. Store photographs flat in boxes.

Store any archival materials on steel (not wood) shelving, away from water pipes or fire-protection systems.

Store videotapes and films upright and away from any electromagnetic fields, such as fluorescent lights, computers, or copying machines. Be sure that you have both a master and viewing copy for all videotapes.

Store all of your archival materials in an environment that has moderate temperature and relative humidity. If the room has windows, cover them with heavy curtains or shades. Do not store any materials on or near heat sources, such as radiators (Dance Heritage Coalition 2002).

Dance advocate Sali Ann Kriegsman has said, "Preserving dance's past/present/future heritage is an act of respect and gratitude for the continuity of human expression and embodied thought. The purpose of preservation is not to fix a dance or a dancer in amber, but to illuminate human experience and those artistic insights that give it an imperishable life." (Deputy 2001, 80)

Dance's Major Preservation Challenge: Surviving the Magnetic Media Crisis

Since the later 1950s, the principal tool for documentation of our dance history has been videotape, and it has served as a powerful medium of artistic expression and visual record, capturing and portraying events that shape virtually all we know about many forms of dance from the middle of the twentieth century. Magnetic media has provided a medium to record and replay our dance history at will, and the popular belief within the dance community has always been that information stored on magnetic media is permanent. As a long-term record for the future, however, videotape is not stable: it is more subject to damage and deterioration, to degradation and deterioration, than could have been envisioned. Magnetic media have a very limited life span, and no tape is safe from the multiple enemies of moisture, dirt, humidity, heat, chemical change, and stretching that occurs every time a VHS cassette is loaded to record or to be played back. Then, too, more than one hundred different formats have been commercially introduced since the invention of videotape recording.

Often, access to taped information can be lost simply because the format is obsolete and a working playback machine cannot be located or can no longer be trusted not to damage a unique tape. As a result, irreplaceable tapes are in peril and there probability is a real of losing *forever* many of the moving images that have become the collective memory of all forms of dance.

Some Preservation Tips for Videotape Preservation. These best practices will help improve the longevity of your videotape collection:

- Familiarize yourself with the formats of your videotapes and create an inventory that describes each by title, format, number of copies, and whether or not it is an original or a copy.
- Improve storage conditions by keeping videotapes in a cool, dry location.
- Store tapes in appropriate archival containers that are hard-shelled and dust- and water-resistant. Do not store videotapes in the cardboard boxes in which they come.
- Keep a minimum of three copies of each tape: the original (the earliest generation); a master (copied from the original and used to make further copies); and a reference copy (for everyday viewing).
- Ensure that playback equipment is working properly before inserting a tape.
- Prioritize your collection for copying and reformatting based on the intellectual (historical, cultural, or institutional) value; the state of deterioration or age of the tape; and format obsolescence (Drazin 2003).

Why Not Reformat to DVD? During the late 1990s, the cost of digital recording devices began to fall, and many turned to DVDs for reformatting at-risk videotapes. DVDs can be an excellent choice for viewing copies, but as preservation copies they have severe limitations. First, they are highly compressed versions of the originals and selective data is irretrievably discarded in making the DVD copy. Second, the variety of encoding systems in use cannot assure compatibility from one machine to another. Third, the life span of this medium is not yet known. Last, failure of a DVD usually ends in total failure; the failure of a tape, by contrast, may involve only limited portions of the tape, making other recovery techniques possible (Drazin 2003, 13). The preservation community recommends that analog tapes be reformatted to Betacam SP. If you make a DVD copy of an important tape, be sure that the original videotape is safely stored according to the guidelines already mentioned.

The Future of Digital Preservation

The Dance Heritage Coalition has taken a leadership role in monitoring the development of digital technology from the early 1990s. The DHC suggested that dance would be an exceptional model for use in addressing the complex issues surrounding the preservation of visual magnetic media. In 2002, the DHC called a meeting at the Library of Congress to design an experiment to determine the most appropriate method of transferring analog videotapes to digital for preservation purposes and using a variety of dance videotapes as the testing focus. In the case of dance videotapes, the digitization process would not only conserve the original object, but would also reduce the further deterioration of and provide access to rare, fragile, and vulnerable materials. By setting preservation standards, the outcomes expected would have enormous resonance not only for the dance community, but for every major archival institution.

During 2003 and 2004, with a grant to the DHC from The Andrew W. Mellon Foundation, a consulting team from Media Matters LLC — a technical consultancy specializing in archival audio and video material under the leadership of James Lindner — investigated various uncompressed and compressed formats as well as container file types that would establish the rigorous standards required by the preservation community. The 2004 report of this experiment concluded that no single compressed solution would be visually acceptable and that only *lossless* compression (no compression) would satisfy the required criteria. To this end, JPEG2000 has been recommended, along with Media Exchange Format (MFX) as a candidate for both preservation and access of archival audiovisual content and records (metadata). The cost of storage, which continues to be a considerable expense in the early years of the twenty-first century, is expected to fall, thus making the reality of digital preservation possible for archives, and establishing an important step toward saving our dance history.

Access to Dance Materials

"Access" is a word used both in the artistic community by those who create and document a work and by the repositories that protect and preserve that documentation. Conflict can develop when scholars and others who draw on the materials for their work find that documents may not be easily available or that access is accompanied by restrictions. As noted in *Images of American Dance*, "Among the barriers to easy access are the incomplete record of what collections exist and what is in them; the inadequate and inconsistent organization of those materials; the conflict between some

214 • Teaching Dance Studies

needs of archive users and the limitations on physical property rights and intellectual rights; and the tension between the need for 'hands-on' and long-term preservation concerns" (Keens, et al. 1991, 5). Indeed, access and preservation cannot be separated. Access can only be guaranteed if the preservation needs of the materials have been met. As a result, libraries are "sometimes seen as unfriendly gatekeepers, withholding information or denying access to it" (Snyder and Johnson 1999, 16). The dance field must continue to advocate that materials stored in museums and libraries be made accessible as soon as possible without jeopardizing any item's physical condition. The future of dance documentation, preservation, and access will be greatly enhanced by supporting the work of librarians, catalogers, and archivists by gaining a thorough knowledge of the issues.

With the development of new technology, especially the increased use and availability of library catalogs through the Internet, access to materials is taking on a new facet. Online catalogs may also provide links to finding aids as well as links to full-text documents. For example, in 1997, the Library of Congress digitized over two hundred of its dance manuals, ca. 1490 to 1926, creating an *American Ballroom Companion*, which provides the full texts, contextual narrative, and video clips of reconstructions (accessible via http://memory.loc.gov/ammem/dihtml/dihome.html). In addition to providing an electronic gateway to libraries and museums, the growth of the Word Wide Web has provided a foundation on which others, through development of Web sites that cover every conceivable aspect of dance, enhance access for all.

Barriers to Access

As already noted, the need for preserving materials often prevents access, as do backlogs in library processing and cataloging. One of the most daunting obstacles to access is copyright, however. Securing licenses and permissions for materials is complex, and, in some cases, the myriad laws jeopardize access to dance's history. The often murky definitions of "educational use" and "fair use" are not clearly defined in current case law. In 2004, the DHC published a report on issues and discoveries that it experienced while securing permissions for its touring exhibition *America's Irreplaceable Dance Treasures: the First 100* (Smigel 2004). Among its recommendations are:

> To initiate a series of talks involving funders, copyright law specialists, dance and music administrators, media technology experts, union representatives, and archivists around the issue of copyright and access.

> To suggest guidelines be adopted within foundation and government grants to ensure or encourage future access.
>
> To encourage the formation of a national clearinghouse, similar to the clearinghouses for music or publications, that can clear dance film and video permissions (Smigel 2004, 2).

The dance community must keep a vigilant eye on copyright and intellectual property discussions in Congress as well as cases that come before the U.S. Supreme Court, making its views known to lawmakers, attorneys, arts administrators, funders, and others when copyright threatens to interfere with access. At the same time, dancers and choreographers need to arm themselves with the basics of copyright law in order to protect their creations from improper use and to become aware of potential liability for possible infringement. Issues include what is copyrightable, definitions of work for hire, fair use, and the advantages of registering work with the U.S. Copyright Office (Dance Heritage Coalition 2003).

Conclusion

Dance literally embodies fundamental aspects of our culture. It tells us who we are, who we have been, and whom we can aspire to be, and it comprises an entire world of spiritual and secular ideas, stories, emotions, and human experience, understood and expressed through movement. The rich history of dance in America serves as both a reflection and a record of this nation's increasingly diverse, dynamic culture. It is imperative that we continue our efforts in documentation, that we secure a safe future for the preservation of that documentation, and that we make accessible the materials that document the artistic accomplishments in dance of the past, present, and future.

Bibliography

Dance Heritage Coalition. *Beyond Memory: Preserving the Documents of our Dance Heritage.* Washington, D.C.: Dance Heritage Coalition, 1994. Edited by Elizabeth Aldrich and revised by Patricia R. Rader and Ann Seibert for online version, 2002.

Dance Heritage Coalition. *Cataloging Moving Image Materials.* Washington, D.C.: Dance Heritage Coalition, 1996. Available in hardcopy and online at http://danceheritage.org.

Dance Heritage Coalition. *Cataloging Graphic Materials.* Washington, D.C.: Dance Heritage Coalition, 1997. Available in hardcopy and online at http://danceheritage.org.

Dance Heritage Coalition. *Cataloging Print Materials.* Washington, D.C.: Dance Heritage Coalition, n.d. (a). Available in hardcopy and online at http://danceheritage.org.

Dance Heritage Coalition. *Cataloging Manuscript and Archival Materials.* Washington, D.C.: Dance Heritage Coalition, n.d. (b). Available in hardcopy and online at http://danceheritage.org.

Dance Heritage Coalition. *A Copyright Primer for the Dance Community.* Washington, D.C.: Dance Heritage Coalition, 2003. Available in hardcopy and online at http://danceheritage.org.

Deputy, Janice M., Editor. *Frames of Reference: A Resource Guide from the National Initiative to Preserve America's Dance.* Washington, DC: Dance/USA, 2001.

Drazin, Barbara, compiler. *Dance Videotapes at Risk*. Washington, D.C.: Dance Heritage Coalition, 2003.

Keens, William, Kopp, Leslie Hansen, and Mindy N. Levine. *Images of American Dance: Documenting and Preserving a Cultural Heritage*. Report on a Study Sponsored by the National Endowment for the Arts and The Andrew W. Mellon Foundation, New York, 1991.

Kriegsman, Sali Ann. *The Living Heritage: Dance*. Washington, D.C.: Center for Arts and Culture, 2000.

Kopp, Leslie Hansen. *Dance Archives: A Practical Manual for Documenting and Preserving the Ephemeral Art*. New York: Preserve, Inc., 1995.

Smigel, Libby. *Report on the "America's Irreplaceable Dance Treasures" Exhibition: Copyright Issues That Affect Access*. Washington, D.C.: Dance Heritage Coalition, 2004.

Snyder, Allegra Fuller and Johnson, Catherine J. *Securing Our Dance Heritage: Issues in the Documentation and Preservation of Dance*. Washington, D.C.: Council on Library and Information Resources, 1999.

Notes

1. Institutional members of the DHC as of 2004 include American Dance Festival; Lawrence and Lee Theatre Research Institute, Ohio State University; New York Public Library for the Performing Arts, Dance Division; San Francisco Performing Arts Library and Museum; Jacob's Pillow Dance Festival; Library of Congress; Harvard Theatre Collection; Dance Notation Bureau; and Anacostia Museum and Center for African American History and Culture, Smithsonian Institution.

CHAPTER 13

Reflections on Educating Dance Educators

SUSAN W. STINSON

I have been teaching dance education courses in higher education for almost thirty years, twenty-five of them at an institution that is nationally known for its teacher education program in dance. Despite this longevity, I claim only experience and reflexivity, not authority; I write this chapter as an explorer sharing my discoveries, not as an expert qualified to tell others what should be done at their institutions.

As a teacher educator (the name given to faculty in programs designed to prepare public school teachers), I have found that our curriculum and the courses I teach within it have developed within a context that would be different for other teachers at another time or another institution. The context includes colleagues and students, available resources, and requirements set by the institution, the state, professional organizations, and accrediting agencies. Throughout my career, I have danced between these influences (the content of which is always changing) and my own values, which also continue to evolve, affected by ideas I encounter in work by other scholars and practitioners as well as what is usually called "life experience." The dance is thus not a solo but a group piece that is constantly in the process of being created.[1] In this chapter, I discuss these factors, and some lessons that I have learned along the way, ones that have the most potential to contribute to others beginning their own journey in developing

217

a dance education program. The emphasis will be on preparing students to teach dance in public education, although readers from states in which there is no dance in public schools will hopefully find useful insights as well. The increasing numbers of new positions for dance faculty in teacher education in the past five years indicate that more institutions are seeing a need for programs to prepare dance educators for public schools.

I have taken the structure for this chapter from a journal assignment I gave for many years to students who were participant-observers in demonstration classes that I taught to public school students of different ages, asking them to write about what they had learned about schools and schooling, dance, students, the teaching-learning process, and themselves. Through teaching, I also have made discoveries in each of these areas. This chapter will address some of the lessons I have learned.

The Institutional Context: Limits and Challenges

During my professional career, the move toward standards and accountability in public education has undoubtedly stimulated some of the greatest changes in my teaching. Like most of my colleagues, I have struggled with this movement and wondered how much further it might go. There are multiple kinds of standards and similar external "rules" affecting teacher education programs in dance. First are those of regional accrediting agencies (ours is the Southern Association of Colleges and Universities) that review the whole institution; anyone in higher education knows that this is a high-stakes review, with major consequences if an institution does not pass. A second level of review is a voluntary one: national agencies that are discipline-specific, in our case the National Association for Schools of Dance (NASD). The third type of review is specific to teacher education programs in our state; we must receive accreditation from both our state educational agency and a national agency (National Council for Accreditation of Teacher Education, or NCATE). This means that those of us in teacher education automatically have considerably more standards to follow and have to prepare twice as many accreditation reports as our colleagues who are not involved in this endeavor.

The next set of standards addresses individuals applying for a teaching license. Each state has its own requirements; ours for initial (undergraduate-level) licensure are based on national standards of the Interstate New Teacher Assessment and Support Consortium (INTASC). In my state, all faculty teaching methods courses must maintain their own teaching licenses, meeting the same basic requirements as public school teachers. At the time of our state and national accreditation reviews, we must also provide documentation that each individual we recommend for licensure meets each standard.

The next level of standards is that for K–12 students in public schools. While the National Dance Standards (Consortium of National Arts Education Associations 1994) are voluntary, my state, like many others, has its own version of these in its *Standard Course of Study* (North Carolina Department of Public Instruction, n.d.), which is, at least theoretically, not voluntary. At the time of our own accreditation, we have to demonstrate how we prepare future teachers to be able to deliver the content within these standards.

Most faculty in higher education do not hold bureaucracy in high esteem, and it is difficult not to feel that the effort to comply with all of the standards is a poor use of our abilities and education. This situation has been made worse in recent years as governmental bodies have passed more and more mandates, some of them illogical and a few potentially harmful. My state has raised standards for students seeking licensure through institutions of higher education, while implementing alternative routes with lower standards and minimal accountability. This trend has worsened due to No Child Left Behind legislation mandating "fully qualified" teachers.

Despite the frustration engendered by this state of affairs, a long-term perspective provides some reasons for optimism. One is that policies come and go, and some of the most misguided ones go first; thus it makes little sense to invest too much energy in angst as we read and respond to the many mandates. Another reason for optimism in dance education is that most of the governing bodies do not care nearly as much about dance as they do about areas of the curriculum they consider more important. When accreditation time comes, we get looked at much less closely by review teams that are not discipline-specific, and, at this point, there are fewer hurdles for prospective dance educators to scale than there are in other fields.[2]

Similarly, there is less scrutiny of dance education in schools compared with most areas of the curriculum. There are no end-of-grade standardized achievement tests for students in dance, so there is no need to "teach to the test." I sometimes remind my students that one advantage of being viewed as peripheral in education is that most principals will not micromanage them to the extent that they will teachers of other areas of the curriculum: As long as kids want to take dance and there are no complaints about what shows up onstage, they probably will be pretty much left alone. Even though our state has a *Standard Course of Study* in dance, complete with grade-by-grade goals and objectives, no outside body comes looking to see whether or not students meet them.

Of course, this is a double-edged sword. Many of those standards that everyone else has to follow, despite considerable gnashing of teeth, do improve instruction. To the extent that we do not have to reach standards, we may be missing opportunities to strengthen instruction. The need for assessment is one of those opportunities. In the arts, we have long resisted developing appropriate means for assessment. One reason is our heritage of thinking about arts education as a no-fail activity, one that is designed to help children feel good about themselves with little regard for what, if anything, they are learning. When we resist for this reason, we are ignoring the reality that competence enhances self-esteem (Hallowell 2002).

There are other good reasons, of course, to feel concern over the current emphasis on assessment. Eric Jensen (2001) notes that too often assessment focuses on what is easily measured, which is usually trivial, and this can easily mean a focus on the trivial within a curriculum. In addition, we may quite reasonably resist assessment because we know that multiple-choice or similar standardized tests do not measure much that is worth knowing, in dance or anything else. The alternative — developing rubrics for evaluating qualitative evidence of student learning — is time-consuming and immensely challenging, but, in my view, also necessary if we are to have credibility as educators (for examples, see Schmid 2003). We must become better at identifying what students are actually learning in dance and describing how well they are learning it. In my own research (Stinson 1993, 1997) I have found that what students perceive they are learning is not always what teachers think they are teaching. Understanding what students are actually learning not only gives us ammunition for advocacy, but it also allows us to further our own thinking about what is worth knowing in dance, and why.

We have the opportunity to consider these and other externally set standards in the same way we do limits set in an improvisation problem, stimulating us to think more creatively and grow in ways we would not have if we could keep moving in our habitual patterns. When mandates have the potential to be harmful to the children and adolescents in our public schools, however, I believe we have the responsibility to take action in solidarity with others who care about the well-being of young people. Our own professional organizations can be helpful here, but as we consider action, we need to get beyond our comfortable territory of dance and higher education and focus not just on what is good for us, but on what is good for the larger community we serve. We also need to remember that decisions about public education, whether K–12 or higher education, reflect political realities, and only rarely will any particular constituency get everything it wants. If we choose to remain apart from such struggles, we will end up as "ivory-tower professors," making little to no impact on what is actually happening in schools. The challenge, of course, is how to do this without losing touch with our most essential values.

There are other aspects of context that influence curriculum in dance pedagogy, too, including the organization and size of one's institution, number of faculty, and different purposes that must be served. At my institution, teacher education programs in all areas of arts education, as well as physical education, are housed within our own departments, not within the School of Education. We have two full-time, tenure-track faculty members and one part-time lecturer involved in the sequence of dance education courses; this is far more than many institutions have.

Most of our courses in dance education serve multiple populations, including those who will teach in commercial and community studio settings as well as public schools. We also serve elementary education majors, who are required to take methods courses in three different art forms. There are some advantages to this kind of student diversity within the same course. One is that students in both elementary education and dance education develop skills of working with those who will be colleagues when they graduate. Because our BFA students are also required to take one course in dance education, some who had never considered public school teaching develop an interest; this is helpful in my state, where there is a shortage of dance educators. For those students who do earn a license, it is helpful to consider aspects of teaching in other settings, because most will do so at some point during their careers. At the same time, serving different populations takes time away from each, because we deal with some situations that are relevant to one group but not another.

Stepping back to the larger cultural context in which individuals and institutions exist, I am grateful that my own institution offers a course on the "institution of education," which gives all of our teacher education students a firm grounding in how American culture affects schools. Students thus bring insights about such issues as racism and "tracking" into dance education courses, where we discuss their implications for teaching dance.

Another part of context is understanding how our own dance education program fits into a larger universe of ways people learn to dance. Certainly there are many people nationally, not just in dance, who sneer at the value of teacher education courses, assuming that all one needs to know is the content of what one teaches; indeed, in many situations, such knowledge will suffice. For example, in professional dance training, usually outstanding dancers *are* the teachers. Their job is to show students what to do and how to do it; if the students are not successful at replicating the movement, it is an indication that they do not have sufficient talent to become dancers. The teachers are not blamed for being inadequate teachers, because professional dancers need to be able to "pick up" movement quickly and accurately.

There are other contexts where people learn to dance without a formal teacher at all. What is commonly called "street dance" is passed on from one young person to another, with individual touches and "new moves" added along the way. Although some studios teach social and street dance, this is not the way most people learn it. Similarly, many individuals learn to dance at clubs, by standing around the edges watching and then gradually joining in. There are many cultures and subcultures in which children learn by watching their elders dance, and begin to join in whenever it is appropriate. Individuals may become very skillful dancers without benefit of any formal instruction. If they do not, there is no teacher to blame; individuals often acknowledge that they are just not very good dancers, or they may say that they have "two left feet."

When dance becomes part of public education, however, there is a major change. It is the responsibility of the dance teacher, like all other teachers, to teach all students; if some students do not learn, the teacher cannot dismiss them by saying that they are just not talented in dance. Instead, the teacher needs to find other approaches so that everyone can learn. Because of this, learning to teach becomes just as important as learning to dance. Our own teacher education program exists in this context.

The Content and Process of Dance Education

We must teach our students both *what* and *how* to teach, and these two facets of the curriculum are related. Most books on dance education present some kind of outline of what to teach in dance; national standards and state and local curricula do so as well. We want our students to recognize that there is not just one way to conceptualize dance content, so we expose them to a number of models, letting them know that each is a creation of its author and that they, too, will create their own understanding of dance curriculum during their careers.

As an example, I share with students my own model, which has been developing during my years of professional practice. It has evolved considerably, but is not a finished work; I share it now only with the understanding that it is not and never will be the "final version." It reflects several of my own values that are not shared by all dance pedagogues, and it includes modeling for students a process of acknowledging and questioning my own values, a process I encourage them to emulate. (Stinson 2001)

My values include breaking down the boundary between creative dance (often thought of as appropriate only for children) and dance technique (often thought of as the "real" dance class for serious students), so that we can simply think about developmentally appropriate content and methodology at all levels. I believe that creativity and skill as a mover are both important for all ages, as is becoming an educated observer of dance, even though limited time means that one cannot cover everything in depth and difficult choices must be made.

Figure 13.1 represents the latest version of my model in visual form. The picture begins with three "spokes of a wheel" that represent three key experiences of dance: dancing, making dance, and watching dance. The three spokes appear separate in the diagram, but in actual dance classes they frequently intersect; for most ages, any dance class or unit of study will include all three. When a wheel is in motion, its spokes are not visibly separate, and ideally this is the case in dance classes, too.

In the diagram, the spokes intersect only at the center; that point could represent a dance lesson or unit of study, but the coming together of these three activities could also represent the "essence of dance" or the person engaging in each of these experiences. I would hope it could be both, bringing together "subject-centered" and "person-centered" dance education.

In teaching dancing and making dance, I present a four-step sequence, which I refer to as *explore, form, perform, evaluate.* This is easiest for students to understand in terms of dance making, because it so clearly parallels their own choreography experiences. One begins by *exploring* movement

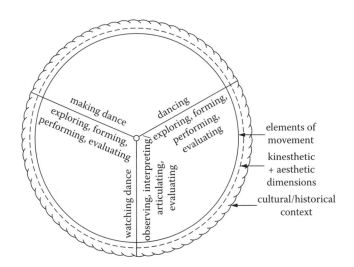

Fig. 13.1 Activities and Processes for Teaching Dance.

possibilities around a particular idea, selecting some to *form* into a composition. One then *performs* the composition (meaning dancing it fully, not necessarily on a stage or for an audience other than members of the class), and in some way *evaluates* it; evaluation may come from others as well as oneself. Following this, there may be revision and re-forming, performing, and more evaluation. The process may continue indefinitely. Of course, these steps are not neatly separated; in young children as well as skilled improvisers, exploring/forming/performing may occur simultaneously. For the youngest children, evaluation may be minimal and come only in the form of descriptive feedback from the teacher, as in, "It was exciting to see the way you …" Again, I think we too often ignore the evaluation phase in creative work, which does a great disservice to our students.

For our students who have learned dance only through imitating teacher demonstrations, thinking about the explore/form/perform/evaluate process in teaching *how to dance* seems more foreign. While students who are good visual and kinesthetic learners may learn to dance very well through imitation of a skilled teacher, this process is not successful for all learners. We thus encourage students to think about a way of teaching basic concepts that includes the four steps, although, again, the steps do not proceed neatly in order at all times. An overly simplified example might be this one involved in teaching arm positions in ballet: The exploration stage could include exploring the difference between an arm that is bent and one that is curved, straight, or stretched, paying attention to how each feels as well as how it looks. Similarly, one could explore what it feels like to extend arms to the side, slightly behind this location and slightly in front of it. This kind of exploration can be followed by forming a *port de bras* sequence created by the teacher, or, back to dance making, students might create their own "arm dance"; in either case, performing (dancing fully) would follow, and then evaluation by the teacher, peers, and/or oneself. Too often, I think, we shortchange students by not developing their aesthetic eye (in observing and evaluating others) and kinesthetic sensibilities (in attending to and evaluating their own performance and that of others).

Watching dance is often part of learning to dance and make dances: students may watch each other dancing and give feedback on the dancing and/or the choreography. When I first began teaching future dance educators, I rarely considered the importance of students' learning how to watch dance other than their own or that of their classmates, and there were few opportunities to do so. Thanks to the development of Discipline-Based Arts Education (Getty Center for Education in the Arts 1985; Clark, Day, and Greer 1987), I began to realize that we need to teach our students how to understand and appreciate dance from the audience's perspective as well as their own, and to understand the importance of dance within their own culture and others; I also began to realize how helping students to see more when watching dance would help them to become better dancers and dance-makers. In the assessment initiative developed for NAEP (National Association of Educational Progress), the phrase "responding to dance" was used to indicate this aspect of the dance curriculum (National Assessment Governing Board 1997). In my model, I have tried to indicate that "responding" is part of all three kinds of dance activities, so have shown *observation, interpretation, articulation, and evaluation* when watching dance to be comparable to the processes involved in the experiences of dancing and making dance.[3]

In the model, there are three circles around these key experiences, representing specific dance content that should be part of all the key experiences. One is the *elements of movement,* which I once thought of as the entire content for the curriculum and now see as only one lens for understanding dancing, dance making, and watching dance. Again, there are multiple ways of understanding the elements of movement, most based on either Rudolf Laban (see, for example, Boorman, 1971, 1969; Preston 1969; Russell 1975) or Margaret H'Doubler (Hypes 1978; Murray 1975), or a combination of these two (Gilbert 1992; Purcell 1994; Stinson 1988). Because the significance of movement elements is covered so thoroughly in so many books on dance education, I will not discuss this more thoroughly here.

Another circle to be drawn around the spokes is that which I call *kinesthetic and aesthetic dimensions.* The kinesthetic dimension in learning dance has already been implied in my discussion of the exploratory stage of learning to dance, in helping students *feel* the movement rather than just go through the motions. Although there is not complete agreement in the field that a somatic approach is necessary in learning to dance (Englehauser 2003), I am convinced that what I have long called "feeling from the inside" is essential to the change of consciousness required to make any kind of movement become dancing. In soccer, scoring a goal is important; how one does it does not matter, as long as it is within the rules. In dance, the *how* is everything, and that involves inner as well as outer awareness. Even the youngest children can learn that dancing is different from just moving around; long before they are ready to learn the word "kinesthetic," they can tell when they are using their inside "dance magic" to turn ordinary *moving* into *dancing* (Stinson 2002).

The second circle includes not only the kinesthetic but also the aesthetic dimension, raising a concept that has engaged philosophers for centuries. There are multiple ways of thinking about the aesthetic dimension, and controversies too complex to do justice to them here. One fairly accessible way to think about this dimension in teaching dance is what one can do to movement to make it more visually interesting to someone watching, such as when we make comments like, "It all looks the same; try to get more contrast in quality," or ask questions such as, "What does the choreographer do to draw your eyes to the stage right?" and, "Why does this look like a duet instead of two solos?" I have argued elsewhere (Stinson 1985) that this is a rather reductionistic way of thinking about the aesthetic dimension, and that it is important to recognize the arts as a lens for making sense of the world, a perspective I share with Maxine Greene (1995). We can help students understand how art works as *art* to communicate meaning by discussing such questions as, "What in the choreography communicates to you that this dance is about the emptiness of life dominated by technology?".

While advocates of discipline-based arts education see art history as one of the disciplines in the arts, I think that the cultural/historical context of dance can be better thought of as surrounding all three spokes, so that students learn this context in dancing (for example, they might learn about Doris Humphrey when exploring fall and recovery), dance making (for example, the connection between chance dance and Merce Cunningham), and watching dance (such as the context of a Trisha Brown dance within what was called "postmodern dance"). Because all these examples are from twentieth-century modern dance, I do not wish to imply that this is the only part of the culture and history of dance that we need to teach, or that cultural/historical context should be brought into every activity for every age. In particular, I find historical references to be not very meaningful for young children who still are trying to figure out how *today* becomes *yesterday* and *tomorrow* becomes *today*, although it does not seem to be harmful for them to see or learn developmentally appropriate dances from "far away and long ago." Most of our university-level students assume that learning history is something one does while sitting, but we encourage our students to use as much active learning as possible when teaching it, just as they experience in their own dance history courses. Thinking about the culture and history of dance as context for dancing, making dance, and watching dance, rather than as a separate discipline, facilitates this even further. My main concern with this approach is that it can relegate historical and cultural context to bits and pieces of factual information thrown into a class, instead of awareness that *all* dance movement exists in, reflects, and has an impact on its place and time, as well as the person creating, performing, or watching it.[4]

In that sense, it is significant that the cultural/historical circle surrounds not only the spokes of dance experiences, but also the other two circles. In other words, the whole idea of this "wheel" reflects not only my own thinking, but also the historical/cultural context in which I developed it. Similarly, considering the elements of movement as part of the curriculum of dance is neither a universal idea nor my particular invention, but rather a cultural construct. The idea of somatic awareness in dance is relatively recent, historically. And most obviously, aesthetic values and practices are culturally and historically situated.

Students as Learners

I teach my own students that what and how they teach should be influenced by the population they are teaching. This means that we must address such issues as child/adolescent development and diverse learners, aspects that our accrediting bodies mandate as well. Similarly, my teaching of how to teach dance is affected by my university-level students, each of whom brings his or her experiences in teaching and learning dance into the dance education setting, and this has a profound impact on how they understand what we are teaching (or what we think we are teaching).

When I first developed the teacher education program in dance at my institution, almost no students came in with experience of public school dance, and few had had any dance experience other than ballet, tap, and jazz classes at their local studios. The curriculum I inherited began with a theory course, followed by supervised teaching experiences at the elementary and then secondary levels. I was amazed to see how little my students seemed to apply the lessons of the theory course in their teaching. In reviewing Piagetian theory (Stinson 1985), I was reminded that learners are more inclined to assimilate knowledge into preexisting cognitive structures, changing the knowledge to fit into what they already know rather than changing those structures. It is far more challenging to help them construct new ways of understanding the world.

With this insight, I realized that students were assimilating everything I was telling them into their mental pictures of what dance education should look like, which mainly involved rows of little girls standing at the barre imitating the teacher and dancing in an annual recital in sequined costumes. It became apparent that because they had not experienced a broader dance education during their school years, they needed to develop a new picture based on new experiences. So I created a new curricular sequence, in which the first course was "experiential foundations" of dance education; I took students with me into elementary and secondary schools while I taught demonstration classes and they were participant observers, learning along with the children. I followed this with a course in "theoretical foundations," and then a more formal methods course and field experience teaching before student teaching.

Over time, however, our students have continued to change. Some of the characteristics of new freshmen are widespread and well documented on a regular basis by articles in *The Chronicle of Higher Education*, while others are more specific to a local context. After twenty years of dance being taught in many schools in my state, many more of our students have experienced dance education sometime during their K–12 schooling. In addition, there are many excellent dance educators in area schools, so that I and my university colleagues in dance education do not have to provide all of the demonstrations. After years of small changes, we implemented a new curricular sequence in fall 2004, one that integrates theory, observation, and methods during the first two semesters, followed by supervised field experience in the third, and then student teaching. We will continue to evaluate our program and the degree to which it meets the needs of our students, and undoubtedly will continue to make changes as needed.

Another aspect of our undergraduate students that we must deal with is their diverse levels of cognitive development and academic skills, as well as their varying strengths as learners. We try to honor different ways of knowing and different intelligences (Gardner 1999), although accreditation standards often make this more difficult. I still find it challenging to teach a class in which some students are concrete thinkers and others have developed the capacity for abstract thought. At the same time, few teachers have homogeneous classes, and intellectual diversity brings new possibilities as well as challenges.

Other kinds of diversity among our students bring richness to our classes, although we have less diversity than many urban public schools. As students share with each other their own stories in relation to a variety of topics in our courses, they become able to see new perspectives, particularly with respect to cultural differences, learning challenges, socioeconomic differences, and differences of sexual orientation.

The Teaching-Learning Process in Dance Education

One is constantly in the process of becoming a teacher; it is a journey rather than a destination. We teach students that they will never become perfect teachers, because no such creature exists. With this long-term perspective, we believe that the ability to reflect critically on one's own teaching, and to problematize and come up with possible solutions, is as important in predicting future success as is the level of accomplishment in teaching that our students achieve by the time they graduate. Because of this, self-evaluation is as much a part of a student's teaching grade as is his or her ability to plan and teach lessons. It is also, ultimately, a source of much of the reward of teaching. Reflecting on one's professional practice, followed by reworking to "try again" and then reevaluating in a continuing cycle, allows teachers the satisfaction of ongoing discovery.

Thinking of learning to teach as a journey reminds me of other relevant metaphors. To travel anywhere in space means that one must go off balance, which can feel scary as well as exciting. This is why it is important to provide support to students as they are experiencing the challenge of the process, especially when they actually begin teaching. For example, I frequently find myself reminding students that teaching dance to a group of twenty-five students is so complex that they can do ninety-five out of a hundred things right and still end up with a class that "doesn't work"; we need to notice our strengths as well as our weaknesses so we can keep up our courage as we continue to learn.

It requires special courage for novice teachers to teach in front of someone who is observing them teach *for a grade*. I remind them of José Limón's admonition to choreographers that "you will compose one hundred bad dances before you compose one good one" (1996, 23), and that the same probably applies to teaching. Thus we encourage all our teacher education students to look for other opportunities to teach, even to a small number of young people, where the stakes are not so high because only their students are watching. Once they begin formal field-experience teaching, we always have them share their self-evaluations first. It helps preserve student self-esteem to be able to say, "You are so insightful in recognizing that you did not do *x*. I agree with you that it would be better to do *y*."

One of the most important demonstration lessons I taught was one that did not go well. I had the good fortune, however, of being able to identify for students how what I had *not* done contributed to its failure, and I was able to go back the next week to reteach it. I told the fifth-graders that I had not done a very good job of teaching the previous week's lesson and I wanted another chance. Fortunately, my analysis was successful, and the second time around it was clear that the children learned what I was trying to teach and enjoyed their success.

I do not always have this opportunity to return and redeem myself. In order for me to feel authentic[5] as a teacher educator, however, I have to take the same kind of risks my students will take and put myself in the position of a continuing learner — more experienced than my students, but still with much to learn. In my department, all of us involved in teaching students to teach take this kind of risk. Exposing our vulnerability and weaknesses to our students is another way of providing support to them. Although there are a number of competent dance educators in the area, we continue to allow students to observe us teaching (live and/or on video) in settings like the ones in which they will teach and critically reflecting on our own teaching, so that they can observe the journey in process.

At this point, I must put up a caution sign: Once students start thinking critically about teaching, they apply it to other people's teaching as much or more than their own. This means that students are very critical judges of those who are teaching them to teach, when it comes time for end-of-the-semester evaluations. Extending this critical perspective, they may become similarly judgmental with regard to other faculty members — my colleagues; in response, I often find myself telling students that there are many ways to teach, and that they have the opportunity to see a number of them, and choose ones that best fit themselves, their students, and the institutional setting in which they will teach. Just as problematic is when students start critiquing the teaching of dance educators in the field whom they observe; it is not helpful to the kind of relationships we need to build with these teachers if they perceive that they are being criticized in our courses. We constantly find ourselves telling students that their role is not that of a critic, but a learner and a future colleague, and that each teacher is on her/his own journey, which involves trying things that do not work as well as ones that do.

It is clear that skills and insights about teaching develop in the context of relationships, with peers and faculty as well as with the subject matter, one's students, and oneself. Some relationships are supportive, while others are challenging. When they are challenging, it is far easier to blame others and sever relationships than it is to figure out how one can learn from them. This is a lesson we try to teach our students and to follow ourselves.

We try very hard to provide support as students negotiate the difficult challenges of beginning teaching, and recognize that students will enter and leave our program at different places on their journeys. Because we exist in an institution of higher education in an age of accountability, however, we are required to evaluate students on how well they achieve the student learning goals of each course, and we are also expected to document that they have met state standards to become certified. While hard work usually increases learning, it does not always translate into achievement in the short run, creating frustrations for students and faculty alike.

The requirement to give grades, not just evaluations, makes our task even more difficult. It has been my experience that most students appreciate feedback on their teaching and want to know how they can get better, but putting them into the "box" of a grade does not feel good unless the box is an *A*. We have not solved this challenge, but, when it comes to evaluating student planning, teaching, and evaluation, we have developed rubrics that include standards students must meet; this allows us to determine points that are added together to become a grade. We accompany this with as much narrative as we can, affirming strengths and potential that may not yet show up in achievement and grades.

Grading students during actual student teaching is even more difficult, especially because it is immediately apparent that some school environments are so supportive that a mediocre teacher can achieve fairly good outcomes, and others are so difficult that even a very good teacher will struggle. We are fortunate to be able to grade student teaching on a pass-fail basis.

The metaphor of a journey can be extended to encompass the overall curriculum in dance education; the various topics are, in some ways, like sights to see and experiences to have along the way. I recognize that I have not mentioned quite a few of the multitude of topics we cover in our dance education courses, including the history of dance in education, current ideas and issues in arts education as they relate to dance, social issues in the dance classroom, student motivation and class management, ethics in teaching, advocacy, uses of technology and other instructional resources, and making connections to other disciplines. This is only a partial list, and it does not include content that students get in other dance courses, including applied anatomy/kinesiology/injury prevention. Like many universities, we also have copies of syllabi on our departmental Web site (www.uncg.edu/dce), for readers who wish further details about our dance education courses as well as others.

Personal Lessons

Being a teacher has taught me a great deal about humility, about the limitations of my ability to achieve all that I aspire to and to fully live what I believe in. I read many books and articles, but good ones about education and the arts get written far faster than I can read them. I am frequently embarrassed when I realize that my teaching reflects as much of my own ego as it does the needs of my students. While I could continue with a lengthy "true confessions" here, I will focus instead on a couple of lessons about myself that I think have relevance for others.

One lesson is that I have only limited control over how students will teach when they graduate. We can teach them as best we are able, and ensure that they do what we (and the state) think they should be doing, before we recommend them for a teaching license and/or write a reference for employment. But they have learned from many sources about what and how to teach, and once they leave us, they will sometimes choose to teach in ways that we find problematic.

At the same time, some students will far exceed our expectations: My ability to accurately predict the future is limited. I can think readily of several students who were discussed at every semester's meeting about "students in trouble," and who barely met minimum standards to graduate but have ended up in leadership roles in the state. I know that not all flowers bloom the season they are planted, and I take special pleasure when graduates exceed my expectations, but, again, it is a humbling lesson.

A lesson I am still struggling to learn is how to achieve the right balance between challenge and compassion. Along with expectations I hold for students, I have long placed expectations for myself on my syllabi. Among them are "to be open and critical in considering your ideas" and "to be supportive and accepting as you share yourself," but I like myself more in the support role than in the critical one. I have to consistently question myself regarding whether I am really being the caring teacher I aspire to be when I readily allow students to turn in work late and earn extra points to make up for poor work. I recognize the obstacles that many of them face in being university students, working far more hours than they should on top of a full academic load, and/or facing personal crises. I know that, in my role as a faculty member, most requirements that I face have a good deal more flexibility than most courses allow students, and so I try to offer them as much flexibility as possible. But I am concerned that there are times when I end up too freely accepting lack of personal responsibility or even cultivating student dependence by helping too much, and I do not think that this behavior demonstrates the kind of care students need. This issue is one that is likely to continue to challenge me for some time.

At this point in my life, I have fewer years of professional practice ahead of me than behind me, and I am convinced that I will not have it all figured out before I retire. I shall simply continue this journey, fully aware that there will always be more to learn. I wish the same for all of my students who have become and will become dance educators.

Bibliography

Boorman, Joyce. *Creative Dance in Grades Four to Six.* Don Mills, Ontario: Longmans Canada Ltd., 1971.

_____. *Creative Dance in the First Three Grades.* Don Mills, Ontario: Longmans Canada Ltd., 1969.

Clark, Gilbert A., Michael D. Day, and W. Dwaine Greer. "Discipline-Based Arts Education: Becoming Students of Art." *Journal of Aesthetic Education* 21, no. 2 (Summer 1987): 130–93.

Consortium of National Arts Education Associations. *National Standards for Arts Education* (1994). Retrieved June 24, 2004, from http://artsedge.kennedy-center.org/teach/standards.cfm.

Englehauser, Rebecca. "Motor Learning and the Dance Technique Class: Science, Tradition, and Pedagogy." *Journal of Dance Education* 3, 3 (2003): 87–95.

Gardner, Howard. *Intelligence Reframed: Multiple Intelligences for the 21st Century.* New York: Basic Books, 1999.

Getty Center for Education in the Arts. Beyond Creating: The Place for Art in America's Schools. Los Angeles: Getty Center for Education in the Arts, 1985.

Gilbert, Anne Green. *Creative Dance for All Ages.* Reston: National Dance Association, 1992.

Greene, Maxine. *Releasing the Imagination: Essays on Education, the Arts, and Social Change.* San Francisco: Jossey-Bass, 1995.

Hallowell, Edward M. *The Childhood Roots of Adult Happiness.* New York: Ballantine, 2002.

Hypes, Jeannette, Ed. *Discover Dance: Teaching Modern Dance in Secondary Schools.* Washington, D.C.: National Dance Association, 1978.

Jensen, Eric. *Arts with the Brain in Mind.* Alexandria, Virginia: Association for Supervision and Curriculum Development, 2001.

Limón, José. "An American Accent." In *The Modern Dance: Seven Statements of Belief,* Selma Jeanne Cohen, Ed.. Middletown, Connecticut: Wesleyan University Press, 1966.

Murray, Ruth Lovell. *Dance in Elementary Education,* 3rd ed. New York: Harper and Row, 1975.

National Assessment Governing Board, *1997 Arts Education Assessment Framework.* (1997). Retrieved July 2, 2004 from http://www.nagb.org/pubs/artsed.pdf.

North Carolina Department of Public Instruction. *Arts Education Standard Course of Study and Grade Level Competencies* (n.d.). Retrieved June 24, 2004, from http://www.ncpublic schools.org/curriculum/artsed/index.html.

Preston, Valerie. *A Handbook for Modern Educational Dance.* London: MacDonald and Evans, 1969.

Purcell, Teresa M. *Teaching Children Dance: Becoming a Master Teacher.* Champaign, Illinois: Human Kinetics, 1994.

Russell, Joan. *Creative Movement and Dance for Children.* Boston: Plays, 1975.

Schmid, Dale W. "Authentic Assessment in the Arts: Empowering Students and Teachers." *Journal of Dance Education* 3, 2 (2003): 65–73.

Stinson, Susan W. "Curriculum and the Morality of Aesthetics." *Journal of Curriculum Theorizing* 6 (1985): 66–83.

_____. "Piaget for Dance Educators: A Theoretical Study." *Dance Research Journal* 17, 1 (Spring/Summer 1985): 9–16.

_____. *Dance for Young Children: Finding the Magic in Movement.* Reston, Virginia, National Dance Association, 1988.

_____. "Meaning and Value: Reflecting on What Students Say about School. *Journal of Curriculum & Supervision* 8, 3 (Spring 1993): 216–238.

_____. "A Question of Fun: Adolescent Engagement in Dance Education." *Dance Research Journal* 29, 2 (Fall 1997): 49–69.

_____. "Choreographing a Life: Reflections on Curriculum Design, Consciousness, and Possibility. *Journal of Dance Education* 1, 1 (2001): 26–33.

_____. "What We Teach Is Who We Are: The Stories of Our Lives." In *The Arts in Children's Lives,* Liora Bresler and Christine Marmé Thompson, Eds. 157–68. Dordrecht, The Netherlands: Kluwer, 2002.

Williams, Margery. *The Velveteen Rabbit or How Toys Become Real.* New York: Avon Books, 1975.

Notes

1. I am especially grateful for the colleagueship of those individuals with whom I have worked in shaping the dance education curriculum at UNCG, including Jill Green, Peggy Hunt, and Melinda Waegerle. I cannot take full credit for the value of the ideas expressed in this chapter, although I take full responsibility for how they are expressed here.

2. As I write this, there is no national PRAXIS II test to measure knowledge for dance educators, as there is in almost every other discipline, but one is likely to be developed soon. A few states have a state level exam to serve this purpose.
3. I am especially grateful to my colleague Ann Dils, a dance historian, for this language.
4. Dr. Ann Dils' comments in response to this discussion are worth citing: Moving toward an understanding of this relationship "means that we can discuss the relationship between the moves students make in class, and how they image themselves in a dance, and images of men and women they see on television and in films. It means we can discuss the differences between others' representations of us (say, how young women are seen in the many music videos or how ballerinas appear) and the images we would construct for ourselves. It allows us to get past saying that a/b/a form lends a sense of completion to a choreographed work and gives us an opportunity to realize why: where else do we see that pattern in our lives? Contemporary dance history is not necessarily a study of the past, but a realization of how dance comes to mean (in relationship to your own cultural and historical experience, your own aesthetic and practical training, the history of the form). And maybe this is a basic problem—not everyone realizes that history has been radically redefined in scope and method by cultural, performance, gender, and sexuality studies" (personal communication, 2004). Dils is engaged with Ann Cooper Albright in a collaborative project known as Accelerated Motion: Towards a New Dance Literacy in America, which is designed to create high school dance curriculum to facilitate these ways of seeing.
5. I recognize the controversial nature of this word, and use it here to refer to my own very personal sense of feeling "real" as a teacher; my sense of being "real" has been informed by the classic children's book *The Velveteen Rabbit* (Williams 1975).

Contributors

Elizabeth Aldrich is internationally known for her work in period dance, especially nineteenth-century social dance, and has provided choreography for numerous feature films, including *The Age of Innocence*, *The Remains of the Day*, *Washington Square*, and *The Haunted Mansion*. She has presented performances, workshops, and lectures throughout North America, Europe, Hong Kong, and Chile. Aldrich is author of *From the Ballroom to Hell: Grace and Folly in Nineteenth-Century Dance* (Northwestern University Press, 1991); the introduction for the *International Encyclopedia of Dance* (Oxford University Press, 1998); a chapter on dance in *Schubert's World: Vienna in the Reign of Francis I* (Yale University Press, 1997). She is also coauthor (with Sandra Noll Hammond) of the accompanying narrative for *The Extraordinary Dance Book T B. 1826 — An Anonymous Manuscript in Facsimile* (Pendragon Press, 2000) and a contributor to the *Grolier Encyclopedia of the Victorian Era* (Grolier, 2004). Aldrich served as managing editor of the six-volume *International Encyclopedia of Dance* (Oxford University Press, 1998) and provided the text and reconstructions for the Library of Congress Digital Library's *An American Ballroom Companion, c. 1490–1920*, which makes available two hundred dance manuals and seventy-five video clips via the World Wide Web. She served as president of the Society of Dance History Scholars (1989–1992) and chair of the editorial board for the Society's publication series *Studies in Dance History* (1998–2002). At present, Aldrich is the executive director of the

Dance Heritage Coalition, an alliance of major dance collections formed to document and preserve America's dance.

Since 2000, **Mindy Aloff** has taught the Dance Criticism course at Barnard College, where she also teaches "The Art of Being Oneself," a section of the First-Year Seminar course in literature and writing for freshmen. She has taught dance criticism and dance aesthetics as well at Princeton and Portland State University. Her writing on dance, literature, music, film, and other cultural subjects has appeared in *The New York Times, The New Yorker, The New Republic, The Chronicle of Higher Education*, and many other periodicals, both in the United States and abroad. She is a past fellow of the Woodrow Wilson and John Simon Guggenheim Memorial Foundations and a past recipient of a Whiting Writers Award. A consultant to The George Balanchine Foundation and the editor of the newsletter of the Dance Critics Association, she is the editor of *The Oxford Book of Dance and Ballet Anecdotes*, forthcoming from Oxford University Press.

Judith Chazin-Bennahum was principal soloist with the Metropolitan Opera Ballet Company when Antony Tudor was its artistic director. She received her doctorate in romance languages with a dissertation on ballet during the French Revolution. Her book *The Lure of Perfection: Fashion and Ballet 1780–1830* will be published by Routledge in fall 2004. She is currently chair of the Department of Theatre and Dance at the University of New Mexico.

Bill Evans was artistic director of the Bill Evans Dance Company (based in Seattle and Albuquerque) for thirty years. BEDC performed in all fifty states and was the most-booked company in the country for several years under the Dance Touring and Artist-in-the-Schools Programs of the National Endowment for the Arts. He founded the Evans Rhythm Tap Ensemble in 1992. He was formerly artistic coordinator of Utah's Repertory Dance Theatre and artistic director of Winnipeg's Contemporary Dancers. He received the Guggenheim Fellowship and numerous fellowships and grants from the NEA as well as state, regional, and private arts agencies. He received the New Mexico Governor's Award for Excellence in the Arts and two Awards for Excellence in Dance from the Albuquerque Arts Alliance. He earned an M.F.A. from the University of Utah and is a Certified Laban Movement Analyst. He is a visiting professor at the State University of New York College at Brockport and professor emeritus at the University of New Mexico, permanent guest artist in the Professional Program of Winnipeg's School of Contemporary Dancers and artistic director of the annual Bill Evans Dance Intensives and Evans Technique Certification Program at Centrum, Port Townsend, Washington. He teaches Evans Modern Dance Technique and Repertory, Rhythm Tap, Laban Movement Analysis/Bartenieff Fundamentals, Dance Conditioning/ Applied Kinesiology, Improvisation, Choreography and Dance Pedagogy. He is a member of the board of directors of the National Dance Education Organization and Produced the 2003 NDEO Conference in Albuquerque. He was featured in the October 2003 issue of *Dance Magazine.*

Susan Leigh Foster, choreographer and scholar, is professor in the Department of World Arts and Cultures at the University of California, Los Angeles. She is author of *Reading Dancing, Choreography and Narrative,* and *Dances That Describe Themselves.* She is also coeditor of the new dance journal *Discourses in Dance.*

Ilene Fox is executive director of the Dance Notation Bureau, New York; Certified Professional Notator; teacher of Labanotation and Certified Movement Analyst. She received a B.A. in dance education from the University of Illinois. Fox has been the notator of works by Anastos, Balanchine, Holm, Joffrey, Limón, Louis, Shawn and Sokolow, among others, and of the Chinese classical dance syllabus for the Hong Kong Academy for Performing Arts. She is also a fellow at the International Council of Kinetography Laban; Advisory Board of the Laban Institute for Movement Studies; and cochair of the Research and Documentation Network of the World Dance Alliance Americas. She is also project director of the DNB's project to develop software to translate Labanotation into computer animation.

Beth Genné, Ph.D., is associate professor of dance in the Department of Dance and of art history in the Residential College at the University of Michigan, Ann Arbor. She is a co-founder of the University of Michigan's Center for World Performance Studies. She is author of *The Making of a Choreographer: Ninette de Valois and Bar aux Folies-Bergère.* Her articles on British ballet have been published in *The Dancing Times, Dance Research, Dance Chronicle, The International Encyclopedia of Dance* and in the Ashton anthology *Following in Sir Fred's Steps.* Her articles on dance in film have also appeared in the journals listed above as well as in *Art Journal* and as chapters in *Envisioning Dance on Film and Video, The Living Dance: an Anthology of Essays on Movement and Culture* and in *Re-Thinking Dance History.* She was a consultant for the American Masters PBS program, *Gene Kelly: Anatomy of a Dancer,* in which she also appeared. She was director of research for Balanchine's Hollywood films for the Balanchine Foundation's "Popular Balanchine" project; her findings on Balanchine's contribution to American cinema were presented at the Film Society of Lincoln Center and the Balanchine Centenary Symposium in St. Petersburg, Russia in 2004. Most recently, she has written an article on the artistic relationship of Balanchine and Josephine Baker for *Discourses in Dance.*

Larry Lavender, Ph.D., is head of the dance department at the University of North Carolina at Greensboro. He holds a masters in dance from University of California, Irvine and a doctorate in dance education from New York University. Lavender teaches courses in choreography, dance criticism, and aesthetic/cultural trends in contemporary dance. His scholarly research and writings are in the area of dance-critical practice and the education/training of choreographers. He has taught and lectured in many parts of the world, and his publications, most notably his book *Dancers Talking Dance: Critical Evaluation in the Choreography Class* (1996), are used in dance departments worldwide.

Dawn Lille, Ph.D., is trained in ballet, modern dance, Labanotation and Effort/Shape movement analysis. She has been a performer, director, choreographer, teacher, writer and dance historian. She holds a bachelors degree from Barnard College, masters degrees from Columbia and Adelphi and a doctorate from New York University. Her articles have appeared in such publications as *Ballet Review, Dance Chronicles, Dance Research Journal, Choreography and Dance* and various encyclopedias. She has written chapters in several books, most recently *Dancing Many Drums,* and has published a book, *Michel Fokine.* She served as head of the graduate program in Dance Research and Reconstruction at City College/CUNY and as director of education at the Dance Notation Bureau. She was the researcher and curator for the exhibit "Classic Black" at the Dance Collection of the Library of Performing Arts at Lincoln Center, and most recently was a researcher for both the "Popular Balanchine" project and the Digital Dance Library project. She teaches dance history at Juilliard and writes regularly for *Art Times.*

Jennifer Predock-Linnell, Ph.D., is professor of dance in the Department of Theatre and Dance at the University of New Mexico. She has been a recipient of an NEA Choreographer's Fellowship, and her dance/video works have been performed in the United States, Australia, France, Portugal, Israel, and New Zealand. She has also been a recipient of a $21,000 Rockefeller Foundation for Cultural Exchange — USA–Mexico. ROSTROS/FACES,

Collaborative Choreographic project between UNM, and UNAM, Mexico City — Utopia Danza Theatro. Her articles have been published in *Siences, Mexico, Psychological Reports: Perceptual and Motor Skills, Impulse*, the 16th and 17th *Volume of the Institute of Psychoanalytic Studies of the Arts, 50 Contemporary Choreographers, Dance: Current Selected Research*, AMS Press, *The International Dictionary of Modern Dance, Research in Dance Education*. She was awarded the Outstanding Teacher of the Year Award for 2001–2002.

Susan W. Stinson, Ph.D., is professor of dance at University of North Carolina at Greensboro, where she teaches undergraduate courses in teacher preparation and graduate courses in research and curriculum. She served as department head in dance for 1993–2002. She has participated on teams writing and/or reviewing standards for K–12 dance students nationally and at the state level, as well as competencies for dance educators. She is past chair of Dance and the Child International. She has presented her scholarly work nationally and internationally and published her work in numerous journals as well as book chapters; her recent research has focused on how young people make meaning from their experiences in dance education.

Jeffrey Stolet has worked extensively as an accompanist for acclaimed dance companies or choreographers from around the world. Stolet has also taught classes about music to dancers at the University of New Mexico and the University of Oregon. He is currently a Philip H. Knight Professor of Music and Director of Intermedia Music Technology at the University of Oregon School of Music. Stolet's compositional work has been presented in America, Europe, Japan, and Australia; it is available on the Newport Classic and Cambria labels. Presentations of his work include major electroacoustic and new media festivals, such as the Society for Electro-Acoustic Music in the United States (SEAMUS) National Conference (United States), the International Computer Music Conference, the Florida Electroacoustic Music Festival, Electronic Music Midwest, SIGGRAPH National Conference, Transmediale International Media Art Festival (Berlin), Boston Cyber Arts Festival, Cycle de concerts de Musique par ordinateur (Paris), the International Conference for New Interfaces for Musical Expression and the International Electroacoustic Music Festival "Primavera en La Habana," in Cuba, and venues such as the Museum of Modern Art in New York, the Pompidou Center in Paris, and the Center for Computer Research in Music and Acoustics (CCRMA) at Stanford University, as well as performances and major exhibitions at venues in Madrid, Barcelona, Seville, and Alicante

(Spain); Paris, Reims, and Beauvais (France); London and Norfolk (England); Milan (Italy); Sydney and Paddington (Australia); Berlin, Cologne, Weimar, and Stralsund (Germany); Grenoble (Switzerland); São Paulo (Brazil); Toronto (Canada); Tokyo (Japan); and New York, Boston, Washington, D.C., Los Angeles, San Francisco, San Jose, Sacramento, Seattle, Portland, Milwaukee, Kansas City, San Antonio, and Cleveland. His most recent compositions include a series of pieces for infrared controllers, Max, Kyma, and the Yamaha Disklavier; a media work for mezzo-soprano, Yamaha Disklavier, computer-generated sound and computer animation, created in collaboration with media artist Ying Tan; and a series of collaborative media performance pieces with artist/performer Leon Johnson.

At the University of Oregon, Stolet has also developed the curricula for a bachelor of science in music technology, a master of music in intermedia music technology, and the curriculum for intermedia music technology as a secondary area for music students pursuing doctoral degrees. Beyond creating new curricula, Stolet has collaborated with the New Media Center at the University of Oregon to transform an original electronic music textbook into Electronic Music Interactive, an Internet-deliverable, multimedia document containing motion animations, sound, and glossary that has received rave reviews in the press, including *Electronic Musician, Keyboard Magazine,* the *Chronicle of Higher Education,* and *Rolling Stone.*

Jill D. Sweet, Ph.D., is professor of anthropology at Skidmore College. She received her bachelors and masters degrees in dance from the University of California, Irvine, and her doctorate in anthropology from the University of New Mexico. Her 1981 dissertation explores the effect of tourism on Tewa Indian ritual dance. She was named a resident scholar at the School of American Research, Santa Fe, New Mexico, in 1979 and again in 2002. Along with numerous articles in academic journals, Sweet is the author of *Dances of the Tewa Pueblo Indians: Expressions of New Life* (1985; 2nd edition 2004), SAR Press.

Linda J. Tomko is associate professor of dance at the University of California, Riverside, where she teaches dance history, theory and methods of dance reconstruction, and Baroque-era movement practices. She is a past president of the Society of Dance History Scholars. Her book *Dancing Class: Gender, Ethnicity, and Social Divides in American Dance,* 1890–1920, was published by Indiana University Press in 1999.

Mary Virginia ("Ginny") Wilmerding, Ph.D., danced professionally for a number of modern dance companies in New York City before moving to New Mexico. She is now an adjunct professor at the University of New Mexico in Albuquerque, where she teaches for both the exercise science and dance programs. Courses include kinesiology, research design, exercise physiology, and exercise prescription, as well as modern dance, ballet, jazz, and conditioning. She teaches modern dance to children at Dance Theatre of the Southwest. Wilmerding is an officer of the International Association for Dance Medicine & Science. She has published original research in *Journal of Dance Medicine and Science, Medical Problems of Performing Artists, Medicine & Science in Sports & Exercise, Journal of Strength and Conditioning Research,* and *Idea Today.* Research interests include body composition, training methodologies, injury incidence and prevention, pedagogical considerations in technique class, and the physiological requirements of various dance idioms.

Index

B

Balanchine, George, 84, 88, 93, 116, 193
Balanchine Foundation, 82
Ballroom round dance position, 109
Banes, Sally, 125
Banking system of pedagogy, 99, 108
Barnes, Clive, 118, 128
Bartenieff, Irmgard, 2, 12
Bartenieff Fundamentals (BF), 3, 6,
    8–9, 16
Barthes, Roland, 97
Baryshnikov, Mikhail, 127
Basso, Keith, 135, 141
Beauchamp, Pierre, 188
Beethoven, 56, 68, 69
Bell, Clive, 42
Benesh, Joan, 189
Benesh, Rudolf, 189, 207
Benesh Notation, 189, 209
Berkeley, Busby, 84
Bey, Theresa M., 165
BF, *see* Bartenieff Fundamentals
BFA students, 221
BIA, *see* Bioelectrical impedance
    analyzer
Bill Evans Dance Company, 4
Bioelectrical impedance analyzer (BIA), 179
Biomechanics, 173
Blackface minstrel shows, 98
BMI, *see* Body Mass Index
Bock, Philip K., 135
Bodies, scrutiny of, 101
Body joints, major classifications of, 171
Body Mass Index (BMI), 179
Body Mind Centering, 3
*Body Movement: Coping with the
    Environment*, 2, 12
*Body, Movement, and Culture: Kinesthetic
    and Visual Symbolism in a Philippine
    Community*, 144
Bollywood movies, 78
Bolshoi, 80
Botticelli, 88
Bound Flow, 14
Bourne, Matthew, 117
Bournonville, August, 88, 116
Boy Scout jamboree, 139
Break dancing, 95
Bruhn, Erik, 127
Bunions, 179
Butler, Judith, 97

C

Cage, John, 70
Calaban, 198
Caloric needs, 182
Canons, 193
Capitalist economic organization,
    oppressions of, 96
Carnaval, 194
Carruthers, John, 150
Casey, Edward S., 40
Cervera dance manuscripts, 188
Change, movement and, 7
Cherry, Christian, 75
Chicago, 84
Choreographie ou l'Art d' Ecrire la Danse, 188
Choreography, *see also* Improvisation to
    choreography
        basis for design, 40
        as critical process, 46
        distinction between improvisation and,
        103
    improvisation and, 36
    origination of term, 29
    training ground, 37
The Chronicle of Higher Education, 228
Classroom lighting, 86–87
Clippinger, Karen, 5
Coalition Planning Group, 204
Cognitive development, levels of, 228
Cohen, Bonnie Bainbridge, 3
Cohen, Selma Jeanne, 92, 206
Coherence of form, 43
Colonial subordination, 96
Communitas, Turner's notion of, 145
Comparison and contrast, 78
Compositional assignments, 48
Compositional prompts, 48
Computer music instruments, 70
Condillac, 29, 30, 31
Conditioning classes, 182
Conscious critical control, 44
Consonance, 63
Coping Efforts, 14
Coppelia, 194
Copyright law specialists, 214
Cowan, Jane, 141, 142
Critical comments, best-working, 161
Criticism, Labanotation and, 194
Croce, Arlene, 118, 120–121, 123, 125
Cultural anthropology, 136
Cultural constructions, 136